One Foot in the Grave
and Counting

One Foot in the Grave and Counting

A novel
by David Renwick

fantom
publishing

First published 2021 by Fantom Publishing, an imprint of Fantom Films
www.fantompublishing.co.uk

Copyright © David Renwick 2021

David Renwick has asserted his moral right to be identified as the author of this work in accordance with the Copyright, Designs and Patents Act 1988.

All rights reserved.

A catalogue record for this book is available from the British Library.

Hardback edition ISBN: 978-1-78196-358-6

Typeset by Phil Reynolds Media Services, Leamington Spa
Printed and bound by CPI Group (UK) Ltd, Croydon, CR0 4YY

Jacket design by Stuart Manning

For Ellie

to whom I owe everything

Contents

Chapter One: From the Underworld — 1

Chapter Two: The Death of Truth — 27

Chapter Three: Edwin — 64

Chapter Four: Yakety Sax and Beyond the Infinite — 122

Chapter Five: The Man in the Cube — 168

Chapter Six: The Suburban Spaceman — 202

Why?

Just about said it all, in Victor's mind.

As a personal philosophy it pretty much covered everything. The distillation of God-knows-how-many centuries' metaphysical discourse and head scratching; and a rather more elegant reworking of his earlier postulate: "What's the bloody point?"

Come to think of it, that doctrine could be boiled down still further, couldn't it? To its purest non-verbal essence …

"?"

Deeper than that you couldn't go. In a world growing ever more polluted by certainties, the question mark was the only sensible brake on our desperate rush towards answers.

Or was it?

Victor couldn't be at all sure.

Which is what makes him something of a hero in our story.

Chapter One
From the Underworld

THE FORECAST WAS FOR blinkered self-interest and bastardry covering most of the country, with occasional spells of humanity developing late in the day. Motorists were advised to take extra care when tearing up behind you like a maniac slinging beer cans out of the window, and only to mow down pedestrians while checking for texts where absolutely necessary.

The dystopian future was now well into its third week and mankind's extinction a done deal. Somewhere in the south-east RAF fighter jets were being scrambled, while the prime minister chaired an emergency meeting of the COBRA committee.

And the nation rejoiced.

For Victor Meldrew then, an average spring morning as he stepped out of his front door for another day on the farm.

In his leafy corner of suburbia the dawn chorus was at its height. A confluence of chattering voices that filled the air, this day as every day, with their simple shrill vocabulary: asserting and expressing themselves in a cacophony of compulsive communication.

So much so, you could hardly hear the birds.

"*It's just coming up to eight-fifteen, it's Breakfast Time, I'm Katty Kelly,* and today we're talking 'man' problems! Our resident expert in all things urogenital is here, Doctor Matthew "Doc" Holiday, welcome Matt – sorry, sorry! I promised not to! Impotence, infertility, anything you don't like the look of on your hubby or feller, lines are open now, do give us a call."

From across the wall in the garden opposite, through two layers of privet hedge, the builders' radio had enough battery power to drown out the cachinnations of Victor's Honda Ballade, as for the third time that week it laughed off his attempts to start the engine.

"Oh I do not belie— ... for God's sake not *again*! That ruddy service department's a joke! I wish I'd never set foot in the place!"

The word slapdash didn't begin to cover it. It was bad enough he'd turned up to find two young mechanics on his roof fencing with old car aerials. And you didn't have to be a conspiracy theorist to tell the vehicle had been recently used to go joyriding. That smell of seaweed in the air filter told its own story.

"Useless rabble."

And so to the ritual inspection of the manual, and the ever-helpful "troubleshooting guide". He had never found one yet that treated the reader as anything but a village idiot. With handy tips like "Check toaster is connected to power supply and switched on" ... "Have slices of bread been inserted?" ... "Ensure product was not recently used as Frisbee by family of gorillas" ...

"Right! What have we got. Battery fine, fuel gauge fine, oil level fine. Vehicle not currently immersed in a river."

With an exasperated yank of the bonnet release he opened the door.

"And! Thrilled to say we're now joined by Sharon in Doncaster. Sharon, you've got a question for Doc Holiday, fire away?"

"Yes hi, Katty, I'd like to ask, is it possible to reverse a circumcision? For the last fourteen years my husband's kept his foreskin in a jar, but to be honest I'm not sure it would still fit."

"Mmm that's an interesting one isn't it, why don't we just hold that thought till we've heard from The Herd. All the way back to 1967 and a very young Pete Frampton, this is 'From The Underworld'."

Not more than a few yards away, some would say in a parallel universe, Margaret Meldrew returned to the front room with two fresh cups of coffee.

"There you go then, Jean. Try not to let this one get cold."

"Hmm? Oh. Thanks, Margaret. That's erm …"

Her friend could barely muster a mumble. The computer screen at which she'd been staring for the last hour had her total attention. And she was, in a sadly non-literal sense, miles away.

Given the choice of having her ears cut off or her broadband, Mrs Warboys might well have hesitated. To a lifelong gossip and eavesdropper, poking your nose into everyone's business was part of the daily routine. But how to cope when an overnight storm has just brought down your phone line? When it is a truth universally acknowledged that life without social media is no life at all.

Happily, the Meldrews' laptop had come to the rescue: that's what good friends were for. And of course she wouldn't dream of imposing for long, that was a given. The minute she was done with her complex matrix of tweets and posts and messages she'd be out of their hair and … but just a second, what was this?

"Ohhh my *God*."

Something on the screen had caused her to gasp.

"Oh Margaret, Margaret, this is *awful*."

"What is it, Jean? What on earth's the matter?"

Slam!

Outside, Victor straightened his back and wiped his hands on a Kentucky Fried Chicken napkin that was nestling in his dahlias. Nothing to report there: no cables uncoupled, nothing hanging off anywhere, no bloodied bits of Jeremy Clarkson from a roadkill clogging up the carburettor.

How immensely irritating.

They say the difference between an optimist and an optometrist is that one is concerned with seeing things accurately. At some point in the past, we can safely assume, Victor had broken his rose-tinted spectacles and found no reason to replace them. If life was not some devious plot, designed to sap your spirit at every turn, then he was a Dutchman. And anyone who disagreed hadn't lately been dumped, like a busted sofa in a lay-by, to "enjoy the fruits" of early retirement. All the gooey cards in the world plastered with golf clubs, yachts and fishing rods hadn't convinced him this would be anything but hell. And so it had proved. Day after day it was one thing or another and usually both at the same time.

"Bugger it."

Time was getting on – there was nothing for it but to go in and fish out the cycle clips.

As Victor stepped through the front door he might well have imagined a pig had been set loose in his house to hunt for truffles. Of course this was not the case, though the sounds coming from Mrs Warboys, as Margaret fed her a succession of tissues, were broadly similar. Sniffling and snuffling through the tears she was all of a dither.

Having slammed down his keys on the sideboard Victor continued into the kitchen.

"On the blink again, ruddy thing, I can't get it started for love nor money. Good morning, Mrs Warboys, are you well. I shall have words to say to that garage tomorrow, I know that much."

"Yes, well perhaps that'll teach you to go buying cars from someone called Honest Sam," was all Margaret had to say on the subject. "And does Jean *look* well? She's just had some very bad news from America. From her penfriend Chesney. The poor woman's in a dreadful state."

"I can't take it in, Mr Meldrew! They've just said – they've just said he's only got three months to live!" Blowing her nose for the third time in a minute she tried to take deep breaths. "Poor, poor Chesney! Three months! This is such a shock."

Victor looked back from the doorway.

"He's in the state penitentiary in Arkansas on Death Row. That can't be good for anyone's life expectancy."

"Victor??"

"Well I know that, Mr Meldrew, of course I do but ... he's always sounded so nice in his emails. And it's been nearly a year now, I suppose I just hoped ..."

"Never in all my puff will I understand, why women do that strange thing. When you said this man was a family butcher I foolishly imagined someone selling sausages. Margaret, where are my bicycle clips, they used to be in this drawer."

"There are *plenty* of things you don't understand," snapped Margaret, as she magically located the missing items. "When to open your mouth and when to keep it shut. And if you want to hang on to this new job you better look lively. Take no notice of him, Jean, you know what he's like."

"No, no, Margaret, I mean I always knew this day would come round. It's one of the first things they stress on the website when you sign up. To become a Friend of a Felon. In the meantime we must all learn to meet contrition with compassion. Whatever these people have done, doesn't mean they're beyond redemption. Remember, it was never proved *all* the fingerprints on the axe belonged to him? Oh what am I going to do. He wants me to go over there now, to say a prayer at his execution."

"Good luck with that then, Mrs Warboys. Tch, how can it be twenty to nine! I'm never going to make it, I know I'm not."

"Sorry, Mr Meldrew? Oh! Well look, I'm just about finished here now, why don't I give you a lift? It's more or less on my way. I just need to let this sink in. And try and get my head together."

For the first time that day Victor's face perked up.

"Are you sure? Well – yes, that'd be a big help, thanks."

"I'll just get my coat – bye then Margaret, and I'll give you a ring later. Oh and have a wonderful meal tonight, won't you, on your anniversary. I've not been to that restaurant myself but I'm sure it's lovely."

"Yes, thanks, Jean. And thanks for the card."

"You can't go by what they say on TripAdvisor. People love to put 'disgusting' when they probably just mean 'average'. That's something I've learned over the years."

"Ye-es. Bye then, and you drive carefully."

"Bye."

As the door closed behind them a strained solemnity hung in the air that would linger for much of the day.

Margaret crossed to the sink to rinse out the coffee mugs and unleashed one of her long, pained sighs. No one could pretend it was easy, maintaining a marriage for forty years. People said you had to work at it but that was rubbish. If you had to force the issue then clearly something was missing to start with. Any way you sliced it life was a challenge. And heaven help the poor souls who had to face it alone: Margaret was strong, but not that strong.

A luminous rectangle on the table reminded her Mrs Warboys had left the laptop running. And before she put it to sleep she couldn't resist, could she, a sneaky glimpse of the man they were just talking about.

A gentle brush of the touchpad and there he was.

Chesney Dubois Pinkerton III. Prisoner # SK9046. The classic mug-shot, front and side view. Young, black, stark, unsmiling. And imposingly handsome, there was no doubt about that. But in those dark penetrating eyes there was something else. A look you couldn't help but recognise, and one that caused her to shudder.

In fact the more Margaret gazed at the screen the more jarring and deeply disturbing it seemed to become.

It was a look of humanity.

By the time they reached Powdrill's Farm Victor's nerves were already starting to jangle.

It's fair to say his driver was not exactly speedy. If the accelerator pedal had been a landmine she could hardly have been more tentative. Tightly clutching the wheel with the scrunched-up face of a burglar in a stocking mask, she was too tense even to notice the cocky schoolkids performing slow-motion *Chariots of Fire* walks in her rear-view mirror. On one hilly stretch they were overtaken by three men pushing a transit van. Like the young Albert Einstein, Victor found himself toying with certain thought experiments: if Mrs Warboys' car was travelling at the speed of light, how old would he be after she'd stopped at six lamp posts in a row to see if her four-month-old puppy wanted the toilet?

Oh, had she not mentioned she was taking her little spaniel to the vet today for a check-up? No, Victor assured her, she had not. Nor that, as the animal had a preference for riding up front, he would be forced to travel on the back seat wedged between a bulk order of dog biscuits and three bags of garden refuse on their way to the tip.

When they finally pulled up beside a row of old timbered barns, Victor did not so much climb out of the car as ooze from it, like a tube of toothpaste. With no feeling left in his arms or legs he could barely stand upright. Very slowly he managed to unlock his spine, and taking a long, grateful breath reacquainted himself with oxygen.

"Thank you very much then, Mrs Warboys, I do appreciate that," he lied. Adding hastily before she could repeat the offer: "I'll probably get a bus home."

"You're more than welcome, Mr Meldrew. And Oscar says a big thank you for being so considerate. He gets horribly carsick in the back unfortunately. Three times in this past week, the poor mite."

"Oh dear."

"I meant to say, not to sit near that soggy patch in the middle."

"Yes well it's been lovely chatting but—"

"Ever since Chris walked out on me, well of course my life was turned upside down, as I don't need to tell you. But this little fellow's been a godsend. The last one in the litter, bless him, and just the most perfect companion I could wish for."

"Very good. Still, I'd better be—"

"Oh, but now! What's *really* fascinating … and I'm not sure I ever told you this, did I, about this amazing gift he's got? And all the rest of his family just the same. Of being able to sniff out bowel cancer in humans? Can you imagine! And totally accurate in about ninety per cent of cases, so they reckon. Yes! Aren't *you* a clever little boy, Oscar!"

"Oh – really? Yes, I think I have read something about erm …"

"And it was quite a regular thing apparently. As a diagnostic aid, the local GPs used to swear by it. I suppose it wouldn't be everyone's cup of tea if you'd just gone down to the surgery, but … it just goes to show, how much we still have to learn from anima— Oscar! Stop doing that! I don't suppose those trousers were clean on today but that's not the point. Come here with you! Sorry about that, Mr Meldrew, I should have put him on his lead. Would you like a wet wipe?"

"Yyy— thank you, Mrs Warboys. If you don't mind I'll just …"

"Anyway, you'll be wanting to get along now, I expect. What is it you're doing for this farmer exactly, Margaret said something about mucking out the pigs?"

"Well that was on the first day. The card in the post office just talked about general odd jobs around the place. He's got me searching through one of his fields at the moment. Thinks he might have dropped a wedding ring out there if you please. Talk about looking for a needle in a haystack."

"Still, as long as he's paying. Should keep you busy for a day or two."

"Yes … I expect so."

A steady drizzle had set in by mid-morning, spattering and softening the heavy tractor ruts in the soil. And the wind from the east, having made its way up Victor's sleeves and trousers, was now engaged in a pincer movement on his thermal underwear. Overnight, a parliament of owls had voted by a comfortable majority for air strikes against the local field mice, so he pretty much had the place to himself.

It was a tall order in anyone's book: tramping across five acres of mud examining every furrow. In the absence of a state-of-the-art metal detector he'd been issued with a long pointed stick; together with an outsize ex-lollipop man's greatcoat to keep him nice and warm. This proved to be more of an encumbrance than a comfort, and would have been easier to button up if it had any buttons. As a result it just flapped about madly at his sides like the wings of a giant albatross, impeding his progress still further.

He'd been told to concentrate on the middle of the field, as that's where Powdrill was "a hundred and one per cent" sure the ring had come loose. A curious assertion that Victor couldn't quite get his head round. If the thing was that precious and you thought it might drop off, wouldn't you just slip it in your pocket to be on the safe side? But then again, he'd long since given up trying to fathom out a world that was run by idiots, where reason and common sense were in woefully short supply.

"Ah ha ha ha!"

Suddenly he jerked to a halt. Poked about for a second in the ground, then bent down and peered more closely. Could that possibly be a gentleman's wedding ring poking out of the soil, chunkily ribbed in glistening 22-carat rose gold?

Or just another sodding earthworm.

We leave it for the reader to guess.

It was in a spirit of adventure they'd decided, for their anniversary meal, to try out a Vietnamese restaurant. Margaret had promised to have a go with the chopsticks if Victor kept quiet about Operation Rolling Thunder.

The decor was smart but spare, with a gentle sophistication that put them quickly at ease. Haunting grooves from a bamboo xylophone mingled with the snap of prawn crackers. And the steady trickle of a water fountain, while reminding Victor of that useless plumber the other week, was soothing to the ear.

A waitress arrived at their table with what appeared to be the complete works of Tolstoy in translation, but turned out to be a menu. Half an hour later, by the time Victor was into his second helping of mi quang shrimp, he had all but forgotten about his dreary day in the field. By the time he was into his third he could no longer smell the manure.

"So how did it go this afternoon, I forgot to ask. With old Mrs Smedley."

"Sorry? Oh come here for goodness' sake! Never did get on with these ruddy things." Struggling to get some purchase on a noodle, Margaret could only curse her ineptitude. But then again, why did we all fall for this stupid custom in the first place? By the same logic you'd use a knife and fork to knit a tea cosy.

"Weren't you taking her out for another driving lesson? Got back in one piece this time at any rate."

"Oh! Yes. Well, making progress by degrees. I've got her to go downhill now without putting her hands over her eyes. But it's a slow old business."

"Don't know where you get your patience. The woman's got precious little sense of direction as it is."

"What's that supposed to mean."

"How many people do you know who sit on a lavatory facing the cistern."

Margaret nodded.

"Still, if it gives her an interest in life. And she's such a sweet old soul. No, actually it was quite a day in the end, I meant to say! We went off afterwards to do a bit of shopping and met a witch."

The beansprout that was on its way into Victor's mouth at that point made a sudden reappearance and careered like a luge down his tie.

"A *witch*?"

"You probably know him. Mr Dimkins? Who serves in the sweet shop?"

"What, the man who sells me my barley sugars? Who told you he was a witch?"

"He did. And he had the head of a dead cockerel in his briefcase. He showed it to us. Anyway we all got chatting, and he went through the Tarot cards, and cooked up some entrails. Said I was going to live a long and peaceful life and you would be visited by a plague of devils. He's a fascinating character and no doubt about it. Oh it's no good, I'm going to have to give up and use a spoon."

"A plague of devils? What did he mean by that?"

Margaret shrugged, as she chomped on her first decent mouthful of rice.

"Something horrible and nasty, was how I understood it. You know, like the wrath of Lucifer."

"Wrath of Lucifer!"

"Oh it's just a bit of fun, stop fretting. How would *he* know you're about to come to a sudden untimely end. And you're the one who's always saying these things are a load of hogwash."

"Is that what he told you? A sudden untimely end? And – did he say when? This year? Next year?"

"He didn't put a date on it. They never do, do they. Just when you're least expecting I suppose. What else would you mean by 'sudden'? Anyway can we drop the subject now, I wish I'd never mentioned it."

"Things people come out with. You'd think they'd have a bit more concern for the effect it's going to h—"

"NO, NO, NO! OF COURSE A HIGH LEVEL OF TOXICITY WOULD MAKE THE PATHOLOGY CONCLUSIVE! BUT WHAT ARE WE SAYING, THAT TWENTY-FIVE YEARS OF

EXPERIENCE COUNT FOR NOTHING? I MEAN THAT'S PATENTLY ABSURD!"

"Ohhhh God, please! I thought we'd got rid of him! Mr Megaphone! I thought he'd gone twenty minutes ago, and left us in peace!"

"Victor??" Margaret hissed across the table. "Will you keep your voice down."

"Keep *my* voice down? You're joking! And we can't even see where he's sitting!"

"WELL, THAT'S A POINT OF VIEW! BUT NOT ONE I HAPPEN TO SUBSCRIBE TO! THE HEPATIC CULTURE WOULD ESSENTIALLY BE REDUNDANT IF YOU'RE LOOKING AT A LIVER THE SIZE OF AN ORTHOPAEDIC MATTRESS! THAT'S NOT SUBJECTIVITY, IT'S EMPIRICALLY SUGGESTIVE – WITHOUT QUESTION!"

"Godddd spare us. So much for a nice quiet evening!"

"Just try not to let it bother you! Some people have got naturally loud voices. If you start getting worked up it'll only send your blood pressure sky high, and what good will that do. Just try and ignore it. And have another sip of wine."

Victor grudgingly drained his glass and poured another. It was a good thing they were getting a taxi home.

"WELL OF COURSE THAT'S NOT NECESSARILY TRUE! AND THAT ARGUMENT IS ESSENTIALLY FALLACIOUS! SO THE HISTOLOGY SUPPORTS THE HYPOTHESIS! BUT THESE ASSESSMENTS ARE NOT MUTUALLY EXCLUSIVE! THE INTUITIVE WILL ALWAYS HAVE A ROLE TO PLAY, ALONGSIDE THE DIAGNOSTIC! DO YOU HEAR WHAT I'M SAYING?"

"They're forecasting more rain tomorrow," said Margaret, in a futile attempt to change the subject. It was a tricky assignment at the best of times, defusing an unexploded husband. "Make it mucky on the farm for you again. I suppose that wedding ring must be pretty valuable. To have you out there every day, hunting about like that."

"Yes. I'm lucky he doesn't think it came off inside a cow, or I'd be up to my elbow in—"

"INCIDENTALLY! I CAN WELL RECALL, SOME YEARS AGO IN TALLAHASSEE, A YOUNG WOMAN, I THINK SHE WORKED IN REAL ESTATE, WHO WHILE BLOWING UP A BALLOON DREW IN TOO DEEP A BREATH, AND INHALED THE BALLOON! SO IT BECAME LODGED IN HER WINDPIPE, AND EVERY TIME SHE'D TRY TO SPEAK, SO THE BALLOON WOULD GO IN AND OUT, LIKE THE THROAT SAC OF A FROG! WHICH IN TURN MADE HER HYPERVENTILATE, CAUSING IT TO BE MISDIAGNOSED AS A GOITRE! HA! HA! HA! HA!"

"Right, I think we've had enough now haven't we."

"Victor!??"

Margaret made a grab but found herself clawing at thin air. Victor was already out of his chair and calmly marching away to locate the source of the problem.

"Ohhhh Godddd." She didn't like it when he was calm. It was flying in the face of nature.

The restaurant was quite a maze with one room branching off after another. And curiously the voice, as Victor approached its owner, did not grow any louder but continued to boom at the same peak volume.

"I REMEMBER I ONCE AUTOPSIED A HYPERTHYROID IN MIAMI! AND UNBEKNOWNST TO ME THE CORPSE HAD BEEN WEARING CONTACT LENSES! LATER ON I HAD OCCASION TO DISCIPLINE ONE OF MY INTERNS, WHO WAS THREATENING TO USE THEM AS DOG BOWLS! HA! HA! HA! HA!"

"Excuse me!"

Having squeezed past twenty tables and gatecrashed half a dozen selfies, Victor found himself addressing a plump, bearded gentleman with a pink bow tie and a pony tail. Extended backwards in his chair at forty-five degrees swilling a large brandy, there was more than an air of Bacchus about him, as he held court to three young wood nymphs. The wood nymphs, who had been rocking with laughter at his story, broke off and stared.

"IS THERE A PROBLEM, SIR?"

"Well, let's see."

From the Underworld

Reaching across the table Victor picked up a small oval container and held it to the light. "Well I'll be jiggered! I could have sworn someone had bugged this pepper pot and wired it up to a 300-watt PA system! But! My ears must have deceived me!" With a deadly glare he slammed it down again. "Why don't you try banging two dustbin lids together, that's another good one! I came to this restaurant for a nice relaxing meal with my wife, not to listen to *your* life story! For God's sake show some consideration for the rest of us, and *keep your bloody voice down*!!"

It was a good three hours before Victor got some feeling back in his nose. The bag of frozen peas had helped to reduce the swelling round his jaw, and by the time they went to bed his mouth was looking a lot less purple.

"Doesn't matter how many times I drum it into you," grumbled Margaret as she wound up the clock. "You won't be told. Carrying on all the while like Charles Bronson, picking fights with every Tom, Dick and Harry. What else did you expect?"

"I didn't expect those three women to attack me with a sodding bronze statue, for a start!" he fired back. "Didn't see *that* one coming, at all!" Flinching at the memory, he reached for a tissue as his eyes began to water all over again. "Worse than the men these days, once they've had a skinful! Don't know how they managed to pick it up! And this is how it is now, Margaret. So much as open your mouth to complain, you take your life in your hands."

"Only you could go out for the night and get whacked in the face by Buddha! One of these days you'll learn to leave well alone."

Victor switched off the light with a grunt.

Of course there was something in what she said, but that was only half the story. It wasn't all self-inflicted. Too many people now, turning too many blind eyes to all the crap in the world. Where was the public indignation and the moral support? Probably never there in the first place.

Half an hour went by but neither of them slept.

In her heart of hearts Margaret knew she was being harsh. It was partly the wine talking; but also a deeper pain, that she knew would crush her if she let it take hold. Attack was her only defence mechanism and those in the firing line are always the ones closest to you.

She thought she heard herself say "I'm sorry", but it was half-muffled by the duvet so she might have imagined it.

Through the gloom she could just make out the vase on their dressing table with the flowers that came that morning. As they had done every May 6th for the last forty years. Twelve red roses. "*From your loving husband*".

Words you could put on a card that felt awkward on the lips.

Margaret wriggled up slightly on her pillow, sensing the pair of eyes that were staring alongside her in the dark.

"You're not going to let that worry you?"

"Sorry?"

"All that stuff about the witch. I just thought you'd find it funny."

"Ohhhh no." Victor twisted sharply to head off some cramp in his leg. "Plenty more to worry about, besides that."

"Well exactly."

The reflective hush continued.

And then Margaret resumed.

"I was just thinking. About that first time."

"First time?"

"You and me."

"Oh. Yes."

"How can it be that long."

"I know."

"And yet, here we both are still."

"I know."

"Doesn't seem five minutes."

Clouds were breaking across the face of the moon, sending a silver glint through the curtains. And somewhere in the distance a car alarm stopped.

"Carol Hawksworth's engagement party. You remember?"

Victor yawned. Then frowned at her vaguely through drooping eyelids.

"At her mum's house in Glendale Gardens. Can see it all now as if it was yesterday. That first moment I walked in. Standing there by the record-player – this dashing young man with a head of thick, golden, wavy hair. I couldn't look at anyone else all night. Spent the entire evening just waiting to be introduced. The way you did in those days. Just smiling like an idiot across the room.

"And then just after midnight there was a power cut. D'you remember? We'd all had far too much to drink. And I just decided to take my chance. Just rushed across and grabbed your hand and dragged you outside into the garden. I remember it took you a hell of a while to get going. You spent half an hour with your hand inside my blouse, twiddling a dead wasp. And then … eventually we both relaxed into it and … well.

"Once we'd got our breath back we got up out of the lupins. Both dusted ourselves down and went back indoors. And when the lights came back on I just stood there gazing at you. And realised I'd grabbed hold of the wrong man. Gregory Birchall, the one with the thick wavy hair, was just leaving with that girl from the hat factory."

From the wistful pause came a sudden snort as Victor jerked his eyes open.

"Sorry?"

"Tchohhhh … go back to sleep."

"No, I heard you."

"What was I saying?"

"Katy Hawksmoor's birthday party. Not likely to have forgotten that."

Margaret sighed but let it go.

"I don't know. Just think it's funny, the way things turn out. How it's hardly ever your first choice you end up with. Or even your second or third. All the people you drive yourself mad about at one time or another. When you're that age. You realise in the end, none of them would have been right for you. So much more to it than just looks."

"Mmm …" Something in the noise he made caused her to swerve.

"Oh and I mean! Look at *you* – ending up with *me*. When you think of who else was around in those days! Ruthie Miles? And Susan Price? Everyone was after *her*. And Shirley Higgs. And that sister of hers, *they* were a pretty pair. Janice Montgomery … Polly … what-was-her-name …"

Her voice tailed off as their faces all drowned in the whirlpool of time.

"You were always my first choice."

"What?"

It was a simple declaration that landed like a stone.

"You've never said that before."

"No? Well …"

"Nnno … well." She did her best not to sound like a Christmas carol. "I suppose there's lots of things you never say. That you think about saying. And then never get round to."

"I suppose."

"In the course of forty years."

"Just human nature."

"And we're all the same."

Another pause.

"Did you put that bag of peas back in the freezer?"

"Yes."

"Might need it again in the morning."

"More than likely."

"Night night then."

"Night night."

Margaret turned over and slid down the bed.

"Happy anniversary."

"Happy anniversary."

There are certain things that no man ever wants to find, and that was one of them. Things you couldn't even show your wife, although Victor had immediately shown it to his. The minute he'd chanced upon it that morning in the bathroom he'd raced downstairs for the medical dictionary, trailing soap and water in his wake, hoping for some kind of reassurance.

All in vain of course.

There were half a dozen explanations listed, only one of which was sinister. But one was enough. To a card-carrying hypochondriac the rarest disease on earth was not rare enough. Fatal conditions as yet unknown to science would one day bear his name, of that much Victor was certain. There was no point pretending otherwise: this was serious.

How long it had been there he couldn't say; though had he been Jewish things might have been different.

Margaret just said it was a spot and would disappear of its own accord.

But what if it didn't? What if it wasn't a spot but that other word – that only doctors use when they want to scare the living daylights out of you.

A lesion.

For a brief, rash moment he'd considered the nuclear option: to see if it came off with Ajax. But certain past endeavours had soon brought him to his senses.

Nor could he take his mind off it when he got to the farm. The sight of an old parsnip, poking out of a sack and rotting away at one end, had caused his knees to buckle. And as he picked his way grimly through the mire for the fourth day running it was all he could do to stay focused.

A gale-force wind was tearing across the field with scant regard for health and safety, billowing the sides of his coat like sails. From high above a lone rook delivered a verdict on his cap before flying back to the *Guardian* features desk.

And that was another thing.

Why did she have to tell him all that yesterday about her dog? What it could sniff out and what it couldn't. Didn't need all that on top of everything else, thank you very much. Granted, he had stopped stressing about his "back end" just lately; ever since the scan last year, which had gone without a hitch. The magic words "clean as a whistle" – he'd been over the moon! Though not before weeks of worry about those positive test results.

And who did he have to thank for all *that* as it turned out?

Step forward Mrs Warboys again.

Calling round with that dollop of black pudding she'd brought back from Germany. Margaret had refused to touch the stuff and how wise she'd been. The very thought of it now made him sick.

The more he dwelt on it the more it made sense. If the wretched creature could detect one problem why not another? Why else would it make such a beeline for his flies? There was no telling what that nose might have picked up in the course of its research. It wasn't like you could call round to his dog basket for a consultation.

There was no avoiding it: he'd have to make an appointment with his GP. And that could take days or even weeks to come through.

"Having fun out there!"

"Sorry?!"

Two hundred yards away a cheery figure had paused at the roadside, with one foot on the ground and the other on his bicycle pedal. A country postman, just finished his round for the day, he probably meant well. But Victor was in no mood for chit-chat, especially at that distance.

"The farmer's wedding ring! Have you found it yet!"

"Ohhh! No! Not yet!"

"No, and you won't either! He's not married!"

The words took a second to carry on the wind, and a few seconds more to cut through the morbid abstractions that were clogging up Victor's brain.

"Yes well that would certainly expl— wh— what are you talking about?"

Screwing his eyes up, he could just about see, though barely hear, a merry little chortle in the distance.

"You can't be that daft! All the others had it twigged in five minutes!"

"I beg your pardon! What others!? What do you mean, had it twigged??"

This time the chuckle was louder and not at all reassuring, as the man returned to his saddle.

"You work it out!"

And off he cycled, whistling, down the road.

Victor watched him go with a mystified look made famous by Oliver Hardy. Some prankster trying to wind him up, the world was full of them. With a sad shake of his head he scraped the mud off his stick and got back to work.

"Mad. Totally mad."

*

Margaret plonked down her bag on the kitchen table and groaned. It had not been a good day from the off.

Settling down first thing with a bowl of cornflakes, she could have done without her husband padding naked into the room to ask if she wouldn't mind casting her eye over something. Prepared as she was to discuss such intimacies, there was a time and a place. However, compassion had won the day, and after a futile search for her reading glasses she'd taken him into the other room, where the light was better by the front window. The rules of farce decreeing, of course, that Mrs Aylesbury would at that minute be coming up the path to deliver an Oxfam leaflet. Whether she heard Margaret tell him to keep it still while she got a cushion to kneel on is not known. But in the field event of jumping to the wrong conclusions their neighbour held a Commonwealth record. And these things spread like wildfire, as Margaret well knew. The public's desire for unsubstantiated smut being one of the great pillars of our society; and the very lifeblood of a free press.

So it was, when she found herself in the post office queue that lunchtime, and caught the words "weird old sod down the road" from behind the partition, her ears immediately pricked up.

Though as it happened Mrs Aylesbury's report must have missed the morning deadline, for this was something much worse.

In hindsight her parcel could have waited another day or two at least. Not for the first time a dress she'd sent off for looked rather less cool without the Pixie Lott double inside, so she'd dashed straight round the corner to send it back.

And that's when she heard it.

The whole sorry story, related with much relish by one of the drivers stuffing his sack. The farmer's field, the wedding ring, the battered old lollipop man's coat. Pieces in a puzzle, she realised now, that had been bothering her for days.

And finally it made sense.

Though not the sort of sense her husband would take kindly to.

Ignorance was more than bliss sometimes, it was a necessity; especially where Victor Meldrew was concerned. Letting him too near the truth was akin to radiation exposure: it damaged him at a cytogenetic level, triggering an uncontrolled growth of misery. He had a hard enough time coping with all the horrors he knew about, so why burden him further?

But then again he would find out in the end. Far better surely for Margaret to do the honours, with more chance of a controlled explosion? No, no, in all conscience she would definitely have to tell him.

Perhaps with a stiff drink inside her, when he got back from the doctor's.

Victor was half way through sliding his trousers down when there was a tap on the door and a young man who looked a bit too much like Bela Lugosi in *Dracula* (1931) stepped into the room. Which is not to say he appeared wholly in black and white or wore a long flowing cape. But he was not someone you'd want to find leaning over your bed in the middle of the night.

"You've no objection to Lazlo joining us?" said Dr Trilling. "He's in his third year at medical college in Budapest, and over here for a month as part of the exchange programme with UCLH."

"We-ell, actually I'd rather he didn't, doctor, if you don't mind. I'm feeling nervous enough as it is. With the rather personal nature of it all. Obviously I don't want to be difficult but perhaps he could just wait outside till you've finished the physical examination?" thought Victor, while replying: "No of course not."

And lying back on his long strip of paper, he watched as the doctor peeled on a pair of thin blue gloves from a box on the wall and lowered the overhead lamp.

Thanks to a last-minute cancellation they'd managed to fit him in that evening, for which he was more than grateful. Arriving straight from his shift at the farm he'd done his best to freshen up in the toilets, and successfully disposed of several things that were still crawling about in his socks.

Trilling was not his regular doctor, who had been off work for six months suffering from the government's new health initiative. Technically retired, he was an affable sort with much of the old school about him, from his peppery manner and pince-nez spectacles to the small jar of leeches he was once said to keep on his desk. (Other accounts had these as blackcurrant wine gums.) And his gently seasoned approach would have surely put Victor at ease if it hadn't been for …

… who, having dragged his chair in close to peer over Trilling's shoulder, had begun jotting down notes with one of those pens that can write in four different colours, while the GP talked through his findings.

Words like prepuce and meatus and frenulum sailed right over Victor's head, back to their home in a dictionary of male reproductive organs on the far shelf. Then followed some scary mentions of squamous and basal cell morphology as Trilling completed the palpation and took out his dermatoscope. By which point Victor, much like the corpse in that Rembrandt painting, *The Anatomy Lesson of Dr Tulp*, had abandoned all hope.

"Well that looks pretty harmless to me," said Dr Trilling as he clicked off the light and began rinsing his hands. "Though I think we should have a urologist check you over. Just in case I've missed something."

Victor wasn't listening. His eyes had just strayed into Lazlo's lap, where it appeared the latter was now working on a drawing. Why this should make him uncomfortable he wasn't sure, though it may have been the way he was using all four inks; and kept holding up his thumb at arm's length towards Victor's groin.

"Mr Meldrew?"

"Hmm?"

"I say, I doubt very much there's anything to worry about. But just as a back-up we'll get it looked at by a specialist. I'll put the referral straight through and you shouldn't have long to wait. You can get dressed now."

"Oh! Thank you. Right."

With which he swung his legs off the bench, flashing a look at the artist, and smartly zipped himself up as if to say: "That's all you're getting today, matey!"

Lazlo responded with a polite smile.

Victor thanked the doctor again, and as he crossed the room to leave stole a final glance at the young man's notepad before it was flipped shut.

It was only for a second but that second was enough.

He could scarcely believe what he had seen.

"Don't be ridiculous."

"I am not being ridiculous!"

"It's just your paranoia."

"It is not my paran— I *know* what I *saw*."

Victor kicked off his shoes and crossed to the fridge for a cold beer. He needed something to steady him after the day he'd had. And it didn't help that his wife wasn't taking him seriously.

"I can see it now as plain as day. *He'd drawn a face on it!*"

"Why on earth would he do such a strange thing."

"You tell me! It was upside down but I could just make out two little eyes on a bald head, and a mouth, turned down at the sides to look miserabl— pardon?"

"I didn't say anything."

"It's not a matter for sniggering, Margaret!"

"Who's sniggering? A pound to a penny it's all in your imagination. And in any case, so what? People doodle. It's not a crime."

"I'll give him doodle. Could tell he was up for mischief the minute he came in and sat down. When the doctor asked if I'd like a chaperone and he said 'Perhaps he's already eaten.' His English isn't that bad, I know. Yes, this is Lazlo, from the department of haematology in Transylvania? He'll be gawping at all your most intimate body parts for the next ten minutes while I examine you. And you don't mind if Ant and Dec join us today for the public's phone vote? If you think Mr Meldrew's got lupus text 1571."

"Yes!! OK, you've made your point, it was all a bit awkward! And so what did he say, the doctor? Are we any the wiser?" There was only so much of this burble she could take before a fuse blew. It was bad enough she was about to add to his woes with that news of her own. Next to which the matter of whether he was going to live or die might turn out to be somewhat trivial.

"Yes, well. As far as he could tell it wasn't anything. But he thinks I should get it checked at the hospital to be on the safe side." Having shuffled off to the front room he collapsed with a swig of lager into his favourite armchair. "So now it's just a race against time, to see if they can fit me in before cockroaches take over the earth."

"Oh. Well. That's ... fairly encouraging then? And more or less what I said?" Meekly appearing in the doorway, she sized up her subject and decided she was pretty much good to go.

The medical crisis, for now, appeared to have passed. Check. He was sitting down. Check. That alcohol would soon be dulling his senses. Check. He was at a safe distance from any large breakable objects. Check.

"I erm ... popped into the post office at lunchtime," she began. "To send back that dress. It was quite busy and I had to wait for a while in the queue."

"Huh. Don't talk to me about post offices." Victor snapped shut his glasses case, ready to cast an eye over the local. "Had one of their lot playing silly buggers today while I was in the field. Trying to put the wind up me for some reason. I couldn't work out what his game was."

"Oh. Really? Yes, well. That might have been him that was talking behind the counter. They all seemed to be having a good laugh about something or other. And when I heard him mention Powdrill's farm, and this man who was out there looking for a ring, naturally I began to pay attention."

Victor's gaze rose slowly from whatever drivel he was reading to zero in on Margaret, who for some reason chose to avoid his eyes in favour of the tea towel she was nervously twisting in her hands. Wherever this was going he knew he wasn't going to like it.

"And anyway. The long and the short of it. This chap, Rob – or was it Ron? I *think* he was called Ron – he and your Mr Powdrill, apparently, are quite good friends. It seems they play golf together and all sorts and – oh, Roy! That was it, Roy! So obviously that's why he was in the know, this Roy, about the whole thing and—"

"*Margaret?*"

"Yes! Right. And so as it turns out, the actual reason … he's been making you go out there every day in that big white coat – which, you know how you said? Hasn't got any buttons so it keeps flapping about all the time? Was in actual fact, according to him, because …"

Would her nerve desert her, at the eleventh hour?

"Was because …"

No, best to just go for it. Like tearing off a sticking plaster.

"He was using you as a scarecrow."

It began with a strange gibbering noise, that quickly petered out to make way for a goldfish-like motion of the lips, from which no sound came. Finally, as if a kink had been removed from his windpipe, a breathless tirade was expelled, the specifics of which need not be recorded here. Suffice to state this news was not well received.

"Oh well that's just *perfect* isn't it! Absolutely perfect! Four sodding days! Slopping about in all that crap, freezing to death! And that's what it was all about? Thank you for that, Margaret. Thank you very much indeed!"

"And I mean, I could hardly not tell you?" Margaret took a step forward, to risk a kindly look. "Said the old wooden ones don't work any more apparently. The rooks just fly down and perch on the arms. And obviously he didn't spell that out to people, for fear of putting them off. Which you can understand."

Victor didn't look as if he understood.

"Anyway. Time's getting on, so … better start thinking about some food I suppose – oh. Who's that going to be?"

In the hall the phone was ringing.

"Toffee-nosed bastard! So that's all I'm fit for now is it, frightening away the birds?" Discarding his beer, he took a glass from the sideboard and unstoppered the whiskey bottle. And to hell with the ice this time. "I mean that has to be my best career move yet, doesn't it! I always said that postgraduate course I did at Wurzel Gummidge College Oxford would pay off in time! That just about puts the tin lid on it. The end to a perfect day!"

Well, not quite.

A minute later, Margaret was back in the room with the unmistakable look of one who has just received bad news.

"Good news?"

"Aunty Ursula's died."

"Oh dear."

"That was her solicitor, he'd only just managed to get hold of our number."

"Poor old soul, was it sudden?"

"Struck by lightning in the middle of *Hairy Bikers*. Wednesday night, during that big storm. Said she'd just got up to put an egg on for her tea and that's when it hit her, straight through the fanlight. Neighbour came in and found her lying flat on the floor with the egg frying on her forehead."

"Tch. Must have been well into her eighties. But still."

"There'll be all that stuff to clear out now. In that big house of hers out in the country. I suppose it'll be down to us, she didn't have any other close relatives."

"One more thing to worry about. As if we haven't got enough on our plates at the moment. Having to trek all the way up to Yorkshire. Still – least we can do, I suppose …"

With a resigned grunt he tossed down the paper and rose from his chair. That glass of single malt was just beginning to do its job: numbing his nerves and muting his spleen; and warping the world to make life seem almost liveable.

It was not to last.

Somewhere – let us call it Under The Rainbow – demons lie. A whole platoon of devils personally assigned to Victor Meldrew with a brief to give him the screaming abdabs. And though already in good voice those abdabs were still a long way from fever pitch.

Victor left the room to hang up his coat in the hall.

As he did so a ghastly visage arose like a revenant from deep in his past, where it had long been slumbering, and stopped him in his tracks.

"Ohhhhh God …"

"Ohhhhh God …"

Margaret had seen it too.

From the kitchen she reappeared, haltingly. Her eyes in a glaze, focused on a faraway phantom that had suddenly returned to haunt them both.

"*Edwin ...*"

Chapter Two
The Death of Truth

To Patrick's ear, Marsh and Barber sounded more like the latest trend among Premiership footballers than a firm of estate agents. But what the hell, their credentials were sound, their rates competitive, and the staff on their website had impeccable teeth. (The result, one presumes, of regular airbrushing three times a day.) Their standards were exacting and progressive; and they had just announced an exciting new raft of workplace offences, with one man already suspended for making an inappropriate sandwich. In short they appeared to have the market at their mercy. So Marsh and Barber it was.

The decision to move was long overdue.

Pippa had been the stumbling block; arguing that things were bound to settle if they only gave it time. There was nothing wrong with the house itself. And could they be bothered with all that upheaval?

But gradually Patrick had worn her down. Through a mixture of gentle persuasion and stress-induced hair loss he had finally won the day, and convinced her it was time to move on.

Three years teetering on the event horizon of 19 Riverbank was enough for anyone. Just to place your ear against the kitchen wall was to journey to the very edge of the rational universe. Beyond lay a world so far removed from reality, even Richard Branson's new quantum tunnelling service, scheduled for spring 2025, would be hard put to cope.

Quite why their new neighbour had attempted to frogmarch them into his bedroom that night when they first popped round to say hallo was beyond Patrick's comprehension. Likewise the disappearance of his ginseng capsules, which had subsequently turned up in Meldrew's rectum. Here was a man who thought nothing of filling his house and front garden with lurid-looking gnomes, or smuggling a live boa constrictor onto a plane in order to cause panic and mayhem among its passengers. And while ever more fanciful tales would be trotted out to explain these events Patrick was having none of it: he knew a sociopath when he saw one.

"So it's Mr and Mrs Trench, is it? Welcome to Marsh and Barber? We spoke on the phone? My name's Derek? I'm one of the senior sales managers? And you're looking to put your property on the market with us? A modern three-bedroom end of terrace? Nohhhh problem."

The man who welcomed them was in his early fifties, but no one seemed to have told him. His grey lacquered hair was carved into tiny peaks like an Artex ceiling, and the gold ring through his left ear vied for attention with a glass eye. Tragically, he suffered from Idiopathic Modern Cadence Disorder (IMCD); though not as much as those who had to listen to it.

"So just booting up the system? Can I get you a cup of tea or anything?"

Patrick and Pippa said that would be nice, and were promptly handed two cups of anything.

"Nohhhh problem. So these are some of the contracts we've recently closed? In your own area? To give you an idea of the purchase price we'd be looking at? Subject to the current volatilities of the market?"

Patrick and Pippa studied the printout and found the figures all met with their approval.

As luck would have it, they had recently stumbled on a grade II listed Catholic bishop who was downsizing to a cell in Parkhurst; and whose cottage, they felt, would suit them perfectly. With the recent boost to their income from Patrick's promotion it was all looking very affordable. Yes, they said, they were more than happy to proceed on this basis.

"Nohhhh problem," said Derek. "So if we could all get our diaries out? And come up with a time when it's convenient for yourselves for me to pop round? And just to make you aware of one or two legal obligations at this time? That you are now, as vendors, required to disclose any factors that could be deemed to have an adverse effect on the sale? No hidden defects you're aware of? Or outstanding planning issues? No long-running disputes with neighbours, or problems or conflicts in that area that might be construed as disruptive?"

Without the ghost of a pause Patrick and Pippa said nothing. Then turned to each other, then turned back to Derek, then both shook their heads with a smile.

Derek smiled back and began tapping his keyboard.

"Nohhhh problem."

And so, having taken the plunge, they sat back and waited. Derek had told them not to expect too much too soon? It was a slow time of year? And things would gradually pick up?

The main thing was, they had got the ball rolling. And the very sight of that board on his front lawn gave Patrick a curious peace of mind. It was a cry for help and a declaration of independence rolled into one. As he'd watched the man hammer in the post a thrilling vision of Dr Van Helsing was evoked; and he had dared to contemplate, for the first time, an end to his darkest days.

"Hey, this looks interesting!"

It was half past eight on a Tuesday morning. And having completed the inspection of his new moustache in the bathroom mirror Patrick turned at the sound of his wife bouncing upstairs. Whatever Pippa had just found in the mail she was anxious to share it.

"Have a listen to this! It's from Mr Hithercroft. You remember, that old bloke with the monocle who came last week? He says: Thank you so much for showing me round your beautiful home on Thursday. It is a truly delightful property, and I would love to arrange a return visit to inspect it more closely."

With a look of elfin glee she flapped the small square of paper in the air and took another slurp of coffee.

"You will not be surprised to learn I am of a generation that has yet to embrace the smartphone or the modern convention of digital cameras. However, I possess an excellent Rolleiflex SL35 still in perfect working order. And I trust you would have no objection were I to bring this along when I next call, as I am keen to take some photographs of you in the nude …"

The elfin glee began to dribble away as she read on …

"I have an extensive collection of World War One gas masks … which if you are agreeable I would propose t— oh dear. I think I feel sick."

Her face had indeed turned a pasty colour. And there was a moment's silence while she returned to earth from cloud nine.

"Mmm. Sounds quite promising then?"

"I *beg* your pardon??!" Impressively hitting a top C, she could only stare as he returned to the bedroom and began lacing his shoes. "Sounds quite *promising*?"

"Well, it's only a bit of fun presumably. And it might make sense to play along. In case he's serious. I mean, we are desperate."

"We're not *that* bloody desperate!" Pippa thrust the offending document into his lap. "And in any case, it's addressed to *you*!"

"W— oh. Really?"

Fast-forwarding through the author's shaky hand, he got as far as the words 'rub each other's thighs with Swarfega' and could take no more.

"Yes, well. Probably not then." Screwing the letter into a ball he reached for his jacket. "Actually, I'd better be getting along. That's if I can find my watch – where the hell did I p— ah! Right under my nose! Isn't it always."

"*Tell me about it.*"

The words came out like a firecracker. With a gist that would be obvious to a five-year-old but was utterly lost on her husband. Certain topics in their house had not been recently broached, and facial grooming was one of them. For best effect she preferred to smoulder in silence.

"Sorry?"

"Yes you're right, come on, chop chop! Mustn't keep her waiting. That would *never* do!"

"Keep her waiting?"

What was going on here?

There seemed to be more and more of this nonsense just lately, but what it all meant was a mystery. It appeared to have started just after the big reshuffle at work. Yet why should all that have upset her? He'd been given a role with a lot more responsibility and a generous pay hike to boot. For the first time in his career he had his own office. His own secretary. His own parking space. His own secretary …

Had he said that once?

No, it was all beyond him as usual.

"Sorry, can I ask who we're talking about here … exactly …"

"Yes, what was her name again? Oh damn! I nearly had her then on the tip of my tongue. But then who hasn't. Carillion is it …?"

"Carillion?? If you mean Carolyn—"

"*Carolyn*! I was almost right. Big firm bust? And where are you taking her for lunch today, somewhere nice?"

"Well I don't know, I suppose we might grab a quick bite in the pub or …"

"Oh yes? Didn't know she was old enough to go in pubs."

The sweetness in her smile was growing dangerously cloying.

"Old enough to be a fan of Ronald Colman though, at any rate?"

"Ronald Colman??"

This was verging on the surreal. Probably all that hormonal choppiness she was prone to on occasion. To most men it would smack of hostility, but Patrick knew better. It was a source of pride that he understood these female phases and how to cope with them. The trick was to just wait and let it all blow over.

"Anyway, look. I need to be off, so …"

Pippa endured his goodbye with a stoic grunt. It was like being kissed by a cheese grater.

"And I'll see you tonight."

"It's possible."

Victor did not have long to wait for his referral to come through.

He had expected to hear nothing before Christmas. Consequently, when it did arrive, bearing the words "This is not a circular", he had tossed it straight in the bin assuming it to be a circular.

An appointment had been made for him at the hospital for Monday June 1st, where he would be seen by Mr Huffenfeffer or a member of his team. As usual he was asked to bring a fresh sample of urine. Like they hadn't had enough from his bladder by now to irrigate the Gobi Des—

Hang on, Monday June 1st? That was next week! Trilling had said he wouldn't have to wait long but this was unusually prompt.

Was that a good sign or a bad sign?

Surely a good sign. It showed the NHS was through the worst of its backlogs and serving the nation as it was meant to. Terminally ill patients were now waiting less than a week to be treated to a barrage of wilfully skewed data; and the survival rate among clueless secretaries of state was the highest in Europe. Greater efficiency was the order of the day and that was something to celebrate.

Or was it?

Why would they have moved so quickly in Victor's case? When Trilling said it all looked fine, what was he keeping back? If it all looked fine where was the urgency? With a thrill of terror Victor imagined his details being rushed across town to this man Huffenfeffer, who had taken one look at his file and put the hospital chaplain on stand-by.

And so it was, when the appointed day rolled round he found himself in the building's spanking old urogenital unit, prepared for the worst.

The tiny side room was bare and functional, with off-grey walls and a fanlight window through which cigarette smoke was wafting from people outside smoking next to a "No Smoking" sign. Some of the paintwork was beginning to peel and a body had been left lying on the bed in the corner. Just above the washbasin was a notice about a prostate support group, with a photo of five elderly men laughing uncontrollably.

The body belonged to Victor Meldrew.

Having undressed and put on his thin cotton gown he had been waiting there now for thirty-two minutes; fretting all over again about what they would find and what could be done about it. He was just studying an extremely thin, long tube that was hanging up in coils, and considering making a run for it, when the door finally opened and a voice said:

"Mr Meldrew. So sorry to have kept you."

The man was younger than expected. Early forties at a guess, with a large square frame and soft features. Hair was dispensed with entirely, in the modern fashion, and he wore a trim white top that buttoned up the back. He was just finishing a custard cream.

"A very heavy clinic out there today, I'm afraid. Two consultants on holiday and one just fallen sick. It creates quite a bottleneck."

"Oh dear."

"I'll be with you in two ticks."

"Yes. Right. Thanks."

Victor began to breathe more easily. Even when the stretchy blue gloves came out, and his gown was drawn gently back, he found the breezy manner quite reassuring.

"My ... GP didn't seem to think it was erm ... but obviously ... you'll want to er ... so I don't know if— Anyway."

Lifting his head from the bed he found he was wittering away to no one, as the gentleman had disappeared. A second later he returned wheeling a trolley.

"Here we go then, Mr Meldrew. This won't take more than a minute. If you want to just lie back and relax."

"Oh right, fine. What won't take more than a minute?"

Having closed his eyes he reopened them, at the sensation of something cold and frothy on his skin. And looking down he discovered his genitals had vanished beneath a sea of white foam.

"Did they not explain the procedures that are being carried out today?"

Somewhere inside the foam he felt it quiver. Procedure on its own was bad enough. Procedures in the plural didn't bear thinking about.

"No? They didn't explain a thing. The nurse just said to lie here and wait. Didn't say anything about procedures. What procedures?"

"Well, I couldn't exactly say, Mr Meldrew. Whatever Mr Huffenfeffer decides is appropriate. He'll need to investigate the whole area. Which may involve a few biopsies, depending on what he finds. But it does mean I need to shave you before he can go ahead."

Returning an aerosol can to his trolley he unfolded a small cut-throat razor and began honing it on a leather strop.

"Ohhh. Right, I see. Yes, sorry. For some reason, I thought *you* were erm—"

"Oh! No, no, no. My name's Brad, I'm just one of the orderlies. The doctor will see you when I've finished."

"Uh-huh."

It would be an exaggeration to say Victor settled back. Does a beetroot settle back when it's about to be peeled? But if ever there was a time to hang loose, he decided, this was it. As Brad set to work, with slow, careful, sweeping strokes, Victor tried to uncurl his toes and not think about sneezing.

"Just like being at the hairdresser's isn't it."

"Well, now you come to mention it – no. I don't know what sort of hairdresser *you* go to."

Brad paused for a second to wipe the blade on a paper towel before resuming.

"Yes, we've come a long way in the last hundred years, when you think of it."

"Hmm? Yes I suppose."

"Modern technology. My God."

"I know."

"Mass communication. Artificial intelligence."

"Oh yes."

"And men on the moon! We take it for granted now."

"Well that's true."

"I was up there myself last week."

"I imagine. Pardon?"

"And I tell you this much. It's a scandal now, the property prices. Don't talk to me about the Dark Side! They must take us all for mugs. Don't you reckon?"

"Yyyy— erm …" All that came out was a croak.

"They call it a space programme but there's not enough space. Nice little studio flat I picked up in '98 on the edge of the Plutarch crater? Fifty Lunar K! Well you couldn't get a bucket of Buzz Aldrin's piss for that now."

"No?"

"The *Mail* have been running a big campaign this week, I suppose it must affect a lot of their readers."

"*Himmm!? Ihhh expect.*"

Reviewing his imminent prospects, Victor went from croak to castrato. While Brad continued, with the air of someone carving a Sunday roast. Until …

Was that the sound of the door creeping open?

It surely was.

A woman in dark blue livery was peeking into the room. Her voice barely audible above Victor's heartbeat.

"Mr Meldrew?"

"Ye-es …?"

"Don't make any sudden moves …"

A redundant piece of advice if ever there was one; as softly she approached the bed. She was slender but steady, and her face spoke of experience and understanding. Behind her was a tall male nurse who looked as if he could be handy when the occasion required.

"Now then, Dennis. If you just want to put down that razor? Do we think that would be a good idea?"

"I've almost finished him now, sister."

"Yes and well done you! In fact I'm thinking that's probably all we need for today? So why don't you pop along now with Oliver and he'll get you a nice cup of tea."

"Erm? Well … all right then. If you're sure?"

With a firm but silken touch Oliver had already disarmed him, and Dennis and his trolley were escorted from the room.

Victor watched them go and unclenched his buttocks.

"Sorry about that, Mr Meldrew," said the sister as she turned to follow them. "The doctor *will* be with you shortly."

"Oh! Right. Thanks."

There was a long hiss of air as if someone had just punctured his lungs. Cupping both his hands he reassured himself everything was still present. Then smoothed down his gown and let out another sigh. Then he gazed at the ceiling, and through the ceiling, and beyond to whatever was up there, and gave thanks. After all this at least he could cope with anything.

Anything?

The door, which the sister had left ajar, was pushed open again and at long last Mr Huffenfeffer appeared. Causing Victor's eyes to spring from their sockets. Really and truly, he hadn't imagined things could get any worse that morning.

But they just had.

All was going well in the land of Integrated Logistics. (Whatever the hell *that* was when it was at home.) And no one could say Patrick hadn't adjusted to his new job as senior creative strategist for digital outreach tasked with the development of day-to-day content analysis and optimising goals for a more streamlined approach to client procurement across interrelated web platforms. At least not without taking a very deep breath.

The work was stimulating, in the way that crunching data on a screen all day long till you're spitting pixels is stimulating. But as previously noted it was not without its attractions.

One of which was currently seated next to him in the Horse and Groom, undoing another button of her blouse as she finished a bottle of mineral water. Those chicken and mango dhansaks had packed quite a punch.

"Phew, I'm hot …"

Patrick was inclined to agree, but let's not go there.

His PA was mature for her years, in mind and body. Beneath the stack of red hair it was all good: from the bright saucer eyes and retroussé nose to the rich flexible lips. If her ample young figure seemed to reference the work of Russ Meyer then shame on you. Crucially, she was sharp and efficient and nobody's fool. And though we should avoid the words warm, bubbly and spontaneous when describing anything but cat spittle, it's fair to say Carolyn Walker had more than your average share of self-assurance.

Yet today she was looking distracted as she scanned the room for an escape route.

"Could we … d'you think, go outside for a bit? And get some fresh air?"

"Yes, no, absolutely. I was just thinking the same thing."

He didn't believe himself. Or her for that matter. The way she'd been constantly twitching and failing to laugh at his jokes had led him to suspect some kind of urinary infection. But her darting eyes betrayed a deeper unease. And as he followed her outside it was clear that something was brewing.

They parked themselves beneath a drooping willow at the far end of the garden where privacy was assured. The hint of a breeze sent ripples through her skirt as she blew her nose on something that used to be a tissue. And Patrick took a long swig of beer to give her some space.

Finally she found her voice.

"No, the thing is, Mr Trench. Oh God, this is gonna sound so naff and girly, it's just … when I feel strongly about a person I've got to say something. You know? I mean you try and bottle up your emotions, what good does it do?"

"Well, I suppose, erm …" Now it was his turn to feel uncomfortable. The passion in her eyes was dangerously exhilarating.

"I mean. I know you're a married man, right?"

There was no point denying it. And why break her flow?

"And obviously I'm living with this guy. I think I told you – Melvin, he works at the ball-bearing. Well. Things have been, how shall I say, a bit rubbish there now for a while. He's been seeing other women, I know that for a fact. Which is just not on, you know?"

"Of course not. No."

"So I'm like hallo? Excuse me, Mel! You want to play that game? It so happens I've got needs in that department as well? I'm only human."

"Well yes … certainly you are …" He gave her what he hoped was a look of benign empathy but came over as an impression of Mao Tse-tung.

"So anyway. To get to the point, Mr Trench … I don't know if I can say it, you'll just take me for a mad person."

"No, no, Carolyn. Not at all. You need to get these things off your chest."

"I know, well. OK. The thing is, I told him, right. The two of us – you and me – were sleeping together. I mean, not sleeping, you know: doing it together. Every night after work in the stationery cupboard."

She was right. He did take her for a mad person.

"In the stationery cupboard? How could you do such a thing?"

"Well, just spread some Jiffy bags on the floor I guess, then we'd both get down and—"

"I mean how could you even suggest it?"

"I know, it's insane! With someone your age? It's *sick*. I know that obviously, but I just wanted to make him jealous that's all. That's all it was. I never thought he'd take it *that* seriously. To say he was gonna kill you."

The spray of Adnams bitter from across the table missed her by millimetres.

"He said *what*??"

"Oh it's all talk with him, don't worry! He's never killed anyone in his life."

"Oh! Good!"

"Not … killed them exactly. I mean he wasn't all that violent before they put him away the first time. Trouble with going to prison, you learn bad habits. And obviously I've told him now it was all a wind-up, but talk about banging your head against a brick wall? So now he's like, I ever see this piece of shit, I swear he's croaked! And I mean it's good in one way, don't get me wrong. It's like he's realised he can't take me for granted? And so we've both agreed we're gonna write off each other's debts, which means we're all square again, but … no, as I say. I wouldn't take him literally, he says all this stuff! Then never puts his money where his mouth is, that's half his trouble."

And thus was Patrick completely comforted by her reassuring words in no sense whatever … as he met her gaze with the waxen face of a cadaver.

Carolyn smiled a helpless smile.

"I know. It's a bit of a mess really. Suppose I could've handled it better but anyway. I thought it was best you knew." Then, with a glance at her watch she rose from the chair. "Ouch. Twenty past two. And you've got that meeting at half past? We should be getting back."

Pippa tapped politely on the back door with her nose and waited.

There was no response so she tapped again. Harder this time with the side of her head, like a budgie ringing its bell.

And still there was no sign of life in the Meldrews' kitchen.

The giant terracotta plant pot she was clutching had been a pain to lift up in the first place and she was in no rush to repeat the experience. There were few enough Pippas to the pound and this thing weighed a ton.

So she waited a bit longer until finally Margaret appeared from the hall.

"Ohhh sorry, Pippa! Sorry, I was just on the phone! Here, let me give you a hand with that. My God, when you said cactus I was expecting – well I don't know what I was expecting."

"Something a bit smaller?"

Pippa grinned as together they shuffled across the floor and plonked the object down in the corner; giving Victor's slippers no time to escape. Pippa took a minute to get her breath while her friend inspected the item in question. It was a good two feet tall but appeared to have seen better days.

"I know, 'cos the saguaros in Arizona grow like trees. This one's still a baby. Twenty years from a packet of seeds but … I dunno, it's not been looking too clever just lately. And if this house move ever comes off I don't give much for its chances. I just thought maybe with your magic touch?"

"Hoh! Well. I don't know about that." Margaret circled the pot and snapped off a few wilting spines. "I'm tempted to say one prickly specimen's enough in this house, but I'll give it a go. Can I get you a cup of tea?"

"I'd love to but I don't know where the time's gone today. I've been online all morning, trying to sort out this wretched christening present for our niece. Think I'm losing the will to live."

"Oh, because your sister's got this thing about vintage toys."

"Well they're antique mad the pair of them. And I tell you, I won't be using eBay again. After that 'genuine Victorian dolls house' made in South Korea. Patrick said we should just keep it and stick a few children up the chimn— sorry, is something the matter, Margaret? You don't seem yourself today."

"Hmm? Oh! Oh, no. Sorry, it's just …"

She couldn't disguise it. The sunken tone and fretful undertow. Her attention was all over the place.

"Just before you came I was talking to a witch."

"Oh God. What, not that bloke in the sweet shop. Who puts sticks of liquorice out in the sign of the pentagram?"

Margaret bit her lip and nodded.

"Goes out with a sister of Satan from the job centre. Well, I ran into him a couple of weeks ago. He said he could tell the future if I wanted, for five pounds so … I just went along with it, as you do. He told me I'd live a long and peaceful life and Victor would come to a sticky end."

"Oh dear."

"I know. If you've ever heard such twaddle. But then, what with one thing and another just lately – I won't bore you with the details. You know how these things prey on your mind."

"It's only natural."

"So yesterday, I'd had a glass of wine, I rang him up. To see if he could be more specific. He said he was busy with an order of Belgian truffles but he'd sacrifice a goat and get back to me. I said oh no, no, not on my account!"

"God, you don't want that! So what happened."

"He said he'd see what he could do with a mummified frog. Anyway, that was him just now. Calling back with a warning. Under no circumstances should Victor go on any long journeys. Because that's when it could happen."

"When … what could happen?"

Margaret shrugged her shoulders. "And now I'm all at sixes and sevens. I mean what the hell am I doing, Pippa, in the first place? Listening to all this tommyrot? We both know it's ridiculous."

"They just like to play on your fears these people."

"Well exactly."

"You believe all that stuff you'll believe anything."

The two of them shared a thin dismissive laugh. Which died a bit too quickly.

"He's *not* going on any long journeys is he?"

"Well that's the thing. He did talk about driving up to Yorkshire next week, to my aunt Ursula's. You remember, the one who's just died. We've got a huge great houseful of junk to dispose of there now somehow or other. All her documents and papers to sort through. All her late husband's clutter from his travels round the world. And that's not to even mention …"

Flopping into a chair at the table she took a long slug of cold mint tea and braced herself.

"… the dreaded Edwin."

Pippa sat down beside her, and although she knew she'd regret it asked anyway:

"Who's Edwin?"

It was nothing that Mr Huffenfeffer said or did when he came into the room that made Victor jump.

His movements were calm, studied and businesslike. As he closed the door he threw a brief smile at his patient. Then switched on the computer to check something. Then took off his spectacles and changed them for a pair that looked identical.

None of which of itself led Victor to pray for a very large sinkhole to appear in the floor and put an end to his misery.

For a few glorious minutes after his previous ordeal he had allowed his guard to drop and begun to breathe normally. The sheen on that cut-throat razor, going about its business between his legs, would very likely haunt him forever. But he had at least come through it unscathed.

And yet … what was that phrase he'd adopted many years ago as his personal mantra – the soddishness of circumstance?

And here it was again made flesh.

"GOOD MORNING MR MELDREW! MY NAME'S HUFFENFEFFER! ROGER HUFFENFEFFER, ONE OF THE SENIOR CONSULTANTS IN THE GENITO-URINARY DEPARTMENT! I HAVE A FEELING WE'VE PREVIOUSLY MET?"

Victor had the same feeling.

"Erm. Yyy— I think, yes. A few weeks ago. There was a rather unfortun—"

"THE BANH HO MINH, IF I CORRECTLY RECALL! IT DIDN'T END WELL! AN UNFORTUNATE CONTRETEMPS WITH MY THREE STEPDAUGHTERS! THEIR BEHAVIOUR WAS UNCONSCIONABLE! FOR WHICH I APOLOGISE!"

"Oh. Yes. Well, I suppose I did say one or two things that were—"

"THE INTERRUPTION JUST NOW WAS EQUALLY REGRETTABLE! THOUGH THANKFULLY RARE! PROVISION AND CARE FOR THE MENTALLY ILL WILL NEVER ADVANCE IN THIS COUNTRY UNTIL WE REASSESS OUR PRIORITIES! THAT A FUNCTIONING SERVICE OF ANY KIND SURVIVES WITHIN OUR CURRENT POLITICAL STRICTURES IS ENTIRELY DOWN TO A LOYAL WORKFORCE OF DEDICATED PROFESSIONALS! AND THAT'S ALL ABSOLUTELY FINE! I'LL LET YOU GET ON WITH YOUR DAY!"

"I know. It's dreadful the way no one seems t— Sorry?"

To his astonishment Victor realised the examination was over. The nimble finger work and flash of a practised eye were so skilful and fleeting they had barely registered. Huffenfeffer was already back at the washbasin.

"NO ABNORMALITIES ARE INDICATED, OR ULCERATION IN THE GLANS! CONTINUE TO MONITOR FOR ANY CHANGE IN SIZE OR APPEARANCE, OTHERWISE I CONCUR ENTIRELY WITH DR TRILLING! YOU'LL FIND IT SETTLES IN A MATTER OF WEEKS! THERE SHOULD BE NO NEED TO SEE ME AGAIN! THANK YOU FOR YOUR PATIENCE TODAY! GOODBYE!"

"Umm. Right, yes, thank you. Goodbye."

Had it not been for a nagging subclinical hernia, staff and patients might well have been treated to the sight of Victor Meldrew skipping up and down the corridor as he left the room.

How easy it was to presume! How tempting to dwell in illusions. Reality rarely toed the line, but this was an unforeseen reprieve from a most unlikely quarter. And it showed you couldn't judge a book by its pink bow tie and loud grating voice.

For the moment at least Victor's raison d'être was restored to its factory settings. Whisper it quietly, he'd begun to feel happy.

So happy that half an hour later he was being arrested for an act of gross indecency in the middle of the hospital car park.

The next few paragraphs contain scenes that some readers may find disturbing, and will therefore not want to miss. The details remain sketchy and given their unsavoury nature that may be a good thing.

Margaret, when she heard about it, had to go upstairs and lie down. And even when her husband was released without charge after questioning it was a while before she recovered the power of speech.

"*Tell – me* – I'm imagining this, it's all some horrible dream ..."

Victor was barely through the back door when the inquisition began. Nose to nose across the kitchen table. It only needed an anglepoise lamp shining in his face. Whatever his wife had heard from the police she was demanding to hear all over again.

"Look, it wasn't my fault. I suppose they've told you that – I was—"

"*DON'T!* Even say the word, Victor! The whole thing is – just—"

"I was trying to do a good thing, Margaret. You can see that? I don't know why it's always me that's in the wrong."

Margaret gritted her teeth. She just prayed her nerves were strong enough to stay the course.

"So let's run through it all again, shall we? You'd finished with the doctor. Which had gone well. You were on your way back to the car ..."

"And I was just passing the entrance to that fertility clinic, when one of the nurses came out and asked if I'd got a minute. Then she started talking about all the work they did, for couples who couldn't have children, and how many of them relied on IVF treatment, as their only hope for—"

"Justtt—! Can we pause it there for a second? You say a nurse came up to you. And you knew she was a nurse because?"

"Well, she had a nurse's uniform on."

"Rrright. And anything else about her? How tall was she?"

"Well— quite tall."

"Six foot?"

"Yy— maybe a bit more, but there was nothing unusual in that in itself."

"Not in itself, no, and nothing *else* unusual that you noticed?"

"Well the dress was a bit short, I'll grant you, and a bit tight but … look, at that stage how was I supposed t—"

"The fact that she had a *beard* … didn't strike any chords at all."

"Yes well that's not the sort of thing you can ask about nowadays is it? She might have started screaming at me. Or reported me or anything."

"*Fine*. So this six-foot-tall bearded person, built like a rugby player in a nurse's dress, is telling you all about IVF treatment and then what?"

"Well then she held up this yellow plastic bucket. With a big slot in the lid. And said they desperately needed donations."

"Donations."

"And would I be prepared to contribute."

With her elbows propped on the table Margaret let her forehead sink into her hands. This was a scenario conceived in Hell.

"I said, what – *now*? She said well, it would make such a big difference to people's lives. Talk about putting you on the spot! I didn't know what to do for the best. I said it wasn't really something I could manage at that minute. So she said there was always a bank I could use, around the corner, if I w—"

"A *bank*."

"I mean what else was I supposed to do? After everything else this morning. You want to try and give something back? So I walked round to where this big vehicle was parked. With NHS IVF on the side. And I knocked on the back doors, and when there was no answer I just climbed inside and …"

"Godddd spare us! And *still* the idea never occurred to you?"

"Well – n— but I didn't—"

"The idea of these junior doctors, all dressing up for the day to raise money for some new equipm— as they do every year? I mean, you must have *realised*, for God's sake??"

"Well it's easy to be wise after the event!"

By this time she was close to imploding.

"So you're inside this van and then what? What was in there?"

"I don't know, lots of bits and pieces. Medical paraphernalia. A big pile of leaflets. And another one of those yellow buckets with a big slit in the top."

(Readers who can see where this is going may prefer to call a halt at this point and seek counselling.)

"I mean we all make mistakes, Margaret! You don't expect some woman to just suddenly open the door like that and look inside? I assumed they all knew I was in there. And besides which, I hadn't exactly got anywhere. I mean all she would have seen was—"

"*Yesss!!* Thank you, Victor! We don't need to go into pornographic detail! I think I've heard more than enough!"

It was all too grisly to contemplate.

"How even your bizarre brain could imagine they wanted you t— Rrrghh!" She was on her feet now, and looking seriously queasy as she headed upstairs. "I shall have to go and wash out my ears with Dettol, listening to that sorry tale!"

Victor sighed as he watched her go. Then rose from the table, with a curious glance at a very large cactus that was now standing in the corner, and set about preparing some beans on toast.

"Bloody junior doctors."

And what the hell had she done with his slippers?

The glorious summer of Victor's all-clear from the hospital was followed by a week of nuclear winter. And how could it be otherwise? Not for the first time an innocent misunderstanding had ballooned up out of all proportion into a hanging offence.

And yet.

Why should he take all the blame? Granted the invitation was unusual for a man of his age. But hadn't they stressed how desperately it was needed? When people talk about a "bank", right outside a fertility clinic, you don't imagine they mean Lloyds or Barclays! And as for that other: it wasn't for *him* to judge a person by her beard, or her shaved head, or her Adam's apple. That sort of thinking belonged to another age. Victor's conscience was clear: he'd behaved like a model citizen. People should learn to be a bit clearer.

Unsurprisingly Margaret took a different view.

Wherever she went, to the shops, to the bus stop, the park, the dry cleaner's, absolutely everyone she saw wasn't talking about it. They didn't need to talk about it. But she knew what they were thinking. There goes the wife of *that man*. The one who was caught "enjoying himself" in the back of a hospital vehicle, on hospital premises, in broad daylight, if you can believe such a thing! Cold fact and context, nuance and nicety, would have little part to play. In the court of public persecution you stood no chance.

The weather didn't help.

Storm Benjamin, which had been hastily cancelled for being antisemitic, was followed by Storm Charlie. What began as a category one hurricane barrelling in from the Atlantic lost force as it was set to make landfall where it was set to rip into coastal areas that were set to be lashed by torrential rain and battered by high winds with the mercury set to plummet. In some areas a month's worth of clichés fell in twenty-four hours.

A few broadcasters, mostly those working in radio, resorted to a primitive form of speech involving "words". But these were in a minority as on-the-spot news teams wearing knotted scarves launched into a frenzied semaphore of elbow-flapping, wrist-flexing and gesturing without which, one assumes, their audience would never keep up.

Amid widespread panic RAF fighter jets were scrambled somewhere in the south-east, while the prime minister chaired an emergency meeting of the COBRA committee.

And the nation rejoiced.

With conditions in the north said to be especially grim Victor had put his trip to Ursula's on hold. In the meantime there was no shortage of paperwork to deal with, concerning the poor woman's death and funeral arrangements and the disposal of her assets. No sooner had they dealt with one set of queries than a dozen more seemed to crop up. And as Margaret tore open yet another Manila envelope at breakfast her spirits were already sinking.

"What's that, more bumf from the solicitors," said Victor as he sat down to butter his toast. "Don't they ever give it a rest."

Margaret scanned the letter and frowned.

"Can't entirely make it out. Seems to be a list of miscellaneous items not covered by the rest of the will. Says if there's anything from the following inventory we wish to acquire to let them know and they'll have it forwarded. The rest will all go to auction and the proceeds will revert to the estate. Just a load of old junk by the looks of it."

"There must be something in there worth having. Surely to goodness."

Margaret licked her thumb and peeled back the first page.

"*One willow-patterned chamber pot. Chipped.*

"*One pair of false teeth. Cracked.*

"*One lace antimacassar. Ripped.*

"*One pair of Hush Puppies. Scuffed.*

"*One stainless steel milk churn. Stained.*

"*One 'souvenir from Stilton' chess board* … or is it cheese board? Obviously a misprint. *Warped.*

"*One china basin. Broken.*

"*One plastic fried egg. Perfect condition.* You want me to go on?"

Victor made a noise through a mouthful of grilled tomatoes. And with a shrug she continued.

"*Four chickens, three ducks and a cockerel.*"

"Real or plastic."

"Real. She had that big field out the back, remember? They kept all manner of livestock there once upon a time when Uncle Dan was alive."

"What else."

"*One gentleman's bathing costume. Right sleeve missing.*

"*One signed copy of the Harold Hare annual, 1954.*"

"Signed by who?"

"Doesn't say. *One cot. Rear leg slightly damaged.*

"*One porcelain rhinoceros. No head.* Ooh! Now then! That might be worth having. Where's my pen."

"A headless rhinoceros?"

Margaret was now busy scribbling something down. "The cot! I remember seeing that as a child in their nursery. Lovely little thing with bluebirds and buttercups all carved down the sides, I think it was early Edwardian. I bet she'd love that."

"Who would?"

"Pippa's sister, for that christening present. For her niece. I told you all about it last week but I knew you weren't listening. Where are we. *Lot three-six-two. Rear leg slightly damaged.* Probably just needs a bit of glue and a coat of paint. I'm sure Patrick could sort that out. Yes I'll get onto that straight away, see how quickly it can get here. That'll really cheer them up, the pair of them."

In that last sentence only the words "the pair of them" would soon be left standing.

It was often Victor's practice when Mrs Warboys began speaking to silence her with a cushion. The larger the better, but that nice squashy one that lived on his armchair was favourite, and had brought him much relief over the years.

She was speaking now, as the three of them met for coffee in town, but Victor had left his cushion at home. This was surely the right decision: a measure that worked well on the phone might be tricky to pull off in the middle of a local tea room.

So he sat and sipped and suffered in silence.

"… and as you know, Margaret, I've never been one for idle gossip or tittle-tattle, but … you remember that Mr Spiller, lived just round the corner from your old house."

"Mr Spiller?"

"He must be well into his seventies now if he's a day. And apparently for the last few weeks he'd been seeing this young woman from the gas works. How he got up there no one knows, but one day he dropped his binoculars, all the way down into her back garden. And that's how she found out."

"Oh dear."

"And of course he's not been right since that dreadful business last year at the hospital. You remember, when he fell downstairs and had to have his whole arm put in plaster? He went back two months later to have the cast removed and there was nothing in there! His hand was there but no arm! I mean what on earth were they thinking of, making a mistake like that? And *then!* Last week, apparently, he fell down and cracked his head open while changing a light bulb, poor man. I don't know, you could write a book."

Margaret tutted sadly and refilled her cup from the cafetière. And in the two seconds it took her friend to draw breath Victor was on his feet.

"Right, I think I've heard enough of this codswallop. If you'll both just excuse me please. People on top of gasworks and empty plaster casts, I don't believe a word of it. And in any case, I'm not sure you can even change a light bulb with only one arm."

"You can if you've still got the receipt."

"W—"

But no, it wasn't worth the effort.

Margaret watched him disappear into the toilet then lowered her voice to a stage whisper.

"So, erm. I hardly dare ask, Jean. If you've heard any more. About …"

"Oh. Yes. About Chesney?"

Margaret nodded.

"Yes well. I was coming to that."

She cast a look round the other tables; at the assorted biddies whose social perspective came all neatly bound up with a big blue ribbon they would never need to untie. Why did she feel so alone suddenly? Even Margaret— well, did she really understand?

"It's not looking good, you'd have to say. As you know, he's always sworn he's innocent, and the whole thing's been one big set-up to frame him. To get this awful governor there re-elected and show he's tough on crime. The lawyers think they may have found some new evidence now that could change things but … oh I don't know, Margaret. If you could read some of his messages … well I'll send them on to you, but … the way he talks, about how much it means to him. To know there's someone out there who actually cares. The comfort he gets every night, just looking at my picture on his wall."

"My gosh, you actually sent him a photo of yourself?"

"I did, yes. Well. In actual fact – and I don't want you to take this the wrong way, Margaret, but …"

"Why would I take it the wrong way?"

"Well. To be strictly accurate, I sent him a photo of you."

"I *beg* your pardon?"

"Well you know me and photos. I thought, that's the last thing the poor man needs, to think he's writing to something an archaeologist just dug up! And as luck would have it, I found a really nice one of you from last Christmas, with such a lovely sweet smile on your face – I think you'd had a few sherries – so I just cropped off Victor and … well I couldn't see the harm in it, after all. And by the sound of things I made the right choice."

"W—y—b— Jean???"

It wasn't often Margaret gibbered. But gibber she did, as she wrestled with the implications and, let's not mince words, bare-faced impertinence of such a deed.

"And you never even thought about *asking* me?"

"Asking you what?"

"If you could send it!"

"I did!"

"No you didn't!"

"No but I thought about it."

"But you didn't ask me!"

"Well what would you have said?"

"I'd have said no!"

"Well that's why I didn't ask you."

This was turning into a routine from *Duck Soup*. And Margaret knew better than to try and out-Groucho Groucho.

"You're telling me a convicted murderer, who hacked to death his own brother and sister-in-law in their bedroom, has got *my* photo on the wall of his prison cell??"

"Please, Margaret? Don't call him a murderer! I know that's what everyone else is saying, but I mean, think of it like this. Four thousand miles away, in another corner of the world, your smile has brought a ray of sunshine into this poor man's tortured soul. That must give you a nice feeling inside?"

Margaret was all out of argument.

"I think we'd better get the bill."

This must have been how it felt during the Phoney War. You knew it was coming. They'd told you it was coming. You were sick with fear about what would happen when it came. Yet every day appeared strangely serene.

According to Carolyn the danger was past. But was Patrick buying it? Having warned him to expect a visit from her murderous boyfriend she had lately begun to back-pedal. The dreaded Melvin was nothing if not mercurial, and all that talk about force-feeding Trench his own bollocks on a kebab skewer seemed to have waned since they settled their differences. Of course she ought never to have dragged Patrick in to start with. There was no excuse and she felt dreadful. The main thing now was to put it behind him. She'd said she was sorry and she hoped he was cool with that.

As it happens, contemplating your own death at the hands of a psychopath is somewhat flawed as a relaxation exercise. Patrick was far from cool and closer to a cold sweat. It was all he could do to sleep at night, imagining this character shinning up the drainpipe with a knife between his teeth. In his fevered imagination even the sound of his wife's hairdryer became a revving chainsaw.

Pippa's only comment – "perhaps you'll be more careful where you stick your wick in future" – was not especially helpful, displaying little sympathy and a poor grasp of the facts. But it was all of a piece with her puzzling remarks about a fat engorged earwig crawling across his face. An allusion, he could only assume, to that Luis Bunuel film she'd recently stayed up to watch. What else but the famous eye-slitting scene would prompt her to keep leaving a razor on his pillow?

In his saner moments he assured himself Carolyn was right: the dust would soon settle on the whole affair and better times were around the corner.

Indeed, a sign this might be the case had occurred only that morning. With a phone call from Derek at Marsh and Barber? Regarding a Mr and Mrs McVitie? Who were looking for a quick sale? On the basis of a cash purchase? Which would mean there was no chain? And perhaps they could get back to him at their earliest convenience to arrange a viewing?

So tomorrow it was, at 2.30 pm. Patrick could "work from home" and help to get the place in apple-pie order. The front lawn would be nicely trimmed, the house all polished and hoovered, and there'd be fresh coffee brewing in the kitchen. Plus the visit should just fit in nicely between Mrs Skimpson's bagpipe practice and the screaming kids at number nine coming home from school to play Mad Max round the bottle bank. Their first choice of cottage may have fallen through, but Derek had come up with another they couldn't wait to get into. So a lot was at stake.

This was the best shot they'd had in weeks, and there was no way they were going to screw it up.

Weird as it was, Mrs Warboys' confession to Margaret was not the most astonishing thing to happen that day.

Victor's car was currently back in the workshop, to have an ignition fault they'd repaired three times in the past ten days repaired again.

This was not astonishing.

The buses were all over the place, with delays and cancellations and a backup at the depot causing major disruptions. As a result, there was little more than a skeleton service operating at the very height of the rush hour.

This was even less astonishing.

And it was not in the least astonishing, therefore, to find Victor and Margaret travelling home that morning on a jam-packed single-decker, amid a jungle of bodies that might have passed for an Antony Gormley installation.

With two stops to go they became aware of a disturbance that was taking place at the other end of the vehicle. A young woman, who was standing, was having words with an older man seated next to her. From a distance it was hard to make out, but her accusatory tone and outrage were evident. The man was on the defensive, apparently fending off some allegation, in a scene that had now caught everyone's attention. The words "improper", "offensive" and "shameful" could be heard, along with much finger pointing and arm waving. Had he accidentally touched her leg? Or brushed against her bottom? Or uttered some lewd or dubious remark?

As her tirade continued, the explanation, when it made its way down the bus, was more worrying still.

The man had offered her his seat.

Having said all she cared to on the matter of gender politics the young woman returned to her iPad to blow up some zombies. Leaving her fellow passenger to stew in his own juice.

Ten minutes later, when Victor and Margaret got off at Woodgreen Common they found the gentleman in question alighting beside them.

Which is where the astonishing bit happened.

"I don't believe it."

"Excuse me?"

Margaret turned, at the sound of a voice that was crisp, precise and calming. The man said nothing more, as if there was nothing more to say. The flicker in his eyes, as he met her quizzical stare, appeared to do all the talking.

But it was a moment before she caught up.

Why was so much so familiar? The regular, chiselled line of the jaw that housed a most appetising smile. The ears that stood slightly too proud of the head, from within a silver mass of thick wavy hair. The slim, compact form that didn't want for authority.

Thick wavy hair. Golden no more. But now that she saw him close up – could it really be?

"My God, Margaret, how long has it been, thirty-five years? And a few more besides?"

"You're joking! All of that! My gosh!"

"So how the devil are you? Is this a coincidence? You don't look a day older. And Victor! Maybe a couple of days older but …"

The chuckle came from somewhere deep down, imbued with its own brand of mischief. Just the way it always used to.

"Victor? You remember Gregory Birchall? From the old days. Funnily enough we were talking about you just the other week!"

"Oh! Yes. How are you. After all these years," said Victor, who could have been shaking hands with the man in the moon for all the name meant to him.

"Really good thank you, as it happens. Well fancy this. First day I come back to my old haunts and …? But no, I should have known. Our paths were bound to cross."

For a few seconds something wistful threatened.

But Margaret was onto it.

"So that was a right to-do then, back there? What are people like."

"Ohhh, no, no, no. I mean it's a fine line. Fine line. I touched a raw nerve, which was never the intention. And let's not forget, Margaret – how all of *us* were at that age? Far too cocksure of ourselves as I recall."

"Well that's certainly true."

"What we were and weren't going to do, in our twenties! To get all politically involved. The whole system was rotten to the core, remember, and *we* were the ones who were going to sort it all out, and change the world."

"Ohhh don't! The things you say when you're young! So what've you been up to all this while?"

"I'm an independent film-maker and writer. Making radical documentaries about globalisation and the repressive policies of Western puppet regimes. What about you?"

"W— oh. Well. Nnno, I can't say I've—"

"Well, no of course! Look at you! Happily married, and why wouldn't you be? That side of things in my case never worked out I'm afraid, but … yes, that's been my life's work. And not too many of us left sadly. The last few years I've been digging around the UK, for a follow-up to my last book, *Inside the Lying Machine*. You know? The death of truth. All the stuff that goes on they really don't want you to know about. Cover-ups, corruption and corporate conspiracy. Complicity in human rights abuse, concocting wars to shore up the arms industry. All the lies and distortions we're fed by the establishment, the press are now too scared to question."

"My God! So who was it told me you worked in a fishmonger's."

"That was a cover. One of many very early on. Trouble in this game, you can't stand still. There's too many people trying to close you down. And you know what, Margaret – and Victor – I'd love for us to stand here and chat, but right now it's difficult. The reason I'm in this area, why I was on that bus – I can't go into details, but … the idea is to present a moving target. Hopefully throw them off the scent. Which just lately is not proving easy."

A steeliness had taken over, as if he had switched to a war footing. His eyes had narrowed and he was gazing past them with a kind of hunted look.

Victor and Margaret turned to stare behind them. But apart from the traffic and a few children playing with a dog there was nothing there.

When they turned back Gregory was gone.

With a speed that flummoxed them both he had vanished among the elms and beech trees of the adjacent parkland. A scattering of pedestrians and cyclists were visible, but he was not among them.

Margaret stood blinking for a moment. The whole episode had an unreality to it though she was not yet ready to let go.

It was Victor who broke the silence.

"What are we supposed to make of all that then! And who the hell's Gregory Birchall anyway?"

"Can't believe that was actually him. After all this time!"

With so many pieces to sift through she was still coming up for air.

"So, from what he was saying, did it sound like someone was after him? Something he must have found out, they want to stop him from writing about? God, the things that go on, it makes you think. We don't know the half of it."

"All sounded completely daffy to me."

"I don't know so much. Look."

With a flick of her head she signalled to where a car had drawn up a hundred yards down the road. A sleek, grey Prius they had failed to notice only seconds before. A man and a woman got out and paused for a second as if searching for something, or someone. The man wore a long black coat, polo neck sweater and skintight gloves. His head was shaved and his face suggested a tragic dental history. The woman was tall and stiff in a short leather jacket, like a diary with a pencil down the back. Her hair was blonde and her legs not for the faint-hearted. Both of them had their collars turned up.

Sinister or what.

"Victor …"

Margaret flinched, as the couple began heading towards them. The intensity in their stride conveyed a darkness of purpose that was all too tangible. Whatever their business she didn't want to be part of it.

"Come on!"

Grabbing Victor's arm she made a dash for the pedestrian crossing, just before the lights changed. And the two them hurried away down the other side of the road.

Mr and Mrs McVitie were the very essence of nice. They were young and keen. They were full of energy, hope and idealism. And it would be some years yet before they turned into Patrick and Pippa.

The viewing was going well. Eighteen Riverbank, it seemed, ticked all their boxes and then some. Mrs McVitie declared it "a little jewel". And Mr McVitie agreed with Mrs McVitie.

But of course Mrs McVitie and Mr McVitie were not the only McVities who were inspecting the property that day.

How would it be, they said, if their ten-year-old son Josh came along to help them decide? As obviously they'd hate to pick somewhere he didn't feel comfortable. "We-ell …" said Patrick. "No problem!" said Pippa. The more the merrier. And why rock any boats they didn't need to at this early stage?

"Ahhh! Now these floor tiles are *right* up my street," said Mrs McVitie, as they stepped into the kitchen. "I've always loved that terracotta look. What do *you* think, Josh?"

"What's this stain round the plughole."

Mrs McVitie crossed to where the little boy was leaning over the sink.

"Whereabouts, pet."

"Oh! Erm – yes!" Pippa was quick to cut in. "I think that's a bit of turmeric from the other night. I did try putting some Domestos down, but ..."

"Maybe you should try again," said Josh. "Once more unto the bleach?"

"Ha ha ha!" laughed Mr and Mrs McVitie.

"Oh very good," said Pippa.

"WTF" thought Patrick.

"Ohhhhh dear! Sorry about that," said Mrs McVitie, dabbing her eyes. "I'm afraid we get this all the time. He is a comedian."

"He certainly is," said Pippa. "For ten years old."

"No, I mean he *is* a comedian. A stand-up comic. That's what he does, in his spare time. Writes and performs his own material on stage, the whole thing."

"You're joking!" said Pippa.

"That's the general idea," said Josh, running his finger along a Venetian blind.

"Gosh, don't they grow up fast these days!" said Pippa.

"Well of course we know ten's a lot younger than most," said Mr McVitie. "But with his uncle and aunt and three cousins and two of our neighbours all stand-up comedians he didn't want to get left behind. It's like playing an instrument, absolutely key to start early."

"We think he could be another Ned Metcalf," said Mrs McVitie.

"Who?" said Patrick.

By which time the youngster was heading back into the hall with the practised lope of a grime artist. The rest of them duly followed.

"Well I'm impressed," said Pippa. "At his age. Where does he do all this?"

"Oh, comedy clubs, and various functions of one sort or another. He's got no fear. Took ourselves to Edinburgh last year, didn't we, for five nights?"

"Wow. And how did that go, Josh?"

"I killed."

"Yes, he did very well. Obviously there'll be the novelty value but ..."

"And then the BBC were on last week weren't they, darling? About doing something for that half-past six slot they've got on Radio Four."

"Anyway!" said Patrick. "If you'd like us to show you the bedrooms."
Josh gave him a look.
"Did you get that moustache from a joke shop?"
"Excuse me?"
"Or have you been eating Marmite. It looks like Hitler gone wrong."
"*Josh*?? Now please. Come on, behave."
"Ohhh God!" Pippa was in hysterics. "I see what you mean! He's *very* quick isn't he? No, he's definitely got something."

"Hasn't he just," said Patrick, resisting the urge to rearrange the child's freckles. "As I was saying, perhaps we could all go upstairs now and have a look at the—"

At this point he was interrupted by an almighty thumping noise consistent with someone pummelling the back door.

"Erm ... and have a look round the bedrooms? And I think you were quite interested in the en-suite shower unit, Mrs McVitie?"

Thump! Thump! Thump!

Crash! Smash!

There was definitely someone out there trying to attract attention. And it didn't take a genius to figure out who.

"... which we only had put in a year ago, so ..."

"Erm. Do you not want to see to that at all?" said Mr McVitie.

"Sorry?"

"There appears to be someone at your back door," said Mrs McVitie.

"Ohhh. Well possibly, yes. Or it could just be the wind."

"The wind?"

"Didn't they say on the forecast? We might be in for some blustery weather."

Smash! Thwack! Smash!

"Little bit of draft excluder. Is probably all it needs."

Draft excluder and a point 45 calibre Smith and Wesson.

Explaining to this nice young couple that he'd recently been hit with a fatwa by a crazed ex-jailbird might take longer than he had left to live. But he couldn't go on stalling for ever.

As the rhythmic pounding got worse, there were sounds of wood beginning to splinter, and somewhere in the mix a man's voice was heard shouting.

"Mr Trench, I think someone's calling your name."

"Rrright. So they are. OK. Well why don't you all go up anyway, to the front bedroom, and … I'll just see what they want and then join you in a second."

Above his head was a very large thought bubble that read "SHITTT!!"

Pippa spotted it and began to shepherd the party upstairs.

"Okey-dokey! Yes, so as I say, the second bedroom at the moment we use as Patrick's office but it should suit Josh to a T."

As the four of them trooped away Patrick returned to the kitchen.

The back door was now shaking on its hinges from the onslaught outside. And any hope that this Melvin person might listen to reason was evaporating by the second. Where were the police when you needed them? Was it too much to ask, for a squad of armed officers on every street corner?

Fiddling frantically with his phone he managed to drop it on the floor where it immediately slid beneath the cooker.

Smash!!!

Good God, the man was now using a battering ram of some kind! Another second and that door was history.

There was nothing else for it but to hope he'd see sense. Once he'd set eyes on his victim he'd surely understand? The very idea of a boring specimen like himself with Carolyn! No one could be that pig-headed.

Smmmmashh!!!

Pig-headed? Or just plain bovine?

The door, he now realised, was not even locked. What kind of Neanderthal was he dealing with here?

As he turned the knob and the door fell open the mad, flaring eyes that stared back at him left the matter in no doubt.

Bovine was definitely the word here.

It was a cow.

"*What* in the name of—!!"

Sidestepping the next lunge, Patrick snapped into that autonomic bullfighter reflex we all deploy when faced with a fifteen-hundred-pound charging ruminant. At which point the cow, deciding that ramming your horns against a door is a creative dead-end, began careering off round the garden in search of another more rewarding form of self-expression.

Crash!!!

And there went the window of the potting shed.

For a ruminant it was not that fussed about ruminating. A thick tattered bandage tied round one of its rear legs appeared to point to some recent injury. But it's fair to say this didn't much hamper its progress.

"*How*??? In the name of—!!"

Switching adverbs was one way to go; but on this occasion didn't help much. *How* it was a cow might be straying too far into the realms of the ontological. It just *was*. And it just was, at this minute, pausing to fertilise Patrick's marigolds before launching an all-out attack on the conservatory.

Some readers, recalling that Patrick's name was being shouted, might imagine the animal had, by some trickery, managed to counterfeit human speech. But the presence of a rough-hewn young man in a smock, hovering by the back gate, would seem a more likely explanation.

"Mr Trench is it!"

"Yesss? *I* am? Who are *you*? What the hell's going on here??"

"One cow, sir!"

"What???"

"One cow!"

"What do you mean one cow? I can see it's a bloody cow! Where the hell did it come from?"

"Yorkshire, sir!"

"*Yorkshire???*"

"Sir. Lot 362, to this address. Those were my instructions. For a Mr and Mrs Patrick Trench."

"W—!! B—!! What instructions? Instructions from who??"

The rough-hewn young man fished into the pocket of his corduroy trousers and began squinting at a crumpled docket.

"Sender – someone by the name of Meldrew."

"Meldr—"

Did he even need to ask? Who else would embark on such a convoluted act of sabotage? Even Patrick had to acknowledge the sheer breadth of sadistic vision required for a stunt like this. The man was a genius in his field.

Crashhhh!!

As predicted, the assault on the conservatory had begun. Accompanied by someone, somewhere, screaming at the top of their voice.

"So if that's all in order then, sir, I'll bid you good day."

With which the man doffed his cap and disappeared.

"Wait!!! You're not going to just *leave* this thing here!? Come back here now! D'you hear me!!! Come back here this minute!!!"

At the bedroom window a freckled face was now staring down; its owner shrieking like a banshee at the marauding beast below. His parents, arriving next to him, took one look at the scene and recoiled in horror.

"Josh??? Oh my God!! You might have told us, Mr Trench? You kept cows?? He's absolutely terrified of them!"

"Come away from there, Josh! Come away, it's OK, it's OK. It can't hurt you! Myyy God, I can't believe this – OK! Right then, Mrs Trench, I think it's best that we left now, don't you?"

There was nothing to say so Pippa said nothing. She simply watched them go and remained frozen to the spot. Bereft and bewildered.

In another upstairs window further along the twitch of a net curtain went unnoticed. Their neighbours, rather wisely, were keeping a low profile. And this time it was Margaret who was on the back foot.

"I don't know what to say. I mean— you heard me when I read it out to you? It definitely said *cot*. I didn't imagine it!"

Victor drew a long joyless breath and shook his head sadly.

"You'd think *someone* might have spotted the mistake? And I can't believe you didn't tell them it was coming."

"Well I ... just thought I'd like to surprise them."

"Yesss. I think we can agree you've managed that. *One cot. Back leg slightly damaged.* I wonder what *china basin* was a misprint for. Chinese bison? Good luck explaining this one away then, Margaret? I'll go and make us a cup of tea."

From the the road outside came the sound of frantic voices and a young child wailing, followed by the slamming of car doors. In the back garden Patrick was attempting to tie a lasso with Pippa's clothes line.

Margaret surveyed the unfolding mayhem and groaned.

"Ohhhh my *godfathers*."

A cup of tea was not quite going to cut it.

That night, with Victor lost in some distant dream, Margaret, too, was a long way from home.

So much to look back on. So little to come. Time to make the most of time. And time perhaps to listen to two voices in her head she found it hard to silence.

Was the truth, as Gregory claimed, no longer fit for human consumption? Wherever you looked there was an agenda that drove the "facts". And those who took us for fools did not tend to miscalculate. His words were persuasive, and never more so than now. Who exactly was trying to "close him down"? The whole thing didn't bear thinking about.

Elsewhere in the swirl of her conscience another presence had embedded itself. A cry in the dark, hypnotic and still, inscribed on the screen of her laptop.

Why on earth she had sent it was anyone's guess, after that exchange in the teashop. But then logic was never Mrs Warboys' thing …

> ----Original message----
> From: cdpink3@aol.com
> Date: 23/06/2020 - 11:29 (BST)
> To: jboyswar@me.com
> Subject: Understanding
>
> Some good news, Jean. Maybe. They just gave me a couple more weeks. While the lawyers submit new evidence to the A-G to corroborate my alibi. My bet, he won't bite, no way. Everyone knows the governor's office are all over this case and that's how it's been from the start. They rewrite the story to make it fit.
>
> No one else here now I can talk to only you. When I read your words it's like I hear your voice. Coming from this other place where things all start to make sense. Every night I look through the bars, and up at the stars, then look into your kind, sweet eyes I know there's a God. He never made the

world perfect so we have to take things as they are. That's how He tests us. If you can accept, and understand, then you lived your life the way He meant you to, and that's the best you can say with nothing to be ashamed of.

I never had a mom to speak of, Jean. But you're just how I'd want her to be. Even though we never met you believe in me. You can't know how much that means in the time I have left. Write me soon.

Chesney.

Yes, well, of course that's just what you'd expect him to say wasn't it. That's how they get away with it over there. The whole blessed lot of them. From the scumbags on the street to the highest office in the land. But unlike her friend, Margaret wasn't buying a word of all that folksy tosh.

Snapping down the lid she put the device back on its shelf and pulled out a tissue. Her hay fever seemed particularly bad tonight.

Chapter Three
Edwin

"WELCOME TO SPRUCE GOOSE Dry Cleaners, for all your everyday dry-cleaning solutions! To assist us today in dealing with your inquiry please take a moment to review the following options. Alternatively, you may find it easier to visit us online at double-u double-u double-u dot goose-spruce dot co dot uk forward-slash dry cleaners, where you will find a full list of our comprehensive range of facilities and services. Please note that all calls are monitored and recorded for quality and training purposes."

"Yesss, as you never stop telling us!"

"If you'd like to know more about how we use and protect your personal data please read our privacy policy, which can be found on our website."

"Yes you said all that last time, and the time before that. God spare us."

Victor shifted restlessly on the spot and transferred the phone to his other ear. He could, ideally, have done with a third ear, to give the other two a break from this turgid ritual, which Torquemada would surely have found a use for. He could feel his life being slowly sucked away into the earpiece as the voice drilled into his skull.

"*Please select one of the following. If you're ringing to check on the progress of a garment or garments, or to inquire whether an item is suitable for cleaning, press One. If you would like to know where to find us, or to enquire about our opening hours, or when the item you placed with us will be ready for collection, press Two. For information about our prices, special offers, and details of our special same-day express service, press Three. To inquire about repairs and alterations, please press Four. If you would like to talk to someone about a bulky article such as a duvet, wedding dress or curtains, or require assistance or specialist advice regarding fabrics including suede and leather, press Four. If you are ringing with any other inquiry, or to register a complaint, then please press Five.*"

"Finally! *Five!* Beggars belief you have to go through this every single time. It drives you up the bloody wall."

From two and a half feet above his head came a testy growl:

"Are you going to hold this stepladder still or not? Jigging about down there as if you've got St Vitus' dance! It won't make things happen any quicker. And it *would* be nice if I could trim this last bit of wallpaper without cracking my head open. Just try and be patient for once in your life."

Victor cast a glance up the wall, where his wife was at work with a Stanley knife. There were slivers of paper all over the floor and the room smelt of fresh paint and paste. He let loose a disgruntled sigh and attempted to brace himself.

"Been through all this rigmarole twice as it is! First time I ended up with the wrong department, second time I waited for ten minutes then the line just went dead. It's more than flesh and blood can st— Ahhh! Hallo?"

"*We're very sorry, but there is no one currently available to take your call. Please hold the line until one of our operators becomes free.*"

"Oh for mercy's sake."

"*Remember, you can always log on to our website, at double-u double-u double-u dot goose-spruce dot co dot uk forward-slash dry cleaners at any time. Otherwise, please hold. We greatly value your custom, and will do our best to respond to your call as soon as possible.*"

"Oh please, nohhh! Not *Night on Bald Mountain* again! I'm sure they all do this deliberately. Yes! Welcome to the Happy Haddock Chip Shop for all your fish and chip solutions! If you're calling about a bone in your gurnet, press One. To report a leaking sachet of ketchup, press Two. If you're sick to the back teeth with all this bollocks and would like to shove a pickled gherkin up th— hallo!"

"Yes? Hallo, sorry to keep you waiting. How can I help."

"Ah! Right. My name's Meldrew. And I'm ringing about a pair of tr— is this a real person?"

"Yes? What can I help you with?"

"Well. It's about some cleaning I've just brought home. When I came to put it away in the cupboard, I j—" Hang on, there was something fishy going on here, wasn't there? "Excuse me, your name's not Mavis is it?

"Yes?"

"But— you were the one I spoke to ten minutes ago! Who told me I'd pressed One by mistake, and said I'd have to call again and press the right number! Which I did, and then waited and waited, with that stupid music going, and then just suddenly got cut off!"

"I'm sorry about that, sir."

"So now I've had to go through the whole thing again! I mean, what's the point of having a dozen and one options if they all come through to the same person?"

From the nerve centre of Spruce Goose came the sound of Mavis Goose raising her eyebrows in despair.

"Sir, you said you had a complaint. And the message clearly states that callers with a complaint should press Five. We have a system here. It's designed to ensure things run as smoothly as possible. Now is there a problem?"

Victor tried some deep breathing. Which never ever worked. It wasn't even this he'd rung up to complain about.

"There certainly is a problem! And it's this note I just found speared to the hook of one of your coat hangers – which I have to say I find deeply offensive!"

"Note, sir?"

"*This garment bore stains of an unusually resilient nature*! What's that got to do with anything? I bring my trousers in to be dry-cleaned! Not referred to the Environmental Protection Agency! Don't need any of that cheek, thank you very much. Next time I'll make sure they're absolutely spotless for you! How would that be? I'd hate to put you to any trouble. Oh! Actually, I have to go now, I've got to jet-wash my nose before I blow it! Good-*bye*!"

On which note the exchange was sharply concluded.

"Are you done now?"

"What?"

"Feel better for that."

"As a matter of fact, *yes*."

Margaret, now back on terra firma, bagged up the last of her scraps and cast an approving eye round the room. The woodwork gleamed back at her, and the pastel patterns were cool and subtle.

"What do you reckon? Once all the furniture's back in place? I think we can be pretty pleased with our efforts. How much was he going to charge, your friend Nobby?"

"Quoted us four hundred originally. Which I certainly thought was pushing it."

"Well there you are then. That's a good two-fifty we've saved, doing it ourselves. And he wasn't even planning to start till today, remember, when he got back from holiday. Still a few bumps here and there, but they'll go down once it's dry. Did you pick up that other book of samples while you were out, for the hall?"

"It's just there," said Victor, indicating a hefty volume propped against the wall. "Oh, and she jotted down the price of those paints for us, if we're interested. Reckoned one big tin would be enough."

"Oh right." Margaret threw back a dust sheet from the sofa and heaved the book onto her lap. With the eyes in the back of her head, meanwhile, she noticed her husband grimace as he checked his watch.

"Yes, you might want to start getting ready soon? The table's booked for seven, and I wouldn't leave it till the last minute."

This prompted a second grimace. Followed by a flinch and a wince.

"I suppose I *could* still cancel." To the grimace, the flinch and the wince was now added an awkward squirm. "I think I can feel one of my jippy stomachs coming on."

"*You'll do no such thing!*" Margaret spun round to face him with a gorgon glare. "After Pippa's gone to all the trouble of setting this thing up for the pair of you? They're moving out tomorrow, it may be the last you see of him. The least you can do is sit down for a nice quiet meal and a chat together. To try and part on good terms."

Victor had his doubts about that. The least he could do, surely, was nothing. But he knew it was futile to argue.

"I don't see why it just has to be me. Why can't you come along?"

"Because it's never been about me or Pippa, has it? As you're perfectly well aware. And besides which I've got my yoga class. Which means I can drop you off first and then pick you up after. And you'll both be able to have a drink."

Victor grunted. "Can't believe it's all gone through so quick. Shows how keen they were, I suppose, that young couple. After everything that happened."

"I know, well. Once it was all explained to them I think they could see the funny side. We did well to get that poor animal rounded up and sent back again. And thankfully no lasting damage was d— *Oh … my … Goddd!*"

"What is it now?"

A small sheet of paper had just fluttered to the floor. And as she picked it up a look of horror crossed her face.

"This list she jotted down for you. The woman in the hardware shop."

"What about it."

"Have you seen what it's written on the back of?"

"Well no, I didn't study it. Why?"

"We're talking about that little dark-haired dumpy woman with the eyebrows?"

"Yes?"

"Because … wasn't it her husband who killed himself. Not more than a month ago? He gassed himself in the car, in his garage."

"Oh that was horrible."

Margaret's hand was visibly trembling as she held up the flimsy document.

"*This ...* is his suicide note!"

"Don't be ridiculous."

"See for yourself!"

"Just as if she'd be so heartless! As to write down the price of some paint on the back of her own husband's suicide n— ... my God. *By the time you read this I will be dead. My life has become such a gutted shell, I have decided to snuff out my worthless existence once and for all. Farewell sweet love. I go now to my grave.*"

"Now turn it over."

"*... Dulux Satin Eggshell, twenty-one pounds fifty, per two-and-a-half litre can.*"

"What on earth was she thinking of?"

"That's definitely not right."

"Can you imagine what their marriage must have been like."

"It's only eighteen-fifty at B and Q."

"What?"

"Well! No! I mean – people. How do you begin to understand them."

And finally deigning to remove his cap he trudged off upstairs.

Margaret slipped the note back in the book, and closed it with a shudder.

"That's made me go quite wobbly."

Pippa's evening so far was all nicely symmetrical. She had sent her husband packing to get on with the packing, and was quietly pleased with her progress. The big stuff was now swathed in bubble wrap, and the rest of it neatly filed away in cardboard boxes like the nation's homeless.

Getting shot of Patrick for a few hours had brought some welcome breathing space, and a chance to take stock of her life along with all those ageing receipts and documents that seemed to breed in the kitchen drawers. Like the goods they referred to, her marriage had long been out of warranty. Some natural wear and tear was to be expected after all these years, and the pair of them had certainly been making some strange noises of late. But fingers crossed, this replacement part would do the trick, and very soon all would be running smoothly again.

Getting the McVities back onside had been a triumph of crisis management. Once it was made clear the cow was not a permanent resident, all parties had returned to the negotiating table and a deal immediately hammered out. There was even some talk of Josh using the incident as a "bit" at the Udderbelly. With cash on the table events had moved at lightning speed. Surveys were waved through and contracts exchanged on the house and the cottage. And although the buyers weren't due to move in for another few weeks Patrick had been all for a quick getaway: before an octopus turned up in his dishwasher, or whatever the hell ghastly treat Meldrew was planning for them next.

The chance of this meal tonight leading to some form of détente was slender at best, though Pippa lived in hope. The two men were, of course, more suited in temperament than either would care to admit; and that was the problem. But the idea was a sound one, and like her neighbour she simply longed to depart with their differences buried and friendships restored.

That was before the text arrived.

It was 10.53, and Pippa was in bed dozing through a novel when she heard the gentle whoosh at her side. Groggily she reached for the phone and instantly wished she hadn't.

"Ohhh hell."

One glance at Margaret's message told her things had not gone well.

The blinds were lightly fluttering in a draft from the open window, as outside she heard a taxi pull up. Narrow ribbons of light crossed the wall above her head and then stopped. A car door opened and closed, and the ribbons moved on. She clicked off her lamp and tried to rehearse a convincing snore. But it sounded too much like a set of farmyard impressions, so she lay there in the shadows and steeled herself.

Wham!

There went the front door. Followed by the thunderous stomp upstairs. With the contents of the house all sealed and ready for transit the place was like an echo chamber. And every thud and thump made

Pippa fear for her fillings. The very fact that he'd declined a lift home told its own story. And it was not *The Further Adventures of Noddy*.

A second later Patrick was in the room. Eyes ablaze in the darkness.

"So how did it go? You have a nice time both of you?" she squeaked with zero conviction. "I erm … got a text from Margaret. She said there was some sort of mix-up with the booking."

Patrick kicked off his shoes with a scowl.

"I've no desire to talk about it, thank you very much!"

"Fair enough." And closing her eyes she turned over.

"But since you ask. Yes. The whole thing was a disaster from start to finish. You realise there wasn't a single person there who spoke English?"

"Yes, well. Whose daft idea was it in the first place? To go to a Turkish restaurant."

"Yours."

"Was it?"

"And correct me if I'm wrong, it was you that rang up to request a nice, quiet little table, where two people could be left alone to discuss some rather personal affairs."

"I can't remember if I used those words exactly."

"Well, whatever words you used, one fact remains, doesn't it. The entire staff and management were under the impression that Mr Meldrew and I were secret lovers. A concept so grisly it curdles the blood."

As he caught himself undressing in the mirror he felt strangely violated. The events of the night had turned his sexuality inside out, and caused him to shiver.

"It was bad enough when they sat us down together on that tiny banquette with a heart-shaped balloon tied to the back. And then brought us a bowl of soup with two spoons. But the true extent of the horror didn't dawn till the next course, when a long, complimentary sausage arrived, which they encouraged us to nibble from each end until our lips met in the middle, like *Lady and The Tramp*."

"Well couldn't you have said something?"

"I'm afraid anything we tried to say was academic, once a band of strolling zither players began to serenade us with Ottoman love songs.

It would have been cruel to just tell them to bugger off. So we told them to bugger off."

"Well I'm sorry about that. I don't know! Always something isn't there."

"*Oh* yes. Though for peak embarrassment it was hard to top the moment when one of the waiters came over, in front of the whole restaurant, and in his rather mangled accent attempted to ask if either of us loved pork. A question that unfortunately emerged as: 'Which one of you has sex with pigs?'"

"Heavens."

"Whenever we got up to go they just doled out complimentary liqueurs and said there was no rush. The only way we got the bill, in the end, was to say we'd promised the babysitter to be back by ten. And we finally left with one of the zither players strumming a lullaby."

"Aaaah. Well that was sweet?"

"Sweet?? Have you taken leave of your senses, woman? Thirty-three people in that restaurant think Victor Meldrew and I are sleeping together! I tell you, the sooner we get away from this place, the better. The man's been a curse on our lives from day one. Twenty-four hours from now, God willing, we'll get back to normality."

Yes, well. God may have been willing, but His flesh was weak.

An hour of perfect posture and prune juice had left Margaret in a good place. Her *chi* was aligned with her *chakra*, and her inner self had attained exquisite mindfulness. As she rolled up the yoga mat for another week and said goodbye to her classmates she was well on the way to enlightened calm.

By the end of the night her sense of *nirvana* would be more of the Kurt Cobain variety.

Listening to Victor jabber on about Turkish waiters all the way home had not done much for her *moksha*. But when they got back she was, at least, still breathing through her diaphragm.

"God knows why I let you talk me into these things," he fumed. "I must need my head examining!"

"No comment."

Margaret closed the front door and slipped off her coat. It was best to just let him get on with it till he ran out of steam.

"And then! When that woman at the next table came over to say there was no shame whatever in a May-December relationship! She did well to avoid a beef dumpling up her nose, I tell you that much!"

"Yes! We're all agreed, it didn't work out." As Margaret wound her scarf tightly round the coat hook it was tempting to wind it somewhere else. "Now what's happening tomorrow? Are you still planning to go up to Ursula's?"

"Hmm? Well, yes, I was hoping to. Now the weather's settled down."

"Good. You get yourself off to the country for a few days, it'll be a nice chance to have a rest."

"Huh. When do I ever rest?"

She meant a rest for herself. But whatever.

"So you just need to check what's there, and make sure the solicitors haven't missed anything. After that last fiasco I wouldn't trust them an inch."

"Yesss … I know what to look for."

"Well be sure that you do."

"I will."

"Well be sure that you do."

"I tell you, if I ever see one of those extra long sausages again I may throw up. I should never, ever have left the house tonight."

On that point they were about to agree.

As she stepped into the front room and switched on the light Margaret came close to a faint. Only her husband, who was following, broke her fall. A groan of disbelief barely made it through her lips, as she managed to steady herself and stood there, staring.

"What's the matter? Margaret? What've you just—"

And then he saw it too.

"*What in the name of bloody hell??*"

How to describe the carnage that met their eyes? It was a scene of mural mayhem; a slaughter of the innocent such as Herod might have wrought, had he feared the ascent of a vinyl wall-covering.

The pastel patterns they had left behind were no more. Ripped from the surface with all the finesse of a very blunt swordfish. Scrapings and scraps of lacerated paper were all that remained on the bare plastered walls. A smell of cigarettes hung in the air, and in the centre of the room were three huge dustbin liners, packed to bursting.

"This is— I d— Our wallpaper!! What in God's name's happened here?"

In the corner, beneath a bucket of murky water, a note had been scrawled on the back of an envelope. Victor bent down and picked it up.

"*Sorry you were out. But thought I'd make a start as promised. Have managed to get the worst of it off, and bagged up ready for the tip. Will come back Monday to start sanding down the woodwork. Cheers, Nobby.*"

"W— are you saying that - I mean, did he just—"

Victor turned again to gaze miserably round the room. He tried to speak, but even his customary splutter refused to come.

Margaret's face was a picture. Sadly it was by Edvard Munch.

"I thought you said you'd cancelled him!"

"Well – I did! A week ago. I told his mate Sid down the pub. I quite clearly explained that we'd decided to do the job ourselves. And to tell Nobby when he saw him to let us have the key back the next time he was—"

"Told his mate Sid?? You mean you didn't tell him in person??"

"Well no, I mean … I didn't know his exact address or number, I didn't know where to get hold of him. I only know him to have a drink with, so—"

"Didn't know his exact address??" The cracks in her spiritual oneness were growing wider by the second, and her *prana* had just about had it. "Why didn't you try Dodge City! That's where all the other cowboys live isn't it? Five days it took to put all that up! I just don't b— !! Didn't know where to get hold of him? I'll tell you where to get hold of him! Round his bloody neck if I catch him!! I'm going to bed!"

As she left, Victor peered into one of the bags and ran his hand through the wreckage of their work. Then he tied it up with a groan, and followed her upstairs.

It was fair to say he'd had better days.

*

Friday morning was dry and clear. And all was set fair for the big recce at Ursula's. Victor's Honda had been duly checked over by the service department, who had given it a clean bill of health. While waiting in the office he tartly declared this was the first car he'd owned that ran entirely on prayer. The manager's retort, that he might need a new Catholic converter, was met with frosty silence.

Margaret had left early for work, wishing him good luck and a safe journey; the warning by Mr Dimkins now seemingly forgotten. There were still some provisions to pick up en route, so he'd be well stocked up when he got there, and the plan was to be on the road by twelve. The keys to the property had been sent in a Jiffy bag, and with the motorways currently clear there was no reason to expect any problems.

No reason in a cosy work of fiction, but of course this was real life.

He was all set to depart and just stepping through the front door when he heard the phone ring. Remembering he'd left it in the kitchen after his diatribe to Mavis, he tramped back through and jabbed the green button.

"Hallo? What? Yessss. No, not yet. Well if you thought I'd be gone by now what was the point of ringing? I've just spent half the morning hunting for that little suitcase for a start. Yes well obvious to you maybe, but strangely I didn't think of looking in the big suitcase. Yessss I did. Yes, right out next to the road this time so they won't miss it. Sorry – why would I remember the cardboard, that's not till next week surely? It was recycle last week, general rubbish this week— oh, no hang on! I tell a lie, you may be right."

It was at this point that a very large vehicle drew up outside, announcing its presence with a hiss of air brakes.

"Bugger it, I think they're here! No, don't worry, I'll go out now and swap them over."

Signing off in a flap, he glanced through the open front door, to discover a huge white lorry was now parked at the kerb. False alarm! It was just those removal men come for next door. With everything else on his mind he'd quite forgotten today was their big day. A shame he couldn't stay to see them off, but there you go. His first priority was the bins and time was getting on.

As he left through the back door two men climbed out of the truck and stood in the road for a moment, pondering some papers on a clipboard.

They were thickset, sturdy individuals, and neither would have looked out of place staggering across the marshes in leg irons at the start of *Great Expectations*. The taller of the two wore a snug black tee-shirt, with an incorrectly spelt tattoo down his right arm, and an erratum on his wrist. His colleague had narrow, probing eyes and a complexion that may or may not have been due to an accident with a blowtorch.

After a few seconds they marched up the front path and rang Victor's doorbell. When there was no reply they waited a minute, then rang again.

Victor, having switched his wheelie bin for the correct one at the end of the alleyway round the back, re-entered his kitchen and was in the process of locking up when the doorbell rang for a fourth time.

"Yesss! Coming!"

The two visitors exchanged looks.

"He say 'Come in'?"

The other one shrugged. The door was wide open, so in they stepped. There were several small chairs, and lamps and pictures, and all manner of items stacked in the hall, while the furniture in the lounge had been squashed together and covered with dust sheets. Rather more oddly, what appeared to be the shredded remains of some brand-new wallpaper lay scattered all over the floor.

"Yes? Excuse me!"

It was not what you'd call friendly fire, and gave them both a start.

"Who the bloody hell are you? And what are you doing in my house?"

"Oh! Sorry! Yeh, morning! You said to come in, so …"

Victor eyed the tall one up and down. He'd had quite enough of this malarky for one week, and was giving no quarter.

"I most certainly did not!" he rejoined. "Is that your lorry out there?"

"That's right, chief. Tunstall and Gridley," said either Tunstall or Gridley, narrowing his probing eyes still further. "Little bit later than we said, it took a while to get through the new one-way system."

Victor groaned.

"Yes well, you've got the wrong house, haven't you? It's next door you want."

"Oh. Really? However did that happen then."

"Our mistake, chief, sorry."

"And if you wouldn't mind just shifting yourselves please? Come on, off you go, that's it. I'm already late this morning as it is."

Victor slammed the front door and watched them both cross the lawn to his neighbour's. It surely wasn't that hard to grasp? The house numbers along this row were consecutive, not odd or even. With his front door wide open you could see how these mistakes happened, but even so. That business last night with the wallpaper was bad enough; he didn't need any more rogue workmen making his life a misery.

All things considered, he'd just got off lightly.

It so happened that Patrick was also heading into town that morning. Which would prove to be one of the worst decisions he ever made.

The removal team were originally due at nine, but appeared to be dragging their feet. This had only ramped up the tension, and Patrick, already living on his nerves, had spent the last two hours peering through windows and checking his watch and wearing out the carpet.

It was a case of so near and yet so far. As long as Victor Meldrew remained physically intact – well, that scene at the end of *Carrie* was never far from his mind. Just about anything could suddenly go wrong and most likely would.

"If you want to make yourself useful why don't you go and get the groceries," was Pippa's solution. "I'll see to everything this end. You can drive straight there afterwards and be ready for when they arrive. You'll be as much use as a bucket of sick round here."

"Thank you."

And yet he needed no persuading. The operation could surely take care of itself without him breathing down everyone's neck. The sooner he left for the Promised Land the better, and the less likely his chance of an early stroke.

Pippa watched him drive off and picked up the phone. They were certainly taking their time, these people, and there was a fair old bit to load up. What the hell was keeping them?

She had just begun to dial the number when a heavy shadow fell across the front room as a lorry pulled up and blocked out the light. She could swear she saw two men get out, but for some reason there was then a delay, followed by a familiar voice moaning about house numbers. Finally her own doorbell rang, and the two men were revealed outside, looking faintly rattled.

"Sorry for the delay," said Tunstall/Gridley. "It's been a bit of a morning so far. And I think we may have upset your neighbour."

"Don't worry, you wouldn't be the first," Pippa chuckled, as she ushered them in. "I'm afraid he's got a bit of a short fuse. Anyway, there you go, it's all yours. The whole kit and caboodle. We've done our best with all the wrapping and boxing up. But I'll leave it in your capable hands. If you're worried about any breakables, there's loads more bubble wrap just there."

"No, no, looks pretty straightforward," said Gridley/Tunstall. "And I guess we can settle up soon as we're done?"

"Yes, eight-fifty I think was agreed?" said Pippa. "Cash in hand?"

"No worries," said Tunstall/Gridley.

"Nice one," said Gridley/Tunstall.

"And I'll just leave you to it."

Patrick had already had a gut-ful of the multi-storey car park. The sign outside had promised him faithfully there were "SPACES", in big green illuminated letters. But of course that was all part of the fun. There were, literally, two spaces, hidden away on one of the thirteen floors among 1,498 stationary vehicles. And at this very minute two men in black ribbed jerseys would be sitting in an office with their feet up, watching him on their screens, and laughing as every so often he slowed down with his hopes raised, only to find a Mini Clubman or Nissan Micra parked hard back against the wall.

After nearly twenty minutes of crawling right to the top and down again, and doubling back and briefly meeting himself in hyperspace (he may have been delirious by this time), he was just on the point of giving up, when all of a sudden – bingo! There it was! As large as life, on the eleventh floor. A nice juicy rectangle of concrete with his name on it, begging to be parked upon.

After all the aggravation he couldn't be arsed with reversing and drove straight in. Switching off the engine he paused with relief, then stretched across the back seat to collect his four bags for life and got out of the car.

The relief was all too fleeting.

If he thought he'd seen the last of his next-door neighbour when the manager of the Dardanelle Grill blew them both a farewell kiss in the doorway last night, he was sadly mistaken.

Like something rising from a swamp, the distant capped figure traipsing up a ramp towards him sent a chill down the spine.

Was there no escaping the man? It was bad enough he'd spent the night dreaming of … well, let's not dwell on the Freudian constructs of that Turkish sausage and the allusions to porcine coitus, which have no place outside the memoirs of an old Etonian. Here he was again, in the flesh, returning to his car with two bags of shopping.

His car …

Oh please, not that wretched Honda that was jutting out slightly, just three spaces along from his own?

The inscription "NOB-END!", written in the dust with someone's finger, confirmed his worst fears. This was taking coincidence too far. The two of them had shared enough awkward silences to last a lifetime; was it too late to dive back into his seat and duck down below the window?

Sadly it was.

Having spotted his very-soon-to-be former neighbour, Victor half-jerked his head in a feeble greeting and attempted to smile. Patrick attempted to smile back and pretended to be doing something with his keys, though he wasn't sure what. This was designed to avoid eye contact as Victor walked past, except that Victor, who had taken a sudden interest in some overhead lighting for the same reason, walked into a pillar and dropped both his bags on the floor.

"Shit!"

Patrick made a brave attempt to ignore it. But with cans of soup and oranges rolling around his feet this was a tall order.

"Oh. Let me … erm."

"Oh! Right. That's very … erm."

Working together they scooped it all up, and along with a dozen farmhouse eggs there was ice broken, of a sort.

"So … today's the er …"

"Sorry?"

"… the day."

"Oh. Yes."

"Yes, I saw them. Just before I came out."

"Sorry?"

"The removal men."

"Ah."

"Be loading up now, I expect. As we speak."

"And you'll be erm."

"Sorry?"

"On your way now. Up to …"

"Oh, yes. Just getting one or two bits in first."

"Uhuh."

"Anyway. I hope it all goes …"

"Yes. You too."

"Need to pop back down again now. Unfortunately."

"Sorry?"

"Eggs."

"Oh yes. Right."

Victor clicked open his boot and stashed his shopping away. The broken eggs he wrapped carefully in another bag to dispose of later. The lid of the boot was playing up again and took three hefty slams before it finally closed. He made a mental note to add it to his list the next time he rang the service department to give them a bollocking. And with a vague valedictory nod he marched away towards the exit.

As Patrick watched him go he heard his phone ring. It was just Pippa, calling with a progress report, but he managed to spin it out for five minutes, to ensure there was no danger of catching up Victor on the stairs. Having signed off he was about to head on down to the mall when a loud metallic *ker-chunk!* drew his attention to Victor's boot lid, which had spontaneously sprung open again.

Patrick did the decent thing and went over to close it. He'd had boots like this himself in the past, and they drove you up the wall. It just needed a really firm hand.

Slam!

Ker-chunk!

No, it wasn't playing ball. Maybe you just had to surprise it, like the top of that swing bin they'd got at home. There was always a knack if you could only master it.

Slam!

Pause.

Kerrr ... chunkkk!

"Oh for goodness' sake."

Something blocking it somewhere possibly? But a quick inspection offered no clues. Time to put some serious wellie into it, and hope that did the trick.

SLAM!!

This time, having slammed, Patrick continued to hold it down with all the strength he could muster. Then slowly, very gingerly, withdrew.

And waited.

There was a long pause. And finally relaxing, he turned to walk away.

KERRR-CHUNKKK!!!

There was no mistaking it now. This was a car boot with attitude. It was quite clearly enjoying itself, seeing how far it could push him. And Patrick didn't like to be pushed.

He reached up to check the catch and found it was working perfectly. It couldn't be the hydraulics or it wouldn't spring up at all. Perhaps those two bags of shopping were interfering with something somewhere?

Patrick leaned in to have a good rummage around. He'd give it one last go and then sod it. This really wasn't his problem.

The knife at his throat, of course, was.

"*Don't even think about screaming.*"

It was not so much a voice as a low rumble in Hell. A sulphurous whisper so close to his ear it might have singed his sideboards. The hot breath stung his face, and he could feel a pulse in his neck that certainly wasn't his own.

A great, brutal weight was applied from behind, pressing him hard against the car. And a claw-like hand was now clamped between his legs, without so much as a letter of introduction. Along with the razor-sharp blade caressing his neck it was more than enough to take his mind off Victor's shopping.

Immobilised with fear, he could scarcely draw breath. And the words "Now quit fooling around" did not readily spring to his lips.

"Ihhh— wwww— yhhhh—"

Was the best he could manage for starters. There was a time and a place for a tracheotomy, and something told him this person would not be calling for medical backup.

"M— Mm— Mm—"

It was slow to emerge, but better out than in.

"Mmm— Mmmelvin ...?"

The face in the wing mirror sneered back at him.

"And you would be the lovely Patrick?"

"Erm ... we-ell."

The question was surely rhetorical.

"Yyy-es, but ..."

With his knife still grazing the skin, Melvin allowed him to step back from the vehicle, and the reflection grew wider.

Patrick had been expecting a typical soap-opera thug: two hundred and fifty pounds of raw meat with scuffed knuckles and a posture perfected in the jungles of Borneo.

He was right on the money.

Between the black beanie hat and the vegan-unfriendly combat boots was a conglomeration of brute brawn and muscle you wouldn't want to mess with. And Patrick, who had never felt more weedy in his life, was not about to try.

"So you and my young lady, is that right? Throwing your dick around in the supplies cupboard at work? A man could have a very nasty accident with a staple gun."

"No, no, no! She must have told you, surely – she made all that up—"

"You calling my girlfriend a liar?"

"Umm."

Careful. This called for some intricate political dithering: an evasive answer to a completely different question. He wished now, he'd paid more attention during Prime Minister's Questions.

"The relationship between an employer and their secretary, in a place of work, is one that demands to be taken seriously at all times, and—"

"Don't give me that load of wank."

Ah yes. The effective supplementary the Opposition never quite mastered. The man would have fared well in an Oxford Union debate.

"Honestly, Melvin, I swear to God – on my absolute life. I never, ever touched Carolyn. As God is my judge, she's a lovely person, of course she is, but I would never think of her in that way, and would certainly never dream of—"

"God is dead."

"What?"

"Grow up, man. All this swearing to God, as God is my judge; I think we both know means fuck all. They never teach you any Friedrich Nietzsche at school?"

Well this was a turn-up. The man had a brain.

"Y— not that I recall, Melvin, no."

"If you took your nose out of her tits for five minutes and read a few books you'd know what I'm talking about. Richard Dawkins, right? Kills it all stone dead. The whole God thing, it's just made up to explain what they can't explain, and don't want to explain. So the logic's all shit. There's no one up there, listening to you, me or anyone else. And no one's gonna save you. So nice try, my friend. Now then. Phone."

"Sorry?"

"Where you're going you're not gonna need it."

"Ohhh dear God."

"You mention him once more—"

"And so ... where am I going, Melvin."

Melvin threw the mobile to the floor and ground it beneath his heel. Then kicked it under a car.

"In the trunk."

"No, no – no please, just give me one minute to explain—"

"*In the trunk!*"

"No, just hang on a sec, please – because – in any case, this isn't my—"

But Melvin was done with dialectic, and done with Patrick's whimperings. The car keys were seized from his hand, and he was upended like a sack of coal into Victor's luggage compartment. And wouldn't you just jolly well know it? This time, as Melvin rammed the lid down it stayed firmly in place, exactly as it was meant to. And no amount of prodding or shoving from within made the blindest bit of difference.

Exactly what was in store for him if he ever got out of there Patrick didn't dare contemplate. It was all he could do to breathe with one knee against his chest and a face full of egg yolks. Had Poe at his darkest ever taken his readers to such a place? This was a horror that knew no name.

A muffled voice from outside sealed his terror.

"Just one sound from you in there. You know what's gonna happen."

There were one or two shoppers now returning to their cars, so Melvin had to play it cool. He was all set to leave with his human cargo when a sign on the wall reminded him payment was required. He picked up the ticket that had fallen from Patrick's hand and made his way to the machine at the other end of the floor.

When he returned he paused for a second.

Now it was definitely the Honda wasn't it, and not the Toyota. No, no, the Honda. Absolutely no question. Or was it that Ford Focus further along? It was a dark, compact saloon, he remembered that much. Or actually ... yes, it may well have been the Toyota.

Thank goodness for remote-control key fobs.

An electronic beep and a pair of blinking hazards were followed by the sound of two doors unlocking to his right.

Ah yes, the Mazda Sedan. Funny how your memory plays tricks. And it didn't help they all looked the same.

Melvin slipped into the driving seat, started the car and eased it out of the bay. A minute later he was heading off goodness knows where to take care of some special business, the nature of which we can all guess. It would only lack a victim, but you can't have everything.

Ten minutes after that, the Honda was also gone: cruising up the M1 with nary a care in the world.

It was coming up to three-thirty when Margaret gave Pippa a call to see how things were going at the coalface.

"Ohhh, don't! It's not something I'd want to do every day, that's for sure. They're just about finished here now, thanks for asking."

The weariness was there for all to hear, along with a medley of clumps and clanks and merry whistling in the background.

"Oh good."

"I got shot of Patrick early on, to save him getting under everyone's feet. 'Cos you know what he's like. He's gonna pick up some shopping, and then collect the keys from the local estate agents on the way."

"So how are you getting to the cottage? On the lorry?"

"You've got to be joking. No, I'll get a cab there, I'll be fine."

"Pippa, you sound exhausted. You sure you don't want some help the other end? Another pair of hands, and a bit of moral support? I never know which is worse, the packing or the sorting out. You could pick me up from here, it's on the way, and Meg'll be fine on her own for the last hour."

In truth she was keen to make amends for all that hoo-ha last night at the restaurant. And with Victor away there was no rush to get home.

"Ohhh well. You sure? I must admit, the moral support would be welcome."

And so it came to pass that having checked and double-checked Tunstall and Gridley had the correct address, Pippa departed 18 Riverbank for the last time. The taxi swung by the shop to collect Margaret, and they made their way to the Trenches' new home in the little village of Thruxton. It was well into rush hour by now but they were driving against the traffic and got there in good time.

The cottage was a decent size, with landscaped gardens and a coffee-coloured dwarf stone wall. White and yellow roses rambled round the exterior beneath a clay tiled roof, and the brief shingle drive led to a roomy double garage. Inside, to complete the charm offensive, there were eighteenth-century beams, exposed brickwork and a fully restored inglenook fireplace. Only one thing, in fact, was missing.

"Where the bloody hell's Patrick?"

Pippa stared out of the taxi window and rechecked her watch. There was no sign of his car, and a quick glance through the garage window drew a blank.

"Well this is ridiculous. He should've arrived by now?"

"You don't think he's got lost?" ventured Margaret.

"Huh. Well."

But further enquiries compounded the puzzle. Wherever he was it had to be a dead spot, as there was nothing doing on his phone. And the local branch of Marsh and Barber confirmed he'd not yet been in for the keys, so a further detour in the cab was required to access the property.

An hour later, as the two women sat cross-legged in the empty lounge, there was further cause for concern.

Where had the removal men got to?

"I don't think the pair of them were too bright," Pippa grumbled. "They'd already had some run-in with Victor over the address. That's why I wrote it all down for them, directions and everything. To make sure they got it right this time."

"Well it can't be coincidence," said Margaret. "There must be some big breakdown or something we don't know about, somewhere or other, that's held them both up."

Pippa crossed to the window and gazed up the road. The light was beginning to dim as clouds moved in from the east. And branches were creaking in the apple tree. She turned to her friend with a shiver.

"Is it getting chilly in here?"

"Does seem to have turned a bit. And they said it would be worse up north."

"Hohhh, what a performance. Makes you wonder if it was all worth the effort."

"Now come on, don't start. You couldn't have found a more lovely place and you know it, so ... oh! Didn't see this here before."

From one of the shelves in the inglenook Margaret picked up a small card.

"Welcome to your new home! Hope you didn't mind us taking the downstairs lavatory seat, but it has sentimental value. And don't worry about all the holes in the front and back garden – that's where we dug up the daffodil bulbs. Also, have removed brass 16 from front door, as our new address is 91 and we can use it upside down. Waste not want not!!! All best wishes, the Pinnocks. P.S. The gas fire in the sitting room will light at the 17th attempt."

"Better give it a go then I think," said Pippa with a groan. "You get the feeling this is gonna be a long one."

What percentage of the public were bastards? It was a question as old as time itself; and one that Victor had often pondered through the course of his life.

In his gloomier moments he'd put it well into the nineties, but surely that couldn't be right. Most of our top surgeons? And all but a few airline pilots?? The country's hedgerows would be piling up with tumours and amputated limbs; and planes would be jumping the queue for take-off, and flying nose cone to tail fin with two geezers in the cockpit window giving the finger. Animal welfare groups would be ritually slaughtered on Boxing Day, income tax would be illegal ("the will of the people"), and emergency vehicles that got in the way would be dealt with by a bastard-approved towing company. And people who thought wars were a bit violent would just get their heads kicked in. No, no, this was silly. The figure had to be closer to fifty per cent, or even forty. It was all too easy to get carried away.

And all too easy, while musing on the above, to drive your car into a ditch.

Aside from that little encounter with Patrick first thing, the day had gone well. His car had made it up the motorway in one piece, which was no mean feat in itself. A few odd bangs and rattling noises, mostly coming from the boot, were par for the course these days, and nothing a little Jazz FM couldn't put to rights. And for most of the drive the weather had held its nerve and remained calm.

Then came the scenery. Sweeping dales of velvety heather and limestone scars; grit-capped peaks and drumlin fields and fells. Hostile, rugged vistas shaped and blasted by an elemental hand indifferent to man.

By the time he'd got within shouting distance of Ursula's these views were blurring big time. A curtain of rain engulfed the car and distant distortions danced in the gale as the blackening skies continued to fissure and shift.

The track that led to the house was full of twists and turns and little surprises; and in conditions this treacherous required full concentration. It was one of life's ironies therefore that Victor, while pondering his public percentage, should have momentarily added to it. Taking one of the bends at speed, and far too wide, he was forced to swerve at the last minute to avoid an elderly woman coming towards him on a bicycle. The elderly woman skidded slightly, but had the best of it as she freewheeled down the sloping lane, screaming back over her shoulder.

"*Bastardddd!!*"

Which you'd have to say was a pretty good shout.

In the sloppy trench where the Honda had come to a halt, Victor got every last groan out of his system, then slipped off his seat belt and clambered out to survey the damage.

"Shit."

His front nearside wheel had sunk deep in the mud, where it was already looking a bit permanent. A set of five long scratches from a hawthorn bush would have come in handy for jotting down a tune, but didn't do much for the car's paintwork. In its capsized position it sat at the same angle as Captain Mainwaring's glasses whenever he'd just risen after a pratfall. And the prospects of it continuing its journey any time soon were nil.

"Shit," he said again, in the hope it would make him feel better.

It didn't.

Such is the permeability of tweed it was now raining inside his cap. And his shoes were already filling up with glop, in affectionate tribute to his active duty as a scarecrow. What was it with him and soggy ruts?

According to the satnav he was only 2.3 miles from his destination. Through a far-off clump of trees two fuzzy gables loomed and blinked in time to the flailing branches: dour and unyielding, imperiously taunting. This was harsh, forbidding country. And as he stumbled, Lear-like, in the storm, madness didn't seem so crazy. Was that wailing, plaintive voice in his head the first sign of derangement? Or through the piteous skirls of the tempest, a lamentation, keening on the wind that tricked the senses?

Or was there someone in the boot?

My God, he was prepared to swear there was! But this was insanity, surely? Could he really have driven half the length of England with a stowaway on board? A few seconds with his ear pressed close to the number plate removed all doubt. Hitchhikers by their nature don't tend to be fussy, but they're more fussy than that. What the words "let me out" lacked in originality they made up for in conviction. And the sounds from within were now growing in urgency.

Victor unlocked the boot and watched it rise.

The underarm deodorant missed his underarms by a good twelve inches, and sent him reeling backwards. Which is not to disparage Patrick's aim, as personal hygiene was the last thing on his mind. Spraying wildly in all directions, his plan was to blind his assailant just long enough to make a run for it. And for several seconds he let the aerosol do its work while he managed to climb free.

"Haarrghhhggghhhh!!!" Victor wasn't sure about the spelling and just went with phonetics. It's safe to say his eyes were not greatly refreshed by that Krakatoa All Day Dry from his shopping bag.

"Whhh— myyyy God! W— what the bloody hell??? What in God's name are y— how long have *you* been in there!!"

"What??"

Patrick lowered his can and peered through the deluge. Having worked himself up into all kinds of panic in a last-ditch attempt to cheat death, he was suddenly confused. Several hours spent lying in the shape of an ampersand had not helped his powers of perception.

"What??" repeated Victor. "What do you mean what??"

"Well, no, I just— what?"

"What the bloody hell are you doing in my car?"

"What? Well I didn't expect you to be driving it."

"What??"

"I didn't think it was you."

"Well who the hell did you *think* would be driving my car?"

"I thought it was someone else."

"*Someone else???*"

"And that's why I just— yes – no – I'm sorry about that."

"You j—" Victor could feel himself tottering in the wind. He'd just driven into a ditch, he was drenched to the skin, and here was his ex-next-door neighbour, having hidden in the boot for four hours to ambush him with a pepper spray, trying to pretend that the last person he expected to be driving Victor's car was Victor! Excuses didn't come much flimsier.

And yet, as he watched his erstwhile passenger struggle to remain upright, and caught the pale, disconnected void in his eyes, he began to sense there was more: the flinty resolve had deserted him, and Victor wasn't quite sure what he was dealing with.

"If you wouldn't mind, Mr Meldrew, I'd rather just …"

"Sorry?"

Opening one of the doors, Patrick collapsed into the back seat. He looked drained and disoriented. Being glad to see Victor Meldrew was a lot to come to terms with. He was, at least, still potentially alive with all his body parts attached; and for the moment just needed to take stock.

With no sign of a let-up in the rain Victor decided to join him. He switched on the engine and got the hot air going to dry himself out. Vapour began to rise from his trousers.

"So what … happened exactly?"

Patrick took a deep breath. And sparing no details, told him. When he was through, Victor really didn't know what to say. So he said:

"I really don't know what to say."

"It's a shame when you came back with those eggs you didn't think to put them in the boot."

"No, well. Didn't fancy buggering about with *that* for half an hour. So I stuck them on the floor. Just by the back s— ah."

"Oh. Yes, sorry. I should have looked where I was putting my feet. Really not with it still, I'm afraid."

"No."

"How far did you say it was to this place of yours?"

"Well – about a couple of miles I'd reckon, across those fields. Does look as if it might be easing a bit out there. For the moment anyway. I mean, if you feel up to it."

Patrick didn't feel up to it. Nor did he feel like freezing to death all night on the back seat of a car.

With a grunt he opened the door.

"So what are they saying, the removal company? Please tell me you managed to get through this time?"

Margaret returned from the kitchen with two mugs of something resembling tea which the estate agents had sold them, just as her friend was coming off the phone. But Pippa's face said it all.

"Bloody answer machine still! That's five messages I've left now. Imagine they've all gone home. What is *happening* to everyone this afternoon? Where is he, Margaret? Would it kill him to try and get to a phone somewhere? Just to let me kn— Hohhh God. It makes you wonder now if … "

"Wonder what?"

"Ohhh, no, no. Nothing, it's just …"

"Listen, you won't have any fingernails left to nibble there before long. I mean, tell me to mind my own business, but is everything all right between the two of you just lately? There's nothing you want to talk about at all?"

Pippa turned away and gazed uneasily into the back garden. If truth be told she was only too glad to have it prised out of her.

"I suppose I have been giving him a bit of a hard time just lately. Over this Carolyn woman. His new secretary at work. You know what it's like, your husband's spending all day with something out of a shampoo commercial, obviously you're gonna get all bitter and twisted, and do everything you can to make their life a misery."

"Obviously. But – you're not suggesting he's gone off for the afternoon, with—"

"Oh it's hardly likely. Patrick's idea of illicit sex is watching Lorraine Kelly with the sound turned down. I doubt he could seduce anyone now without a map. No, it's more this thing with her boyfriend. I mean, until now all that stuff – I didn't even bother to take seriously, but … what if there *was* something in it, after all?"

"Something in what? What *are* you talking about? Pippa?? What thing with her boyfriend?"

As a child Victor had been warned never to accept sweets from strange men.

It was advice he'd followed faithfully until a month ago. Then one day as he was coming out of Tesco, his guard was down and like an idiot he'd walked right into it.

Strange men didn't come much stranger than Ranjiv, who was ringing from somewhere east of the Khyber Pass to see if he was well today and could he spare two minutes to answer a few questions? Victor thanked him for asking and said he wasn't *that* well, having been sick three times in the night after eating some dodgy pork, which Ranjiv described as jolly good, in which case how would he feel about the chance to save money on his phone bill? The "sweets" in this case being a super new bundle that for just £9.99 a month extra gave him unlimited minutes and texts with free calls after six, an upgrade to 4G and a chance to double his data to a cool 800MB. (It may be noted, incidentally, that Ranjiv, like most of his peers, was being treated for IMCD? That's to say, "treated" as in copping a big fat commission for his sales patter?)

And Victor had bought it. Metaphorically and literally. And lo and behold, no sooner was the contract signed and put into operation than his mobile reception was just as bad as before almost overnight.

He'd had this problem before when visiting Aunt Ursula. Then as now he found the only way to get a signal was by leaning out of a certain bedroom window on the top floor. And after their cross-country trek, through waterlogged scrubs and pasture, this was not an attractive option; especially once that downpour got its second wind.

A traveller in that antique land would have likely savoured the Gothic tableau: the stark Victorian edifice, with its ridged slate roof and grey brick turrets, gabled on its southern elevation and girdled with a wrought-iron balustrade; where, from an open window atop the taller tower, a lone tormented figure could be seen raging into the storm.

"What!!?? No, I told you! This is the best it gets! The phone line's off, and obviously this weather's not helping! Hallo?? Are you still there?? Yes, a lot later than planned, what with one thing and another! The car went off the road, and on top of all that …" He took a deep breath and screwed up his eyes against the spray. "I mean I don't even know where to start."

In the bare, gloomy sitting room at the other end Margaret listened in stupefied disbelief. Then she put Pippa on. Then Victor put Patrick on. Then it was Patrick's turn to get wet shouting out of the window while Pippa listened in stupefied disbelief.

So first and foremost, had he informed the police? Well, not as yet. Why ever the hell not? Well, he wasn't sure if it was a good idea. Why ever the hell not? Well, because Melvin would deny the whole thing, wouldn't he, and then what? It was only Patrick's word against his, and he might come after him and turn a damn sight nastier. Pippa couldn't believe what she was hearing! Of course she was glad he was safe – but for goodness' sake!! You'd got a homicidal maniac out there, driving around in their car? The whole thing had to be reported. And if he didn't do it, she would.

Patrick begged her, before she rang off, not to call the police.

Pippa rang off and called the police.

The police said they would definitely put an alert out for Patrick's car and for the man answering Melvin's description. But obviously they couldn't promise anything. Unless Patrick could prove he'd actually been stabbed he wasn't yet technically a victim of knife crime. And the way things were these days they had to prioritise. Pippa said she perfectly understood, and in that case she'd ask Melvin if he could see his way clear to hacking her husband's head off next time, and she'd get back to them. Would they need to see a video of this? Or would just the severed head in a bag be sufficient?

When she came off the phone she was red with rage, and quivering from head to toe. The day just seemed to be getting worse and worse.

It was not about to get better.

A sound at the front door caused them both to look round. Through the frosted glass it appeared that a truck had arrived! Anxiously, Pippa darted into the hall, and Margaret sighed with relief as she mentally rolled up her sleeves.

But a second later the truck had driven off. And Pippa came back into the lounge looking baffled.

"What was that all about? I thought—"

"So did I, but evidently they'd just come to deliver this. Stuffed through the letter box." In her hand was a bulging A4 envelope. "It's addressed to you."

"Addressed to me—"

Margaret tore open the package and slid out a small sheet of lined paper with a message written in capital letters.

"Dear Mrs Meldrew. Enclosed please find eight hundred and fifty pounds as agreed in cash settlement. With compliments, Tunstall and Gridley."

Reaching in further, she produced a thick wad of banknotes secured with two elastic bands. The pair of them stared in silence for several seconds.

"Tunstall and Gr—"

Margaret's brain was whirling nineteen to the dozen, as motes of logic began slowly to coalesce.

"They d— ... when that van came this morning, and you just ..."

Her hand holding the note fell away, while her fingers squeezed the money as if to throttle it.

"Ohhhhh Goddd ... no??"

"Eight hundred and fifty? That's what the removal firm were going to charge us. Sorry Margaret, I'm not getting this. Why's this been sent to *you*? Here? And who are Tunstall and Gridley when they're at home? Whatever's going on??"

There was work to do at Aunt Ursula's, but that could wait till tomorrow.

The first job was to put their wives in the picture. This had now been ticked off; not entirely painlessly. Next up was the small matter of getting comfortable for the night in a creaky old house that was neither warm nor welcoming.

Following Ursula's death the utility company had immediately cut off the electricity. Three days later it was reconnected in response to an email from Margaret, then disconnected two days after that by a man in a different department who had just got back from paternity leave and was not yet across his in-tray. Several more emails and phone calls were required to sort out the mix-up, during which the supply was reconnected, disconnected, reconnected again and then disconnected again. Finally, there was an absolute assurance the power would be back on in readiness for Victor's arrival on the 27th.

The power was, of course, off.

To say the house was like a fridge is not to imply the basement was filled with an enormous salad crisper, or there was a half-eaten chicken on the landing. In fact there *was* a half-eaten chicken on the landing, but as we shall see, this was not the most peculiar feature of a home whose owner had grown increasingly eccentric over the years.

"Yes, I should watch where you're stepping," said Victor, as they crept along slowly by torchlight. "It's a bit of a museum. The pair of them were great travellers. All over the world, here, there and everywhere. What with that and all their animals. You couldn't move round here once, for stray cats … dogs, goats, horses …. it was a job to keep track of them all."

"Yes, though not so hard to keep track of when they're charging round your back garden demolishing everything in sight," said Patrick, with a painful wince. To his dying day he was not buying that story about a misprint on the paperwork, which had "dodgy dossier" written all over it. "Still! Lots to look forward to here in the meantime, would you say? Banged up for the night in an Addams Family theme house, with no light or heat. Completely soaked to the skin and freezing half to d— ohhhh myyy *God*. Mr Meldrew? Drop the torch! Now! Would you please? I'm sorry, I'm sorry, it's just that I can't—"

"Can't what? What's the matter? What's happened?"

They had come to the top of a staircase, where Patrick suddenly froze, as if he'd just walked into an invisible wall. A spasm of pain appeared to shoot up his neck as his head jerked away through ninety degrees. And shielding his eyes he stepped into the darkness.

"*Up there*, Mr Meldrew! In front of you! Don't make me turn round."

"What do you m— up where? What are you talking about?"

"On the *wall*, Mr Meldrew?"

With a strangled hiss he threw out his arm in the direction of Victor's torch beam.

Victor stared ahead blankly. The wall, like every wall in the house, was busy with memorabilia: masks and maps and photos and engravings, and artwork and artefacts from every corner of the globe. Here was a shrunken head from Peru; there a hand-carved hand from the Ivory Coast; and below them an old sepia print of Ursula's great-grandfather, posing with his foot on the neck of a Moroccan waiter.

Centrally placed at eye level was an imposing watercolour of a bird-eating spider from the Amazon rainforest, proudly nestled on a bed of lush vegetation. As hirsute a specimen as ever graced a crate of bananas; and so lovingly rendered was each hair on its furry legs, they seemed to follow you round the room. Along the bottom of the frame lay six dead flies, whose hearts must have given out at the Machiavellian glint in its compound eyes.

"Ohhh right." As Victor stood gazing at this image the penny dropped. "You mean this picture of a spi—"

"*Don't!!* Even say the word! Please!"

"What – spider?"

Patrick shuddered and clicked his teeth. "Yesss! *Thank* you for that, Mr Meldrew. Very much indeed."

"Yes that's one of her wildlife studies. Quite a few of *them* dotted round the place. Of course once the arthritis set in, I don't think she was able t— sorry, are you all right then, or …?"

As Victor swung the flashlight round Patrick managed, finally, to face him, blinking in the glare.

"I can't take them, I'm afraid. It's just one of those things. I've had it all my life. I can't look at them, I can't talk about them, I can't even think about them. When I was four I had to be rushed to hospital after reading Little Miss Muffet. That's not a joke, it happened! So if you could possibly refrain from shining a spotlight on the thing."

"Oh right. Oh dear. So you mean, like in that film – did you ever see that at all? *Arachnophobia*."

"Yes, I'm hardly likely, Mr Meldrew, suffering from a pathological fear of spiders, to have gone to see something called *Arachnophobia* am I? Any more than someone with hay fever would stuff a dandelion up their nose."

"No, I suppose not really."

"Perhaps at some point you could take it down, and hide it away somewhere. I'd very much appreciate it."

"Right, yes. Well. Why don't I do that now then. If you want to just hold the torch for a second?"

There was something shifty in his tone, though Patrick was too far gone to notice. It was all he could do to give Victor some working light as he stood there with his eyes clamped shut, fighting to control a panic he knew was irrational. However lifelike, it was after all just a painting, and he had to get a grip. It wasn't like the dreadful thing was there in the flesh, prowling about the house. Now that *would* be a reason to freak out!

As he transferred the picture to a nearby broom cupboard Victor paused, before shutting the door, to gaze at a small embossed plaque on the lower edge of the frame; then glanced back at Patrick with a frisson of guilt.

Anyone who can't guess what was on it should really try and keep up.

It bore, simply, the name "Edwin".

"Have you done with it yet?"

"Sorry?"

"Is it safe to open my eyes?"

"Oh! Yes!"

Victor's own eyes were everywhere it seemed, as he took back the torch and began to aim it at the skirting board, then back and forth across the ceiling.

"What are you doing?"

"What?"

"Will you keep that thing still? I'm feeling wonky enough as it is."

"Yes! Sorry. Just erm … interesting lampshade."

"What? Look, I thought you said there might be some old clothes round here somewhere, in one of these bedrooms, we could change into?"

"Oh yes. That's right. You still feeling a bit damp?"

"Damp?? In case you hadn't noticed – yes!! Just a little on the moist side? I'd be hard put to say, Mr Meldrew, when I last got this wet. In the amniotic sac perhaps? For the love of God just point me to a towel."

Having found another torch in the garage Victor left Patrick to search through some wardrobes, while he went away "to see to a few things downstairs".

It's fortunate Patrick was so preoccupied with drying out that he failed to spot those inverted commas, or he might have guessed Victor was up to something. He might, for example, have secretly followed him to the conservatory, where the storm had just caused a heavy branch to crash through the roof. And he might then have noticed, as Victor did, a large glass tank in the corner, full of rocks and plants, one side of which was now shattered. Why this should have caused Victor to spin round with his torch like a lighthouse while speaking in tongues might not have been obvious, but it would surely have set him thinking.

Half an hour later he arrived in the kitchen doorway just in time to watch his neighbour fly across the room and upend a colander over the remains of an old feather duster that was lying on the floor.

Bizarre behaviour? For your average sentient being. But you had to remember who you were dealing with here. And so, with no more than a raised eyebrow, Patrick simply asked:

"What's going on?"

"Hmm?? Oh! Nothing, just doing a bit of tidying up. Seeing what's what. How about you. Did you find anything in that bedroom?"

"I did, though sadly most of the corsets and bombazine frocks were a little snug around the hips. And of course the hats up there are so last season. I couldn't find any of her husband's stuff anywhere. I mean, where should I be looking, the place is like an absolute rabbit w— Oh my God. Oh my God."

"What?"

Patrick let out a low, fearful gasp. Light from the torch in his hand threw his face into lurid contrasts and his eyes were now flaring.

"No, I just thought! Suppose it got out somehow?"

"What!"

Victor's heart skipped a beat. He was already living on his nerves, for reasons he didn't care to divulge. And this was too much.

"Suppose it got out? That you were coming up here, to this house? And the second he realised he'd got the wrong car … he'd just put two and two together, and …"

"Ohhh! Right! Well … no, no, I don't think that's very likely do you. In many ways you're probably safer here than anywhere. Now look, erm. I've just noticed the oil-fired stove in here's still working, so that's a bit of luck? So er … why don't you go back up, and try that door right at the end of the first landing. It's a bit of a lumber room, if I remember. And you might find a few bits and pieces in there."

Patrick paused before moving off. There was a sense he was being sold some kind of dummy, though he couldn't put his finger on it. And maybe it was better not to try. The psychoanalyst had not been born who could fathom out that brain.

Victor watched him depart and closed the kitchen door. Then he switched his torch off and listened. If anything was there in that blackness, looking for trouble, might it now be tempted to show itself?

In the room there was no sound beyond a soft drizzling patter on the window.

No sound except …

A subtle, rhythmic pulse that began to rise from the shadows, pitched high above the rain. Distinct from the chirp of a cricket, this was more of a hiss: produced, as anyone who knows about these things will attest, by the stridulation of densely bristled legs being rubbed against the abdomen.

To be clear, we should say this was not a practice Victor Meldrew was wont to indulge in.

Which left only one possibility.

"Ohhh where the hell are you hiding, you little— come out here and show yourself!"

Somewhere on the floor above Patrick flinched as he opened a trunk full of old shirts. The noises from below were growing more baffling by the minute. A series of partially muffled clumps and thumps was followed by an almighty clang, and then a loud metallic cascade, consistent with a number of saucepans falling off the wall. Then a door was violently thrown open as something like a police chase got under way, with the sound of feet galloping up the stairs and along the landing. Then another door was slammed shut, and it all went quiet.

Patrick groaned and tried to put it out of his mind. There would be an explanation of some sort; there always was.

Except when there was no explanation.

Let's face it, spending the night in a deserted old house with Victor Meldrew was never going to be fun for all the family. If he could only hang on till morning, all would be well. This was not the time to lose it and end up loping round a maze with an axe. He had to believe he was stronger than that. In the meantime …

In the meantime, he was still desperate to get out of these soaking wet clothes and into something dry.

The options before him were not tempting. Pairs of shabby old trousers, which admittedly looked quite funky since the moths had been at them, were way, way too short, suggesting their owner may have shared a tailor with Archie Andrews. The sweaters and cardigans were threadbare, and the shirts and vests a veritable wildlife kingdom in 50% cotton. An air of mould and decay hung over them all: could he really bear to have this stuff next to his skin?

One thing he did know: the toilet was calling. He'd not given it much thought since they arrived, but all of a sudden the need was urgent. All that dampness and anxiety had brought things to the fore.

Remembering he'd passed a bathroom earlier on, he stepped out of the door and made his way along the cobwebbed passage.

When he got there he found a thin streak of light was spilling out beneath the door.

There could only be one occupant. But what was going on? Why would he not use the cloakroom on the ground floor? And why had he come hurtling upstairs in that frantic manner?

Ignoring his every instinct to leave well alone, Patrick bent down and peered through the keyhole.

It was not an edifying sight.

With a torch held aloft so he was lit from above, the man in question was kneeling against the toilet, *whispering* into the bowl! A casual observer might have taken him to be at prayer; except that his eyes were wide open and he was making various cooing sounds over the rim. At one point he reached across to the handle, as if threatening to flush; then sharply withdrew and whispered something else, while wagging his finger in a scolding motion. There was then a pause while he set down the torch on top of the cistern. A second later he produced a pair of long-handled salad tongs, which he began clicking together as he lowered them into the pan.

Patrick had seen enough. There were certain recesses in the human psyche too dark to penetrate, and one more second at that keyhole, he felt, could scar him for life. Besides which he was now close to bursting.

Straightening up, he rattled the handle and loudly rapped on the door.

"Mr Meldrew?? Excuse me! How long?"

From inside there came a hasty expletive and the sound of a toilet seat crashing down. More scuffles followed, and the door was opened, no more than a few inches, as Victor's face appeared in the gap.

"Yes?"

"*Yes??* Well – can I come in please?"

"What for?"

What for? In the name of sanity, what sort of question was that?

"What do you mean what for? What do you think for? Mr Meldrew, there's already enough permafrost in my underpants to keep a leg of lamb fresh for a month! And standing at the toilet passing icicles is not high on my list of favourite sensations. So if you don't mind, I really need t—"

"Erm!"

Patrick made a move to get past, but Victor was having none of it. With his foot jammed squarely against the door he continued to block his path.

"There's another one upstairs."

"What?"

"I don't think this one would suit you. It's a bit temperamental. If you know what I mean."

"Temperamental?"

"It may need a new ballcock."

Patrick was already hankering for that axe. Which was not a good sign. With a higher spec bladder he might have stayed on to argue. But life, and his patience, was short.

"Where is it?"

"Where's what?"

"The other toilet."

"Oh. I think, directly above this one."

Patrick shot him a look that would be illegal in a few years' time, and then beetled away to the top floor. Now was not the moment to lose his nerve. The night was yet young, and there was a long way to go. Though barring these little outbreaks of tomfoolery, surely the worst was behind him now?

Behind him, and getting closer by the second.

By ten o'clock that night tensions were beginning to ease.

Patrick had fallen asleep on Ursula's bed, and for an hour and a half the day's horrors were sweetly forgotten.

Victor had been busy in the kitchen preparing one of his spaghetti specials; which Patrick had initially declined, until it was pointed out to him (by his stomach, no less!) that he was absolutely starving.

A ready supply of logs and kindling had enabled them to get a merry blaze going in the lounge. And with a dozen or more candles twinkling away in dangerous positions round the room it wasn't long before they were breaking into the bottle of bourbon Victor had bought earlier, and barriers were gradually coming down.

Having completed their trawl through Uncle Dan's wardrobe, and deciding that neither of them favoured the look of a recently exhumed corpse, they had settled on a pair of long quilted dressing gowns that literally suited them down to the ground, and enabled them both to channel their inner Noël Coward.

"Well isn't this all tickety-boo," said Jack Daniel's, though that was just the alcohol talking.

Victor agreed. With his hands wrapped round a glass tumbler he leaned back in his big leather chair and chuckled. There was a sparkle to his eyes, and his cheeks were glowing with a rosy hue common to many forms of eczema. He wasn't chuckling about anything in particular, but just because, all of a sudden, he felt like chuckling. Often enough people had accused him of finding nothing funny. And he was certainly finding it funny now.

"Yes, tickety-boo and a half. I must say. Now we've had a chance to spend some time together? Not like that awful to-do last night. Balloons and sausages and zimmer players and whatnot – we won't be going *there* again! I mean, it only goes to show, would you say? That people aren't always as horrible as you think. Underneath it all. D'you know what I mean by that?"

With another sip of liquor he slid down a further inch in his chair. Six more sips and he would be horizontal.

Patrick, too, was feeling quite mellow. Viewed through an alcoholic gauze the world was more fuzzy and frivolous. He returned Victor's blether with a serene nod and closed his eyes. After all he'd been through today this Tennessee sour mash was hitting the spot.

"No, because I was just saying to Margaret, only the other morning. D'you know, I'm going to miss Pappa and Pitrick because … Pickwick and Patter … Pinprick and P— what is it?"

"Patrick and Pippa."

"That's right! I knew you'd know. Paprick and Pitta! Sounds like a Hungarian sandwich! If you ask me …"

The mirth this produced in the speaker was contagious, and even Patrick had to smile. Victor's fit of giggles might, indeed, have continued for several minutes if he hadn't at this point noticed a "Missed Call" alert on his phone, which was certainly not there half an hour ago.

"Oh now! What have we got here. A bit of a fluke by the looks of things, my wife trying to get through? I wonder what that's about." But when several attempts to call her back came to nothing he rose, reluctantly, to his feet. "Better go and see, I suppose. And don't forget now, to help yourself."

Plonking the bottle in Patrick's lap he crossed unsteadily to the door, and two minutes later was back at the top-floor window yelling into the gale.

"So what's it like now where you are? Still chucking it down this end! But we've had a bit of grub now, both of us, and got a fire going, so ..."

"*Never mind the bloody fire!!*"

The rasping voice that tore into his ear took him quite by surprise. It was also blindingly effective in sobering him up. Margaret, it appeared, was not in the market for small talk.

"Two hours now, I've been trying to get through! Do I gather that, after I left for work this morning, two removal men called round, and you sent them next door because they'd got the wrong address?"

"Ohhh God, don't remind me! That was another cock-up narrowly averted. If ever there was one."

"It *wasn't* a cock-up!!"

"Well of course. Because obviously they w— ... what?"

Between the wailing of the wind and the thrashing of the trees he couldn't be sure he was hearing right. What was she banging on about?

"*It wasn't a cock-up!!* They'd got the *right* address! And they *weren't* removal men!"

"Weren't remo— what do you mean?"

"They were the people I rang up three days ago, about Ursula's! Don't you remember? We went through half a dozen of them in Yellow Pages, and they were the ones we settled on! *Tunstall* ... and *Gridley!*"

"Tunst— ... and Gri—"

Struggle as he might, nothing was coming.

"They were a *house clearance firm!!*"

"A hou— cl— f—"

"I didn't go into any details at the time, the girl on the phone was a bit of a drip. But she said she'd try and get 'the boys' to call round one day this week. To see exactly what kind of th— Rghhhhh!!" Whenever she made that noise you didn't want to be anywhere within strangling distance. "The *real* removal truck broke down first thing, and didn't get there till mid-afternoon! And the texts never came through till tonight, when we went to the pub for some food, and Pippa finally got a wi-fi signal. What else was she supposed to think when those two dimwits turned up? If we had their bloody mobile number it would be a start! The whole thing's a complete nightmare – they could be anywhere by now!!"

"Oh. Right."

Ten minutes later, when Victor returned to the lounge it's fair to say the spring had gone out of his step. Patrick was squatting by the hearth, feeding some more logs onto the fire.

"How are things back at base camp. All tickety-boo?"

"Hmm? Well, yes. Fine, fine. Basically fine. Though there has been one *slight* hiccup. Apparently. Erm. With your removal operation, as it happens. It appears that, due to a misunderstanding on my part, the people who took away your furniture this morning weren't, in actual fact, removal men after all. They were from one of those house clearance outfits. Of all things!! And it's proving a bit tricky, finding out where they've got to at the moment. To try and sort it all out, so …"

"Ohhh right. I see. Good God, what a relief."

"I'm sorry?"

Behind the thick damask curtains rain continued to pound the windows and the ivy bristled with indignation. Victor, braced for another storm indoors, was thrown off-balance as his companion stoked up the fire and then settled back in his chair.

"No, for one awful moment it was just like all this was happening! And you were actually in the room talking to me! Even though I know full well, I'm still upstairs on a bed fast asleep … it's completely as if I'm physically *here*, sitting by the fire. And I've just been told a couple of junk dealers have waltzed off with the entire contents of my house! Which I'll probably never see again. Where does it all come from? I'll never understand. And even though I'm now *thinking* all this, on some weirdly meta-conscious level, it's still going on. Just have to keep floating through it, I guess? And then eventually I'll wake up."

"Yesss …" murmured Victor, as he reached for the whiskey bottle. "That's what I'm afraid of."

Now then, to digress for a moment. You know when you hear a song on the radio, and you just can't get it out of your head for days on end?

Well, that had never happened to Victor Meldrew.

Until a few weeks ago, when he found himself in the car one day tuning in to the famous Welsh anthem *Cwm Rhondda* (Guide Me, O Thou Great Redeemer) performed by a male voice choir. While lovingly rendered with much brio, the words, he noticed, had undergone one or two changes. For example, the chorus that ran "Bread of Heaven, Bread of Heaven, feed me till I want no more" had become: "Victor Meldrew, Victor Meldrew, he can stick it up his bum"; suggesting he was not in fact listening to *Friday Night is Music Night* at all, but to a specially recorded disc someone had planted in his CD drive.

The production quality was beyond dispute. And considering this was the work of non-professionals the *a cappella* harmonies were especially impressive.

"Sodding car mechanics, I'll break their bloody necks!" was the verdict of one reviewer, while others felt the recital deserved a wider audience. And indeed, when a subsequent version was posted on YouTube it immediately went viral.

The lyrics in full (which remain the intellectual property of H. L. Foskett Ltd Auto Repairs and Body Shop) ran as follows:

There's a bloke we can't stand any longer,
Always on the bleeding moan.
Every time we mend his bloody Honda
He's back grousing on the phone.

First we fixed his car's ignition,
Checked his brakes and clutch and then
Overhauled his whole transmission.
He just brought it back again.

(tutti)
Victor Meldrew!
Victor Meldrew!
He can stick it up his bum,
Up his bum!
He can bugger off till kingdom come!

If the intention was to piss off the listener to high heaven (which it was), their efforts were not in vain. More maddening still was the dreadful earworm that remained, with Victor continuing to sing and hum the bloody thing in his sleep till he was sick of it.

He was not best pleased, therefore, when the two men who turned up to tow his car out of that ditch, having recognised the name, began trilling the song to themselves in his presence. And tempting as it was to declare he wasn't paying good money to listen to ruddy Simon and Garfunkel, he just let them get on with it.

When at last the vehicle was dragged from the sludge he was amazed to find it started first time. Indeed it appeared quite refreshed by the whole experience, with his faulty suspension – dismissed by the team at H. L. Foskett as "knackered beyond repair" – now totally cured.

Some more good news of a sort came from Margaret at midday. Patrick's car had been found by the police, abandoned in a lay-by, and she and Pippa were off to collect it and hoped to reach Ursula's by nightfall.

In the meantime Victor stayed well out of Patrick's way. After all they'd been through it seemed like the safest option, when there was always a chance his guest might stumble on the family's collection of antique bone saws.

There had been little rest for Patrick that night. When he did manage, briefly, to forget that real life was real; and with Cartesian logic to cease to think therefore he wasn't, he had succumbed to dreams that served only to spook him further.

Through the gloom of the bedroom one of Uncle Dan's toupees, seen earlier that day in a drawer, had somehow come to life! And in his nightmare he had watched aghast as the thing began – *of its own volition* – to glide up the sheet towards him, before plopping to the floor and scuttling away across the carpet. In the name of God, to what deviant end within our subconscious were such ghastly fancies forged?

The mantle of dusk was fast descending when a dark grey Mazda Sedan turned in through the gates and pulled up among the sprouting weeds at the front of the house.

Margaret and Pippa had shared the long drive between them and both looked exhausted.

Patrick emerged from the door and made a beeline for the car. His clothes still felt like clingfilm but were dry enough for travel, and he didn't aim to waste any time. Victor said they were both welcome to stay on for the night as it was already getting dark, and Patrick said he'd sooner stick his head up an elephant, which seemed to settle the matter.

Margaret and Victor watched the two of them drive off and closed the front door. In the sitting room Margaret plonked herself down on the sofa with a long weary groan.

"Hohhh God! I don't know how much more I can take. Is there anything left in that bottle? I'm just about done in."

"Tell me about it." Having locked up for the night Victor collapsed in the chair beside her. "And no more news, I suppose, about those two characters and their lorry?"

Margaret cocked her feet up on the stool as she poured out what was left of the whiskey. "Well, I got through finally to that droopy drawers on the desk, who said she'd do her best to get hold of them, but she reckoned the whole lot might have gone off to auction this morning in Bury St Edmunds."

"What, already?"

"Said they work to a very quick turnover, apparently. Still, I suppose we should be grateful for small mercies. At least you managed to head off any upsets last night with you-know-who."

"Huh. With a lot of jiggery-pokery. I eventually got him cornered in the upstairs toilet. Left the door closed and the window open all night, and when I went in this morning – no sign. So fingers crossed he's now left the building. I don't know, the things people keep as pets."

"Yes. And from what Pippa was saying he might have had a seizure or goodness knows what. People get these phobias, it's more serious than you think."

"Chances are he'll be up a tree or something by this time, somewhere in the grounds, and well out of harm's way. So let's not worry on that score. I think we can rest assured, Margaret, that we've definitely seen the last of Edwin around here."

*

There was a case to be made for Patrick and Pippa just hitting the gas that night and getting as far away from Victor Meldrew and his cranky relatives as possible.

It was not a very strong case.

Yesterday's storm had left the rivers and roads in a right two-and-eight. Banks bursting apart and chaos from collapsing branches – it was like 2008 all over again! After backing up for twenty minutes down a narrow country lane where a tree was blocking the way, and then performing a thirteen-point turn at a flooded bridge, Patrick was already starting to lose it. And an hour into the journey they were still only five miles on from their starting point.

And so the decision was made to cut their losses and seek out a hotel for the night. Tomorrow was another day, and they could set off nice and early, refreshed and revived, with a fighting chance of actually seeing where they were going.

As luck would have it (good or bad we shall shortly discover) they came upon one of those jaunty roadside boards which read: "*Aw! Sorry you just missed us! You just passed The Stranger's Rest Hotel and Restaurant. Luxury Accommodation and Family Dining, 500 yards back on your left.*"

"What do we think," said Patrick. "Give it a try?"

"Go on then," said Pippa. "We'll be driving round here in circles otherwise, for ever more."

There was a vagueness about the night sky when they turned round, as the gibbous moon slipped back behind a cloud to decide if it was waxing or waning, and the countryside vanished from view.

The entrance to the hotel, when they got there, was marked by two brick pillars with carriage lamps and a set of fancy filigreed gates that appeared more frivolous than functional. Through an avenue of larches, oaks and Scots pines a rough gravel track snaked its way up through the grounds. Along the way, rabbits that had long since learned the lunacy of freezing in headlights could be seen lolloping for cover. And in the undergrowth a million tiny life-forms were involved in acts of sex and violence, claiming it was good for the garden.

Perched on a central summit was The Stranger's Rest. An odd kind of building with tall, massive wings that towered above the centre, it appeared to be squatting on its haunches ready to pounce upon the unwary visitor. Two high circular windows, which were lit as the car began to approach, seemed to stare down suspiciously for a while, then went black. And apart from a faint orange glow through the front door the building was plunged into darkness.

"Ah! Furniture. That brings back memories," said Patrick as the two of them stepped into the lobby. He was referring to a couple of Chesterfields, a long glass coffee table and a writing bureau upon which lay a small laptop. The colourless paintwork had been carefully chosen to match the music that was playing on a sound system somewhere in the mid-fifties, and on the walls were a number of landscape paintings by a local artist who should have known better.

The room was currently deserted, but the sounds of chatter and drinking nearby suggested a party was going on.

Patrick picked up a small handbell from the bureau and gave it a ring.

Much to his surprise an adjacent door immediately opened and a woman stepped out. There was quite a lot of her, and quite a lot she was keen to own up to. Quite a lot of woman and not that much blouse, if you get the drift. If that wasn't a wig on her head it was a strange place to leave a blancmange, and as for the posh country manner and snorting laugh, let's just say her height was about fifteen hands.

"Good evening, welcome to the Stranger's Rest! My name's Lorna? And what can we do for you nice people this evening – hang on, let me just go and close these. So we can hear ourselves think."

Crossing to a pair of double doors at the back she pushed them both shut to dampen the noise. Her perfume never left the desk, and her high heels took no prisoners in the carpet.

"There we go, sorry about that," she said, sailing back. "We've got a private function on tonight. People come here for a good time and we try to make sure they get one. So would you be looking to stay with us tonight, or …?"

"If possible," said Pippa. "We've got a bit of a drive ahead tomorrow."

"Well you've come at a very busy time as it happens. The only thing I've got left is the honeymoon suite."

"Oh, really? Oh, right. And what exactly would that erm …"

"Well it's a little bit special, as you can imagine. If you're romantically inclined." Was that a mischievous wink or a false eyelash come loose? "Let's just say we've never had a complaint from the couples who've stayed there."

Pippa turned slightly to Patrick, then slightly to jelly. There was plenty of sub-text here, most of it not that sub. But what the hell? They were only young once. And that was ages ago. Maybe with a can of petrol and a box of firelighters the old spark could yet be rekindled.

"All right then," said Pippa. "That'll be fine."

"Sound good? *Ohhh* kay, let's see if we can't sort you out a special rate."

If this all seemed too good to be true it's a pretty safe bet that it was.

Spoiler alert: a comic twist was on its way. Though not so comic if your names were Patrick and Pippa, and you'd just been shown up to a grand set of rooms on the top floor and told to "have yourselves a ball!"

"Well! This is a bit good isn't it," said Pippa, as Lorna was heard clopping away to the lift. "Cut above your bog standard, and no mistake. I wonder what they usually charge?"

Patrick, who had popped into the bathroom for a freshen-up, called back through the sound of running water: "Well I suppose this time of night it was just going begging! My God, there's a lavatory in here that seats four – I tell you, plush isn't the word!"

In fact plush *was* the word. Marble pillars and Regency chaises longues strewn with velvet cushions; a Louis the Fourteenth HDTV (or so the cabinet would suggest); and a vast circular bed with satin sheets. I mean, vast circular bed, what was *that* all about? You'd need Mercator's Projection to find the hot water bottle!

The rest of the furnishings were well up to snuff, with classical portraits and elegant draperies, and along one wall a huge antique mirror with a jewelled ormolu frame that seemed to double the size of the room.

Pippa slipped off her shoes and sat down on the bed. Lorna had put on some Miles Davis, and the muted horns were soothing and cool. A German white wine stood beside a large bowl of fruit, along with a box of Belgian truffles. She peeled off the cellophane and popped one in her mouth. Then her eye travelled to the pillow, where a lacy white camisole in silk had been draped across, with a card that read "*To enhance your pleasure*".

"Wow. They don't call it a honeymoon suite for nothing then."

Picking up the card she read on: "*Anything else you may need is under the pillow.* My God. You don't think ..." And yes! A quick glance confirmed it. "Blimey, they *have* thought of everything."

If there was any upside to all the crap they'd been going through, they were at least going through it together. There was nothing like shared misery for restoring relations. And they'd still got each other. Just. For the first time in months she remembered why she'd married him.

"Listen ... Patrick. I know I've been a complete arse for the past few weeks. What with one thing and another. It's not been nice and you didn't deserve it. But I mean, here we are now – in this amazing place? It feels like, I don't know, something's telling us to get our act together. If you know what I'm saying? And listen, I'll even turn a blind eye to that ridiculous—"

"Sorry?"

She turned at the sound of a door opening, and from the bathroom stepped a man who looked quite like her husband. There was something missing that she couldn't put her finger on; mainly because he'd washed all the bits down the plughole. That little blue razor on the tray of toiletries appeared finally to have jogged his conscience. And in truth he felt like a new man; while his wife, who had felt like a new man for the past two months, found herself going all soppy and soft.

"It's been a long while since we spent the night in a hotel."

"It has."

"And they've left us a lovely bottle of wine."

"You think we could be tempted?"

"I think *I* could be tempted."

They had moved in quite close at this point and ... steady on! They were kissing. Long, soft and liquid with a note of spice. When they broke Patrick picked up the bottle opener and did the honours. The wine fulfilled its duty. Crisp and tangy. A welcome intoxicant. The mood, the bed, the night were all suddenly full of potential.

"Might be an idea to fill up this ice bucket?" said Pippa. "While I um … just go and sort myself out?"

("Just go and sort myself out" of course being code for "Stay where you are, I'll be right back." And "Stay where you are, I'll be right back" being code for "Give me two ticks while I pop to the bathroom." Beyond which we refer you to Bletchley Park.)

Now, the events that came next may be hard to credit in this day and age. And yet they happened all the same.

Patrick was standing by the ice machine at the far end of the corridor, watching his chips cascade into the bucket, when the lift doors beside him slid open and a gaggle of partygoers spilled out with much raucous laughter. They were mostly middle-aged and mostly drunk, and most of them were carrying glasses or swigging from bottles and generally behaving like arseholes. Which was only right and proper as that's exactly what they were.

Patrick did his best to ignore them, but as he collected the ice and turned back to his room he was caught up in the tide of bodies, which were all heading in the same direction. And his attempt to break free was foiled by a lady wearing various bits of dead animal round her neck, who linked her arm through his and dragged him back into the throng.

"Hey, hey, hey! Where d'you think you're off to?" she cackled, in one of those fruity voices that doesn't come cheap. "You're going to miss all the fun!"

Further along, where the passage branched off to the right, people were disappearing through a doorway. It had all gone very quiet, and one or two women were removing their shoes, as muffled smirks and devious looks were exchanged.

Some poncey party game or other. Why would Patrick be interested?

"Look, I'm sorry, but I've really no desire t—"

"*Ssshhhh!!!*"

The lady in the furs thrust a finger to his lips and mimed a zipping action along her own. A second later he was propelled into the room. Two seconds later someone had found him a chair to sit on. And three seconds later he was undergoing the most embarrassing experience of his life.

The space in which he found himself was cramped and dark, with four rows of seats facing the wall. It resembled, in fact, a tiny viewing theatre, in which the guests were now gathered with a growing sense of excitement.

The reason was clear. In place of a screen was a giant two-way mirror. Beyond it, a bedroom, in which a woman was carefully applying some lipstick. Leaning in close to her audience she blotted her lips on a tissue and performed a slow, sensuous pout. This went down a storm, with people all sensuously pouting back and fluttering their eyelids in exaggerated pastiche of Minnie Mouse.

When she stood up and crossed to the bed there were several delighted gasps. While not quite naked she might as well have been, for all that her flimsy nightwear concealed. Wisps of lace and not much else clung to her body for dear life, revealing a set of curves that were not entirely where they ought to be.

Pausing only not to consult a Gideon Bible in the drawer, she spread herself across the bed like Marmite: sinuously and provocatively flexing her limbs in readiness for things to come. Unlike Marmite this was definitely to everyone's taste behind the glass, as a celebration in dumb show took place, with arms being thrown in the air and one man jumping onto his chair to pant like a bloodhound.

Imagine, then, the crushing dismay as suddenly the whole tableau went black, and a man carrying an ice bucket came tearing into the room and killed the lights. Amongst the frantic jabbering that followed, the words "Get your clothes on, we're off!" caused the greatest outrage, with many of the spectators booing and others demanding their money back.

For the first and only time in their lives, Patrick and Pippa left a hotel without paying the bill.

There were seven bedrooms in Ursula's house and they all smelt of boiled cabbage. Air fresheners made no difference, nor incense or perfumed candles, nor *pot pourri* or the power of prayer. And over the years Victor had had to throw away five pairs of pyjamas when he got home.

Once, in 1988, Uncle Dan had fallen asleep with his pipe still alight and set fire to the bed. Attempting to smother the flames with a rug he had set fire to the rug. A minute later the whole room had gone up. Firemen fought the blaze for an hour, and what remained was a blackened shell full of ash. When they removed their breathing apparatus all they could smell was boiled cabbage.

Sleep was the only known cure, and Victor and Margaret were just dozing off when that loud rapping on the front door went and spoilt it all.

"Good God, the things that go on in these places!" said Margaret, as she traipsed back in from the kitchen. She put down an old paraffin lamp and took off her dressing gown. "Makes your hair curl, just the thought of it."

"Don't tell me it's that pair come back again? I thought they'd be half way down the M1 by this time." Victor blinked at his wife through the gloom, then fluffed up a handkerchief and wiped his nose on the pillow case. "What's happened?"

"You wouldn't believe me if I told you."

"What?"

Margaret told him.

"Myyy God. What are you s— the two of them were actually both ... in the middle of—"

"I don't think it quite got that far. But I mean! If he hadn't gone out there for that ice – can you imagine?"

Victor did his best not to.

"Pippa's still shaking like a leaf down there. And Patrick's face seems to be stuck in a strange grin like a ventriloquist's dummy. Hopefully that'll pass, but ... I made them both some cocoa, and said they could have that room on the top floor. You know, where Great Aunt Gertie used to live, before they got the court order."

"What about the fingernail marks down the wall."

"I think those were all filled in, weren't they? When they took the bars off the window. Anyway, I could hardly turn them away. After all they've just been through."

"I suppose."

Victor was already drifting off by the time Margaret slid in beside him. She turned off the lamp and wriggled back down the bed. Five minutes later she, too, was fast asleep.

Somewhere outside among the trees a presence was stirring ...

When Patrick and Pippa had finished their cocoa and every last crumb of humble pie they began their ascent to the bedroom.

The contrast with their previous suite could not have been more stark. As Pippa lit the candles she'd been given by Margaret a dismal chamber was revealed, with a scruffy old four-poster standing against the far wall. Whether the wall was holding up the bed or vice versa was unclear, but the false leg being used as a brace at one end did not inspire confidence.

On the ceiling a text had been scrawled with a crayon tied to a broom handle. (We know this because the writing implement was still propped up in the corner.) A message of hope and humanity from one who had gone before, it read simply: "Try not to step on the woodlice."

Down in the grounds the presence prepared to seek out its prey.

Patrick tried the mattress with his hand, half-expecting it to crumble to dust.

"Hard as rock. But better than nothing I suppose. At least there are no mirrors in the room. Obviously Meldrew would have taken them all down, as he has no reflection. I tell you, the first sign of daylight tomorrow we're off. Please God we can grab a few hours' sleep in the meantime."

"Talking of which, don't tell me I left the toiletry bag in that sodding place! I could've sworn I put it back in here before we left?" But a frantic rummage through the holdall she'd just plonked on the chair was to no avail. "*Bugger* it! And there was a full packet of valium in there as well. Unless it fell out on the back seat maybe, as we were coming back? It's no good, I'm gonna have to go down and look. Hand me that torch."

"If the valium's still in there, save some for me."

As Pippa returned to the car Patrick began his preparations for bed.

The doors to the house were all locked and secured, but with a little ingenuity the presence had found a way through.

The flare from Pippa's torch came bobbing down the staircase and into the hallway. Behind her in the blackness, scurrying legs went darting up the steps with barely a rustle.

In the bedroom Patrick draped his shirt and trousers over a chair, then threw back the covers on the bed. Somewhere beneath the dust were two pillows, which did not look especially tempting.

On the landing outside, the presence was closing in.

Patrick crossed to the window and lifted the sash as high as it would go, then peered down into the gloom.

Directly below was a lean-to conservatory whose roof had been speared by a massive branch from an adjacent ash tree. Collecting the pillows, Patrick leaned out and began whacking them together with a force that did the North of England's asthma rates no good whatsoever. The resulting draught extinguished several candles, and feeling his way back to the bed he began groping around for some matches.

To his horror he came across something large and warm and hairy.

"Ohhhh ... my ... *Godddd*."

It was a human hand.

Worse still, it was a human hand attached to a human body. And although the face was in darkness Patrick had a pretty good idea what it looked like.

"Ohhhh ... my ... *Godddd*," he repeated.

The shape was in shadow. Savage and simian. Then it slunk into a flickering light beside the door, and bared its teeth in a snarl.

"Mmm— Melvin? Howww— did you—"

"Oh! Well! I rang the coppers, didn't I? Obviously, 'cos I was worried sick. Worried sick about my poor missing brother-in-law? And how helpful were *they!* Give me the address and directions, absolute stars. Incidentally, d'you know you've got a lot of broken glass around this place? That could be a real security issue."

"Ohhhh ... my ... *Godddd*."

"And will you give that bollocks a rest? Can you still not see the paradox? If there *was* a God he'd be far too smart to believe in himself! There's your Omniscient Being fallacy right there! So I d— ... can I smell boiled cabbage in this room?"

Patrick laughed for six seconds in a bid to ease the tension. Which is not easy when your assailant's holding a harpoon.

Yes, a harpoon. It was that sort of house, remember. There was a whole glass case full of them downstairs, but this one was was fine for Melvin's purposes.

Patrick briefly considered grabbing the false leg and attempting to sword-fight his way out. But then sanity prevailed as an idea flashed into his head of quite breathtaking brilliance.

He fell to his knees and began begging for mercy.

"Please, please, please! *Please!!* Won't you believe me!? There was no truth whatsoever in all that stuff she said! No truth of any kind!"

"Keep going, it's good to see a man dig his own grave."

Had Patrick literally been digging he would shortly have come to a pair of slumbering figures in the bedroom beneath. One of whom convulsed with a noise like a startled chimp, as the overhead ructions grew louder.

"What the hell's going on up there!? Sounds like they're having a right old ding-dong."

"Mnnnhhh? Whahh? Ohhh go back to sleep."

"Chance would be a fine thing? Listen to that! Can you hear that? Ruddy racket, coming from those two upstairs! You can't tell me that's not keeping you awake, Margaret! Margaret??"

Margaret snapped out of her foetal position with a yelp.

"Wha—?? Yesss! I'm completely wide awake now! I can't imagine why!"

"I mean just listen! I thought you said they were all luvvy-duvvy again, after that set-to over his secretary? It doesn't sound much like it."

And indeed the fracas that followed seemed to confirm this.

"No, no, no! Please! Please put that thing down? I can understand, obviously, you'd be jealous, but there's no cause to be! Honestly! There was *nothing* went on between me and Carolyn – I sw— Oooofff! Nghhh!! Ohhhh *shittt!!*"

"My God, what the hell's she doing to him? You think one of us should go up and see what's happening?"

"*Absolutely not!* Just leave them to it!" Margaret grabbed his arm and yanked him back. "It's not for us to interfere! They've got to sort this out for themselves."

As the two of them stared at the ceiling the cries and the clumps and the clatters suggested some kind of pursuit was taking place around the room, with Patrick protesting and pleading and knocking over furniture.

Strangely, there was nothing heard from Pippa in all this. Perhaps she had nothing left to say, or decided that actions spoke louder than words. All the same it was odd not to hear a peep from the supposed victim in the affair.

Until …

All of a sudden the most ear-piercing female scream rang out from above!

"*Pippa???*"

Upstairs, the door to Great Aunt Gertie's room stood open. Inside was a tableau of mayhem lit by candles and torches that contained something for everyone. For fans of *Spartacus* there was a man with a crayon-tipped broom handle flapping a blanket about to ward off his opponent, while a man with what looked like a whaling lance kept jabbing away at him, in homage to *Moby Dick*. For good measure, a taste of *Psycho* was provided by a hysterical young woman shrieking in terror at the top of her voice.

Whatever Melvin was playing at with his sadistic taunts could be no more than foreplay. That thirst for revenge would be quenched only by Patrick's blood. As the latter fell back on the bed and became caught in the drapes his attacker moved in for the kill. A candle was knocked over and immediately died. Cocooned in shadow, the two figures continued to flail. To a soundtrack of sneers and squeals and imprecations an arm went up and a flash of light caught the barbs of that bloody harpoon.

It was all over in seconds.

From the other end of the room Pippa let fly with the only missile at her disposal. Her aim was too high and the toiletry bag hit the roof of the bed, raining its contents over Melvin's head. And Melvin, momentarily forswearing his beliefs, went full-on apeshit.

"*Myyyy Goddd Allll-mighty!!!!*"

And no, it wasn't the flannel or the dental floss or the embarrassing ointment that triggered this reaction. All of those and more he could have coped with. But even a deranged hitman has a tipping point.

And for argument's sake let's say that tipping point was a ruddy great tarantula landing on your face.

Regular viewers of *Alien* will have no trouble picturing what followed: a man literally blinded with panic as a monstrous life-form clamped its eight spiny legs around his eyes, nose and throat, releasing, for good measure, a salvo of urticating hairs and a shot of venom just in case he got too comfortable.

The first rule for dealing with a spider sting, as any Boy Scout knows, is to drop your harpoon. This Melvin did but it wasn't much help. And as he reeled and staggered with the pain and frantically clawed at the thing and stung himself even more his whole balance went for a burton. And with your back next to a tall open window that was asking for trouble.

The fading yell as he tripped and plunged was capped by an almighty crash of glass far below. Pippa ran across with her torch and shone it down into the void.

The ground, as they say, had broken Melvin's fall and he wasn't moving very much.

Victor and Margaret had arrived in the doorway, a bit late in the day. But they got the gist of it. And Patrick, having freed himself from the bed, joined his wife at the window.

"You OK?" she asked.

"Yes, I'm OK." he said. "Are you OK?"

"Yes," she said. "I'm OK."

Melvin didn't look OK. But then whose fault was that? As he twitched and groaned amid the wreckage of glass and timber on the conservatory floor it's safe to say his campaign of vengeance had run its course.

Meanwhile, the black mass that was attached to his face like an all-over beard took a moment to get its breath back and slowly regrouped.

Phew. That free-fall stunt just now had been really scary. And yet kind of cool at the same time. You could see the appeal of these extreme sports, but no way would you risk that kind of thing without a man's head for protection.

Delicately unclipping each leg, one by one, it detached itself and picked its way through the debris towards a big glass tank in the corner.

It was fun to travel. It broadened your mind. And the last two days had been quite an experience: exploring new places, like the inside of that toiletry bag, and the bathroom window ledge, and the saucepans and shelves in the kitchen; and making new friends in the lavatory. But let's be honest, you wouldn't want to make a habit of it.

As Edwin settled down among his rocks and his plants, and helped himself to a late-night snack from his stash of dead beetles, he felt a sweet glow of contentment, knowing he was back where he belonged.

There was no place like home.

Chapter Four
Yakety Sax and Beyond the Infinite

WITH THE PASSAGE of a hundred trillion years the supply of gas required to initiate the formation of new stars throughout the cosmos was gradually exhausted, resulting in the domination of black holes which through countless aeons all slowly expired from the loss of thermal radiation. Depleted of dark energy and subject to the laws of dynamic fluctuation and recurrence, the universe was thus reduced to a state of irreversible entropy, in which all material form and life and spacetime finally ceased to be.

But we are getting ahead of ourselves.

The following morning Victor woke up with a bugger of a headache. This was hardly surprising as it was half past ten and he'd only been asleep an hour. The events of the previous night had left him distinctly fragile, and in no immediate hurry to take trampoline lessons. As he lay there trying to remember how to open his eyes the sights and sounds of the last twelve hours were not readily forgotten.

The police had been there in minutes: assessing the scene with calm precision and those dislocated speech patterns that TV cop shows always get spot-on.

"Been having a bit of bother then tonight, have we, by all accounts?"

"Tried to attack you and got a bit too clever for his own good this chappie, did he?"

"Fancied yourself as a bit of a harpoon expert sir, did you? But not quite able to get your act together when it came to the crunch by the looks of things, were we?"

"Ah now! Recognise that face anywhere, don't I? Charging him soon as we get back to the station with a string of other related offences with which he's also wanted in connection this gentleman then, shan't we set about?"

"Pardon, sir?"

What was left of Melvin would be shortly repaired and sentenced to fifteen years in clink, from which he would return to the community a changed man: fully skilled in bomb making, arson and cybercrime and radicalised by all manner of nasty politics.

Somewhere in the south-east RAF fighter jets would be scrambled, while the prime minister chaired an emergency meeting of the COBRA committee.

And the nation would rejoice.

Patrick and Pippa went home to lick their wounds. Which is not an image we'd care to dwell on, through a two-way mirror or otherwise.

And as for the hero of the hour, it would not be long before he was taken in by a home for rescue spiders, where he was fed and looked after, and encouraged to express himself with creative web-work and line dancing.

Margaret was in the kitchen buttering some toast when Victor finally made it downstairs. For the first time in a week the sun was out, and the glare through the window was dazzling. Shielding his eyes he pulled down the blind and fished out a cereal bowl from the cupboard.

"If you're thinking of having porridge we're out of milk. Unless you want powdered."

"Powdered will do."

"We're also out of porridge."

Victor put back the bowl and sat down. He'd got precious little appetite anyway.

"Hohhh God, what a night. I can't believe it's all over."

"I know. And when you think what could have happened. Talk about touch and go. Looked for a while as if he might have been right the other week, that bloke. I should had known he was talking rubbish."

"What bloke the other week? Who was talking rubbish?"

"Him in the sweet shop. That Dimkins character. You wonder if he's even a real witch in the first place. Stringing people along like that."

"Oh. Right. Forgotten all about it."

"All that guff about you coming to a grisly end if you went on a long journey. I've a good mind to ask for my money back."

"W—"

Victor struggled for a moment to see where she was coming from, but didn't much like the direction of travel, so he let it slide.

"So what time are you off this afternoon? I suppose you don't want to leave it too late."

"No, and we've got some big floral displays to get ready tomorrow, so I'll need to be in early. About two o'clock, probably. You'll be all right here on your own till Friday? What you haven't got sorted by then'll just have to go to pot. Oh, and I rang the electricity. They promised faithfully you'll have it back on by the end of today."

"Huh. Where have I heard that before. Anyway, think I'll just go down and check the post box. Be enough crap in there by now to sink a battleship, I shouldn't wonder. Get a bit of fresh air at least."

With which he collected some keys from a hook on the wall and went trudging off through the front door.

He had not been long gone when Margaret's attention was drawn to a distant sound of hammering and power tools coming from the southern boundary of Ursula's land. She glanced out of the window but could see nothing beyond a screen of thick laurel bushes. Someone, somewhere, industriously beavering away. Perhaps she'd get a better view from upstairs?

Ah yes. It was that new neighbour Mr Sheldrake, working on some kind of enclosure for his ducks and chickens. Or rather, adding to the one that was already there between his two wooden sheds. Was it her imagination or were those sheds a bit closer to the house than they used to be?

By all accounts it was only a month since he'd moved in, but he seemed to be making his mark on the property. A leathery-looking gentleman, rather tautly put together, he moved with the gait of a statue come to life, earnestly driving home each countersunk screw as if it was his last. You had to admire the work ethic, but it was a noisy affair. And with all the drills and bangs and clucks and quacks she very nearly didn't hear the tubular bells in her cardigan pocket.

"Hallo, Margaret Meldrew?"

The number meant nothing, so her tone was terse. If this was about an accident that wasn't her fault, or a once-in-a-lifetime chance to consolidate all her debts, the caller was in for a mouthful.

"What? Nohhh ... I think you must want one of the farms. There's no peccary here. I beg your pardon? Ohhhh *Gregory*!! No! Sorry, there's a bit of a racket this end, and I can't move far from the window or I'll lose the signal. I'm actually in Yorkshire, at my aunt's house, who's just died, it's a bit of a story. So how are *you*?"

The voice in her ear was like a warm breeze. Smooth and beguiling, with just enough edge to dilute the intimacy.

"Margaret, I hope you don't mind me tracking you down like this? I rang round some florists, and spoke to your colleague. And I would have called sooner, but things have been fraught. God knows what you both thought of me that day, when I took off through the common. That man and that woman ..."

"Oh! Yes! I think we saw them."

"It's like, wherever I go they're on my tail, you know."

"Tchhh, God! But – so who are they working for then, these p—"

"Let's just say they mean business. The way things are, I can't drop my guard. It's a long and sorry tale, I'm afraid, that goes back to Fallujah, sixteen years ago. I mean, I won't bore you, but ..."

"No, no! You won't bore me?"

"Well, we were right there in the thick of it, you know? Trying to find a way through the western propaganda machine. I was in a jeep with a three-man film crew. Bunch of government goons haring down on us, firing at our heads. We hit a rock, the jeep went over, my cameraman was killed. Somehow, to this day I've no idea how, I managed to drag myself out and get away. A load of stuff we'd found out, I posted online. Very conveniently, it's all since disappeared from YouTube. And I tell you, they don't give up these people."

"I can't believe what you're saying to me, Gregory! All this time, all these years, and all these dangerous places? It sounds like you're lucky to be alive."

"I'm making it sound melodramatic. You just try and do your bit. Whether it's in Gaza, or Mosul, or Yemen. To get the human race to take a good hard look at itself. And as long as I keep my head down, and don't do anything stupid … but listen. I'm calling, obviously, to apologise for waltzing off like that. And before I leave town next week I thought perhaps, I don't know, we could all meet up for dinner one night. If you wanted to come here, to my hotel. And we could pick up where we left off. Go over those old times together. What do you reckon?"

"Oh. Well the thing is, Victor's going to be staying on here till Friday, doing a bit of an inventory on everything, and …"

"But *you'll* be around?"

"Erm …"

Why the hesitation? The answer was simple enough, surely.

"I'm not quite sure, exactly, what our plans are going to be as yet, but …"

"Well have a think anyway, and let me know. Last time it was all too brief, that's for sure. You've got my number now, so … I'll wait to hear from you, OK?"

"OK."

"You take care, Margaret. We'll speak again soon."

"Yes. Bye, Gregory. And for goodness' sake look after yourself."

The line went dead and she felt a sudden emptiness, though she couldn't say why. Because there was so much of him, in a sense? And so much to digest? A ghost from the past who was somehow much more than the sum of his parts. And Fallujah, for God's sake! That was a hell of a long way from Carol Hawksworth's house.

As she lowered the phone she let her hand relax finally. She hadn't noticed how hard she'd been pressing it against her ear, and now her fingers had gone numb.

Well of course, all that noise coming from across the way had made it difficult to hear.

Talking of which …

Before he found a wasps' nest in the post box Victor had been in quite a good mood. There was a lushness to the grass and the trees after all the rain, and the sun on the pine bark drew out a heady scent that was most agreeable. Ambling along through the ragwort and buttercups was more than enough to mellow the soul, even one as tortured as his. And as he stepped out through the front gate onto the roadside an astonishing sound broke upon the air: one of the rarest in nature, at this time of year or any other.

Victor Meldrew whistled.

He was likely unaware that he whistled, and if challenged would have strenuously denied the charge. But whistle he did; lightly and blithely, with an involuntary nonchalance that left his defences down just when they were needed most.

The small cast-iron tower that stood on the verge was already half-obscured by a drooping lilac tree, and the buzzing traffic through the slot at the top not immediately obvious. Consequently, as Victor bent down to unlock the door he was unprepared for the onslaught that followed.

For one brief second he caught sight of a solitary white card lying at the bottom inside. But there was no chance at all of retrieving it.

From within came an airborne attack whose political roots would be one day traced to a grievance over squatters' rights, but which basically involved getting mad at anyone who came near. An unseemly slanging match ensued, with the wasps, who didn't much like being yelled at by some old git with a shiny head, responding in their native tongue. Zigging and zagging around his head and up his sleeves and down his collar, they were everywhere. All over his body and inside his clothes the joint was jumping. There went the first stab of pain, on his left shoulder! And there was another! Just inside his waistband!

Waiting for them all to die of old age didn't seem an option. And so, before you could say Clark Kent he had torn open his shirt and tossed it aside. The subsequent image, of Clark Kent dramatically removing his trousers and wriggling them off, tends to get less coverage. And with good reason: it took Victor a good twenty seconds to undo his shoes, and then his belt, and clumsily pull down each leg while hopping about in a jig of hysteria.

As he raced back to the house, leaving his clothes in a pile by the gate, the wasps did a collective high-five and returned to their nest to fight another day …

… while Victor, as he entered the kitchen, was fresh out of self-congratulation.

"*Bloody things!* That's all you need, isn't it! Can you believe that, Margaret? What was inside that ruddy th—"

But Margaret, as we know, had left the room, and his words were wasted on the air. What she would have made of her husband exploding through the door in his underpants can only be imagined. But it's fair to assume she'd have batted an eyelid.

"Urh."

Victor sat down to inspect the damage. Remarkably, after all that, he appeared to have got away with only two direct hits. But they were both giving him hell.

"Ffffhh!! What are the chances of finding some vinegar in here, I wonder? Or is that for bee stings, I can never remember."

Whatever. The jury was still out on that alkali/acid debate anyway. All Victor knew was that ten minutes later, after dabbing it here and dabbing it there much of the pain had eased, and he was ready to have another crack at that post box.

From what he'd seen there was one single item inside, nestling at the bottom. But it had the feel of something important. And as he'd learned to his cost, all too often, you can overlook these things at your peril. He hadn't come all this way to miss out on some vital notification that might affect the house sale or the disposal of the contents. He just had to be better prepared this time.

And so, wearing a pair of thick leather gardening gauntlets and some swimming goggles, and with a scarf tied round his face, he returned to brave the swarm.

Yes, there it was beneath the nest: a small white rectangle, slightly soggy at the edges, bearing a red Royal Mail logo.

This was not going to be easy, by a long chalk.

Once his arms went in he was working blind. The gloves gave him no sense of feel or direction. But for several minutes he stuck at the task, while the natives grew more and more angry. And after much groping and fiddling he had his reward. With the card gripped precariously between two fingers, he drew out his hand and backed away to safety.

Off came the gauntlets and goggles. Then a brief fumble for his glasses.

There was no name or address on the front. Just the usual small print about options for redelivery.

On the other side was a handwritten note in thick felt-tip pen.

It read:

"*WARNING!! This post box is full of WASPS!!*"

And underneath, in letters that grew more tiny as they went along so as to fit on the card:

"*Will leave all future mail in a black bin liner behind hawthorn bush. Postie.*"

Outside the gate, the corporate hum seemed to break up, briefly, into several hundred diminutive guffaws.

You might well ask, who would have thought such a simple idea could fly? And the answer would be: Victor Meldrew.

Yes, Victor Meldrew, and many like him, were never in doubt that a bloody great rubbish bag was the ideal home for all the junk that's shoved through our letter boxes. Brochures and pamphlets and puffery, hermetically sealed in guaranteed hedgehog-asphyxiating plastic that outlived its usefulness the day it came off the press, and without which our lives would be not one jot poorer.

A good hour it took him, to complete his trawl and consign what he could to Aunt Ursula's recycle bin; by which time it was just coming up to half past two. Yet when he tracked down his wife to one of the upstairs bedrooms he found her kneeling on the floor, intently studying what appeared to be some kind of vast architectural drawing spread across the carpet.

"What's happening, I thought you were supposed to be off by this time?"

"What?"

"It's getting on for quarter to. What's that when it's at home."

Margaret picked up a large old-fashioned magnifying glass and buffed it on her sleeve. Then leaned in close to inspect some faded writing.

"It's a plan of the house and grounds. You remember? The solicitors sent it back after they'd taken a copy. And that boundary's a good ten yards past the ditch, according to this. So he is *well* out of order! And if he thinks he's getting away with it he's very much mistaken!"

"Who's well out of order? What are you going on about now?"

"Sheldrake – is his name? Have a look out there. You see where he's knocking up that great long fence, next to our dried-up stream."

Victor crossed to the window and peered into the distance. A lot of hammering was going on, and he could just make out some kind of wooden stockade, with what looked like some chickens and geese running about. A middle-aged man in a jerkin was pausing to light his pipe before picking up a chainsaw.

"What about it?"

"Don't you remember her saying? The last time we spoke on the phone. About some people who'd just moved in next door, who were putting up these new sheds she reckoned were slightly over the line. And if you look at these plans you can definitely see it. As plain as day, what he's up to."

Victor eyed her curiously. There was a strange fire to her voice that didn't quite fit. As if she'd just had an urge to reboot her conscience. Though for what reason he couldn't guess.

"Up to?"

"They think they can go round building these illegal settlements, they've got another think coming!"

"Illegal settlements?? For ducks and chickens?"

"That's how they get away with it, isn't it! By exploiting the weakness of others. *She's* just an old woman in her nineties, how's *she* going to stop us? Well it's high time someone had the guts to stand up to these people. So off you go then."

"Yes, well I daresay y— what do you mean?"

"What?"

"What do you mean, off I go then? Off I go where, to do what, for goodness' sake?"

"Well what do you think!?"

Having joined him at the window she rapped a finger on the glass and raised her right eyebrow, as if to brief him on his mission. But still he was none the wiser.

"*What??*"

"Go and *talk* to him! Show him these plans, and tell him he's overstepped the mark! He needs to dismantle those sheds and take back that fence, and withdraw to his own land. It's the least we can do, after all the years she spent here."

"Why does it have to be me?"

"Because *I* need to go and get ready in a second! And he'll take more notice of a man. You know what these stuck-up country squire types are like."

Victor wilted. Those wasp stings were still throbbing and he was just looking forward to a nice sit down with a cup of tea. But when Margaret was in this sort of mood resistance never got him very far.

"Right, well that sounds like a good idea. Let's declare war on the neighbours over some fenceposts! What if he's got a gun?"

"Oh just *do* it. I've got to go now, and pack my things."

Smacking him in the chest with the plans, which she had just refolded, she left the bedroom. Something had got her goat, but he wasn't sure what. And he had the sense that Sheldrake was just a minor player in this drama.

Still, if there *was* any funny business going on with the boundaries it made sense to get it sorted now rather than later.

So long as he didn't have a gun.

As she stuffed all her bits and pieces back in the holdall one by one, Margaret realised she'd mislaid her moral compass. She'd mislaid it, to be precise, more than forty years ago. But fancy it turning up now.

And how to make up for all that lost time? You could only do what you could do. The world was a cauldron of pain and injustice, in which righteousness merely bubbled around on the surface. It was so easy to overlook; so hard to acknowledge. And harder still to make a difference. But then what were we good for in this life, if not to try?

Of course she didn't consciously think all these things. Like most of what burns inside us they were felt on an abstract level; as if she had something to prove, to herself if to no one else.

But now, time was getting on, and she couldn't afford to dawdle. Slipping on her jacket she gathered up her bags and searched around for her car keys.

Downstairs she heard the back door slam, which meant that Victor had left the building. Hopefully to put this person straight, as instructed. He was not, after all, a man to mince his words when the need arose.

Returning to the top-floor window she watched as down below he set off across the wild, untended grassland. After a few seconds he disappeared from view beneath a canopy of elder and chestnut trees, then reappeared in miniature as a distant figure approaching the spot where Sheldrake was working.

Visibility was hampered, so she hurried across to one of the bedroom cupboards, where she remembered seeing a pair of Uncle Dan's old birdwatching binoculars. The lenses were scratched and the image slightly blurred, but there was Victor, pausing beside a large roll of chicken wire, to bellow up in the air, as if to someone in the sky.

As she panned slightly to the left Sheldrake was revealed, sitting astride the roof of one of his sheds, nailing on a sheet of felt. Pausing in his work he glanced down as Victor called up, gesticulating first towards the fence and then towards the ditch. And to give him his credit, he did seem to be making a forceful case: striding backwards and forwards and jabbing at the plans with his finger.

Sheldrake listened for a bit, then cocked his leg over the side and climbed down a ladder to join Victor on the ground. Somewhat to Margaret's surprise the two men then shook hands and began to exchange some light banter.

A moment later the door of the shed opened, and a woman stepped out who appeared to be Sheldrake's wife. She had long brown hair and a short brown skirt. And a short waxed coat and long waxed legs. In her mid-fifties for sure, and like her husband and all of their class with no further need to evolve. At her age, it was strictly against the law to look that stunning. Or would have been if Margaret had anything to do with it.

Viewed in a grainy vignette that was all wobble and no sound, the whole thing brought to mind an old silent comedy, without the comedy. What the hell was Victor saying to this woman now? Whatever it was made her rock with laughter. Which in turn made her look even more delicious, as she tossed back her hair and crinkled her eyes, and the tip of her tongue poked out cutely between her teeth, like it would just bloody well have to, wouldn't it. Then Victor laughed back, and then Sheldrake joined in, and *then* – if this didn't take the biscuit – the latter brought out some folding chairs from the shed, and all three of them sat down, in a curious nod to the 1945 Yalta Conference.

Could this get any worse?

It certainly didn't get better. Lifting up a large rucksack, Sheldrake feigned a magic pass with his hands and pulled out a bottle of wine as per a rabbit from a hat. This was met with much gaiety and clapping, and a minute later they were all sipping from plastic cups and chatting away as merry as you please.

What Margaret muttered under her breath was perhaps not worthy of her. But then she was currently prey to some complex strains of inner conflict and emotional dissonance, which the sight of her husband handing round a bag of M&M's did nothing to assuage.

Still less was her delight when Mrs Sheldrake began suddenly choking as one of the chocolate-coated nuts appeared to go down the wrong way, and jumping to his feet Victor rushed across to help. It was one of his long-standing boasts that he knew a thing or two about the Heimlich manoeuvre, memorised long ago from an episode of *Magpie*; but the vision of him tightly gripping this woman from behind and performing heavy rhythmic thrusts while she gasped and shrieked was really more than Margaret could bear.

Where were all the professional snipers when you needed one?

As with the best silent comedies there was more to enjoy in the second reel. When Margaret returned after a brief toilet break she found that events had taken a more mind-boggling turn.

Having tragically survived her gagging fit Mrs Sheldrake appeared to have got a second wind, and more besides.

To say that she had Victor over a barrel was no more than the literal truth. For there he was, pinned hard against an old water butt, while the lady in question unbuttoned his shirt and copped a languorous feel up his back.

It's fair to say that Margaret was no lip-reader. But even she could see the words "Stop that immediately" were at no point uttered. What was it with men when they didn't know they were being watched? The words hanky-panky didn't get near it. And as for this woman's husband: what kind of sleazy *ménage* were we looking at here, as he sat there apparently egging them on?

It was a miracle those binoculars were still in one piece after she'd flung them across the room. The three china ducks on the wall were not so lucky; but such were the casualties of war.

Margaret was half way down the M1 when the accident occurred. And all because she lost her concentration, just for that one split-second, and wasn't looking where she should have been.

For the past three hours, whenever the name "Victor" came up on her dashboard she'd flatly ignored the call. He could ring and ring till he was blue in the face: she wasn't in the mood. After that tawdry display outside, God only knows what he'd got to say for himself. Whatever it was could damn well wait. In the meantime she was content to spend her journey home rehearsing the interrogation to come: a kind of mental dress run in which she rather handily got to play both parts. And no prize for guessing who came off worse in *that* exchange.

But then somewhere around Junction 10 she began to think about fish fingers. Were there still enough left in the freezer for tea? Or would she need to stop off somewhere soon to do a bit of a stock up? And if so, would she go for those chunky *Taste the Difference* or just the regular?

And that was how the accident happened.

With her thoughts elsewhere she completely forgot to screen the call, and by the time she saw his name flash up it was too late.

"Hallo?"

"Hallo, Margaret?"

"Who's this?"

"What do you mean who's this – who do you *think*!"

"Victor? Oh. Sorry, the line's a bit crackly."

"What's going on? I've been trying to get through to you all afternoon!"

"Really? Well I must have just lost the signal."

"What, five times?"

"Well *I* don't know! So you're back then now are you, finally?"

"I got back ages ago. I must have only just missed you."

Margaret doubted that. And made a low grunting noise that signalled as much.

"So what did *he* have to say for himself in the end, the Fiddler on the Roof. I saw the two of you shaking hands over there. All very pally."

"Fiddler on the roof?"

"Your new friend Mr Sheldrake."

"You know he's not Jewish?"

"When did I say he was?"

"No, they're both from east Lanarkshire, apparently. And seem like a nice couple. He reckons there's actually two ditches along there and we may be getting them mixed up. But he says he's happy to look into it and if he's wrong he'll either move it all back, or see about doing a deal for the extra bit of land. I mean he couldn't say fairer than that really."

"Sounds like you all got on a treat."

"I know! And that Cressida's certainly a character. Nearly came a cropper, as it happened, with one of my chocolate peanuts. Though luckily I remembered that technique, you know? Of how to unblock someone's passageway when they're choking."

"Yes, you wouldn't want one of your nuts to block her passageway."

"Sorry?"

"I'm sure she was most grateful."

"Oh, and then she said if I was interested, she'd got this special gel..."

"Oh yes?"

"... that was brilliant for wasp stings. And touch wood, since she put a bit on my shoulder, I can't tell you, the relief!"

"So quite a success then all told."

"And plus they've invited us both round there tomorrow, for afternoon tea. Of course I said you wouldn't be here, unfortunately, but ..."

"Oh but you can't let Cressida down. No, no, you just go along and enjoy yourself. I'm sure you'll have a whale of a time. Now look I'll have to ring off, I've got to buy some fish fingers."

"Oh. All right then, bye."

As excuses go it sounded pretty damn feeble.

Which of course was exactly the point.

Another night, another flight from reason, time and sentience. From the moment that bedside lamp went out your fate was sealed. Dreams, dreams and more dreams. Autonomous and unforgiving, without respite, a lottery of virtual worlds and otherness that showed no mercy.

Sometimes you could dream you'd woken up when you were still dreaming; and sometimes you could dream you'd just dreamt you'd been dreaming; and sometimes you'd even dream you'd been dreaming that you'd just dreamt you'd woken up, when in fact that too was a dream. And sometimes ... well, you get the idea.

So thank God for the fact that, by hell or high water, at the appointed hour, that radio alarm always put the matter beyond doubt.

"... and now with the time at 8.39 let's take a look at today's papers.

"And yesterday's horrific bloodbath at a clothing factory in Nuneaton is given a cautious thumbs-up by the Daily Seizure, which devotes most of its front page to Princess Eugenie's latest wardrobe malfunction. Under a detailed diagram showing how one of the sliding door runners came away from its metal housing, the paper carries news of a brand-new app that can reduce climate change, which has been ruled unconstitutional by the US Supreme Court. According to research it says 'the human genome is much the same as the garden gnome, just pronounced differently.'

"'The most vile and repulsive man in Britain' is how the Daily Thompson describes its new star columnist Dreg Grisly. In his first op-ed piece for the paper, Grisly argues that a recent injunction restraining the press from bringing back the death penalty is further proof we're sleep-walking into a police state. Is it any wonder, he says, that our children can no longer spell their own names, or master the basic skills of selling lethal arms shipments to repressive Middle Eastern governments?

"And finally, the decision to publicly crucify a schoolteacher who winked at one of her ex-pupils on his twenty-first birthday is hailed as a victory for common sense in today's Nightmare World of M. R. James, and a kick in the teeth for the 'batty barristers' who produced irrefutable evidence she'd just got something in her eye. 'Three cheers for the mums and kids on the Jury of the Damned', it says, under a photo of them all posing with the stars of Gogglebox. 'Now we know there's nothing wrong with a tin of good old-fashioned British treacle for breakfast, we can sleep much easier in each other's pyjamas—'"

Margaret awoke from her delirium with a start. In exactly that way that people never wake up suddenly in a film or on TV: by not jack-knifing upright directly into camera.

It was small wonder you had all this gibberish swilling around in your head.

What happened to all her usual dreams; where she was in a bath full of snakes, or being chased through a wood by Malcolm Muggeridge?

This was all Gregory Birchall's fault. With his one-man war of words and blasted heroics. He had no business invading her psyche like this.

Though she had to admit, it was fun to be twenty-one again.

As she stood there at the cooker that morning, stirring her porridge, she tried to imagine her own husband in a jeep careering down a dirt track with a local militia squad firing at his head. But no, it wouldn't come. He'd be stopping every five minutes to get out and tell them they didn't own the bloody road.

And what was so wrong with meeting up for dinner anyway? A chance for two old friends to sit down and unwind. Swap a few stories and share a few memories. Have a few laughs together.

In his hotel.

And what of it? Goodness knows, she'd never crossed *that* line before, in forty years of marriage. At her age the very idea was ridiculous. All the same, she didn't need this carry-on with Cressida Sheldrake to muddy the waters.

Not since that night Victor gave a naked woman a lift home in his car had she felt so rattled. The fallout from which had lasted a week; and it didn't take much for all the sordid details to come flooding back. OK, a pedant would argue this lady wasn't actually naked in the car. But that was only because she'd put some clothes on. The merest technicality in Margaret's eyes. She was, by her own admission, a nude model, having only just posed for Victor at his art class. And what he'd seen he could hardly then un-see, it stood to reason. To this day she'd not forgiven him for those nipples. There was *trompe l'oeil* and there was just plain vulgar.

But enough.

It was another nice morning, and time to be making a move.

Thank God for the precious calm of her workplace and its mellow distractions.

Amid the scented bouquets and sprays of the florist's she could file away all these obsessions for a later date.

And then came the curious case of Mrs Staveacre.

It was quite a job dismantling the edifice of someone's life. And after six hours of sifting through all the clutter in Ursula's study Victor was beginning to wish he'd never started. So much that had once meant everything, and now meant nothing. Trappings of an existence that were all set to die the death of a thousand skips. And the only heart they would break now lay cold in the grave. It was fair to say his afternoon tea next door couldn't come quick enough.

The Sheldrakes' house was imposing and Georgian, and Victor sensed it had a bit of an attitude. Cressida was at the front door to greet him when he arrived, and led the way into the drawing room. She was wearing something light and skittish in cotton and some jangly jewellery. Having sat him down on a hard striped chair she poured some Earl Grey into a bone china cup. Victor noticed that she'd now tied her hair back and found himself comparing her neck with the spout of the teapot. Her husband was still in the back yard cutting up some logs.

"Well, do give our love to Margaret won't you," said Cressida, picking up a small tiered stand from the table. "And let's hope we'll all get a chance to meet again before the two of you sign off up here."

"Well yes, I hope so," said Victor, selecting something that might one day grow up to be a sandwich. "She sends her apologies."

Cressida then sat down facing him and began to talk about Islamic pottery. This completely threw Victor, who had come along expecting to reprise their conversation about ditches and boundaries; or how his wasp stings were getting on today, or how was her throat feeling.

But Islamic pottery it was; ranging from its birth in the seventh century in Mesopotamia to its later influence on Byzantine tiles and ceramics. He had a vague idea this derived from a comment he'd made about a vase on her table, but couldn't be sure. His concentration having waned after the first six words, he was already entering a catatonic trance.

Then, to his utter alarm, he realised she'd stopped and asked him something. And he had no idea what it was.

Could he possibly ask her to repeat it, after he'd sat there for five minutes with a big wide grin on his face, apparently hanging on her every word? He'd look like a simpleton. Better to try and bluff it out with some all-purpose blether.

"Hah! Well! Yes indeed. That's the sixty-four-thousand-dollar question."

"Excuse me?"

"Sorry?"

"I just asked where you were from, originally."

Ah. Nope. He'd have to pass on that one. For the moment at least. Where he was from ten minutes ago he could just about manage: it was that big house next door. But this was a real brain freeze. And how long would it be before his face got stuck in this rictus grin? He could already feel the muscles going into spasm. What if he couldn't break out of it, and she started to talk about the massacre in Tiananmen Square? The jig would be well and truly up.

In the awkward hiatus that followed, a terrible truth dawned.

He had absolutely no conversation left.

He'd used it all up the day before without realising. Every last word. And now he was running on empty. Yesterday had been frothy and superficial and fun. But this was a whole different ball game. This was serious social interaction, with someone from another planet. And from that look on her face, it was only a matter of time before she called for the men in white coats.

But as luck would have it fate was on his side, in the shape of a sudden horrific accident.

Mumbling something he didn't quite catch, Cressida rose from her chair and crossed the room to open a window. As she did so the low background spurts of her husband's chainsaw grew immediately louder, and she had to shout to make herself heard.

"Darling!? You *do* know Mr Meldrew's here? Have you got much more of that to do before y— *oh my God!!!*"

From outside, the shrill engine noise went briefly into overdrive and then cut out, accompanied by a sudden shriek that sent a shockwave through the room. Victor was out of his chair like a spring, while Cressida seemed to crumple on the spot.

"What is it? What's happened—"

"It's Roger! He's just cut his foot off!"

It was a page from last Thursday's *Herald*, and it very nearly went in the bin. Having just clipped the ends off two dozen gypsophila stalks Margaret was in the process of scrunching up all the bits in the paper when her eye was drawn to the following story:

OAP'S BEDROOM 'TURNED INTO LAVATORY' BY CRUEL PRANK

A ninety-year-old widow was the victim of a sickening practical joke this week when a number of packages delivered to her home were found to contain blocks of frozen urine.

> The incident occurred on Monday at the River's Bank nursing home in Cadogan Crescent, where the boxes in question were left unattended in the resident's room for several hours while the central heating was on maximum.
>
> Mrs Kitty Staveacre, who was in hospital at the time recovering from a hip operation, was thankfully spared the disastrous effects of the deed.
>
> Said the manager of the home Mr Larry Spikings: 'We can't imagine who would have done a thing like this. She had no enemies in the world. When the boxes arrived, addressed to Number 19, we never dreamed what was inside. We can only thank heaven she won't be back for another week, so we can at least try and repair the damage.'

Margaret shuddered. It was frankly incredible what people would sink to these days. Though why you'd want to target a harmless old woman like that, for no apparent reason, was anyone's guess.

If truth be told this was just the kind of elaborate "jape" she'd had to put up with herself on more than one occasion, when her husband had managed to upset someone or other. In fact, if she didn't know better ...

But no. Surely it couldn't be?

Suddenly her mind was doing somersaults.

Number 19 River's Bank?

And it wouldn't be the first time would it? Ever since this new place opened last year: letters and deliveries going the wrong way. Who else, in the normal course of events, might expect to receive a consignment of urine through the post, frozen or otherwise?

There was an ominous echo of something here that she couldn't shake off.

It had all taken place about a month ago: in the long-running war between Victor Meldrew and The Rest Of The World, a minor affray that appeared to have passed without consequence. Though in hindsight perhaps they should have realised there was more to come.

The worst of it had been the lyrics.

Blasting through the walls of their house across a thumping bassline and taking the phrase "lack of decorum" to a whole new level:

Hey yo, motherfucker, no brother gonna shit wid me
Check it man, no cuck ain't gonna hit on me
Now I got emancipated I ain't constipated or subjugated
Take a dump how I want it's not complicated
Now they bustin' my hump to get me investigated
By some cats wanna put me in da can
An' paint me black and white man, like a soup can by Andy Warhol
Gettin' shit from Interpol an' I need some paracetamol
Cuz it's critical you gotta rise up be political
An' put your neck in a noose it's the only truth
No pussy nigga cop get to inspect me
I'm-a pull da trigger watch him pop till he learns to respect me
Dudes on the spectrum jizzin' in the rectum
It's counter-factual till it gets contractual

The effect of which was to send Victor off to investigate, while his wife kept her distance in the front doorway.

Outside in the road an ice-cream van was parked, around which three toddlers were jigging about, licking 99 Flakes. The vendor, now apparently taking a lunch break, was slouched at the wheel with his knees bent up and feet on the dashboard: the illusion that he had just trapped a small armadillo between his teeth dispelled by a Greggs paper bag lying scrunched in his lap. On the passenger seat was an empty Foster's can, on the first leg of its journey to Mrs Aylesbury's rose garden. The windows were all down and the CD player was dialled up to full volume.

Those who recall the earlier events in a Vietnamese restaurant may get a sense of déjà vu from the dialogue that followed:

"Hey you!! What the bloody hell d'you call this on a Sunday morning??"

"What?"

"You think you could turn that up a bit louder please? I'm not sure they can all hear it properly in Papua New Guinea!"

"What's *your* problem?"

"What's my problem? You!! This is supposed to be a quiet residential road, in case you hadn't noticed! Not *Listen With Mother* on acid!"

The young man blanked him out with a glassy stare. As someone whose cultural horizons were largely confined to the testicle he wasn't quite tuned in to Victor's frequency.

"Ah go wind your neck in and stop taking the piss!"

"I'll take the piss as much as I want! Whenever I want, and wherever I want, if it's all the same with you!"

"Is that right! We'll see about that then, won't we!"

"What's that supposed to mean?"

"We'll see how much you can take the piss! I know where you live mate, so don't push it."

"Are you trying to threaten me?"

"Fuck off."

Yes. That was pretty much how Margaret remembered it all; from what she'd been able to hear for herself, and from what Victor had told her afterwards. A lively little exchange, but in the rough and tumble of these routine encounters there was nothing there you'd take literally.

Or was there?

Over the years she'd learned never to underestimate the power of a grudge.

And it beggared belief what people would put in those ice-cream freezers.

Cressida Sheldrake sat beside the hospital trolley nervously biting her lip. The paramedics had got there in record time and done what they could on the spot, but now it was down to the specialist skills of the A & E team. The extent of the damage was still to be verified, but thus far the signs were quite hopeful.

In charge of the assessment was a tiny Sri Lankan lady who was ideally placed to specialise in knees. Returning through the curtains after consulting a colleague she rechecked the patient's heart rate and shone a light in his eyes.

"Still unconscious from the trauma. This is not uncommon. While we're waiting to send him through for a scan, perhaps I could take a few more details from you, is it Mrs ...?"

"Yes, Sheldrake. Cressida Sheldrake."

"And the gentleman here is your husband."

"Good God no."

"I beg your pardon?"

"His name's Meldrew. M-E-L-D-R-E-W. I think that's correct. His address I don't know, I'm afraid. I know he doesn't live locally."

"Oh. I'm so sorry. I thought—"

"No, no, I believe one of his relatives died up here recently, and he's been looking after the sale of their house. We'd just invited him round for some tea, my husband and I, and when he saw that Roger had chopped his foot off with the chainsaw – out like a light I'm afraid! Took a real crack to his head as he hit the wood burner, I'm just hoping it wasn't serious."

"Errr – no." Dr Sanganachelvayakam looked suddenly flustered. "We're not expecting the CT to show anything, from what we've seen so far, but ... I'm sorry? Your husband chopped his foot off?"

"I know! Second time in six months, what's he like!" Cressida rolled her eyes to the ceiling and flicked the palm of her hand forward. "I mean, because – well I just think the false leg's so obvious now I've stopped mentioning it. A lot of people take it for arthritis. And the way he's up and down those ladders! Ten years ago that went, when he crashed the Jag. And now he's got this habit of using it to rest the saw against, every time he goes to pick up a new log. Nightmare! I don't know."

"Uh-huh. I see."

"Urghhhh ... ghhhhh ... ohhhh myyyy *Goddd*."

Beneath the red blanket something was stirring.

"Victor?"

For the first time since he was rushed into the building, in scenes reminiscent of *Supermarket Sweep*, signs of life were beginning to emerge.

The gash down his forehead looked mild enough but had taken its toll. Where in the name of Hell was he? In some liminal space between life and death that was all dazzling lights and strange far-off bleeping sounds, and where one and a half women were standing leaning over his face and staring down at him.

"Mr Milldroo. How are you feeling now, sir?"

Dr Sanganachelvayakam peeled back one of his eyelids and let it spring down like a roller blind.

How was he feeling? As if he'd just taken part in a new game show where contestants rest their neck on the edge of a lavatory while two teams of comedians take it in turns to slam the lid down. (With big cash payouts for their chosen charities.) Unfortunately, all that came out was:

"Wurrhhhh … ohhhh … wurrhhhh …"

Cressida took over. Speaking slowly and precisely and ever so clearly.

"Victor, listen carefully. You had a bit of a shock at my house. And it caused you to faint. And bang your head. Quite badly. It left you unconscious for about an hour. But now you're in hospital. And they're going to come along in a second and pop you into the scanner. Just to make sure you're OK. Do you understand all that?"

Yes … yes, that all seemed to make perfect sense to him. There was only one thing he wasn't quite sure about.

Who was Victor?

Now isn't it funny the way those mood swings always catch you off-balance? Turning anger into anguish and back again in the twinkling of an eye? Just when you think you're not hopping mad, it's just an aberration, you find the real aberration is the aberration and you *are* hopping mad after all.

For the last day and a half, like little video clips on a loop, those scenes by the shed kept replaying in Margaret's mind. M&M's and wasp stings, and you rub my back and I'll squeeze yours, and let's all get together at my place (sorry to hear your wife's not around, but hey) … it was a pretty potent mix. And what sort of name was *that* in any case? Cressida. I mean please! She probably had a parrot called Grenville. And let's not get started on the dyed hair.

What with all this and the row leading up to that business in the nursing home, Margaret had had more than enough to chew on since she got home. All that remained was to seethe and make plans to give her husband hell the minute she next spoke to him.

And then in an instant everything changed.

It was coming up to midnight and she was just about to put the light out after reading. There had been no word from Victor all day, and up to this moment she'd hardly given it a thought. After their last exchange in the car perhaps it had dawned on him that a cooling-off period was in order, and he'd decided to keep his distance.

But then how realistic was that? Knowing Victor, those snarky comments likely went in one ear and out the other; especially on the phone where her laser-sharp withering gaze would be sadly wasted. And to give him his due it was most unlike him not to ring all this time. For one thing he'd be firing off questions about all the stuff he was sorting through. What did she think about this, and what should we do about that? And was any of this rubbish worth keeping? Plus it was hard to imagine him coming back from that tea party and not immediately wanting to share the details. If she served no other function in life she was the sounding board upon which he relied to keep himself sane. The prop that held him up, through good times and bad.

All of a sudden she was getting a dreadful feeling, things weren't right.

Alone in that great big house, with its ailing structure and dodgy timbers, there were a dozen and one ways to come to that sticky end she was warned about. What if the prediction was still active? What if that man with the harpoon had some accomplice who shared his thirst for violence? Or what if her husband was walking back down the lane and a tree fell on him? God knows there'd be plenty enough that were weakened in the storm.

Uncertainty turned to panic. All this time she'd been mentally browbeating the man, and there he was, like as not, lying in a pool of blood somewhere fighting for his life.

Where was her phone? Please God he was somewhere in range of a signal! As anxiously she tapped away on the screen she was already berating herself for all those festering suspicions that she knew were unjustified. Victor and Cressida Sheldrake? For goodness' sake, get real!

"Hello? Victor Meldrew's phone?"

The voice was soft, husky and breathy, and almost certainly horizontal. It was a voice laced with intimacy, wispily confidential, purring in an unseen darkness.

"Whooo ... is this?"

As if she had to ask.

"Oh! Margaret, is that you? Sorry let me switch the lamp on. Just a tick, it's on the other side of the bed. Victor? Wake up, it's Margaret."

Dimly, through the hiss of the phone Margaret thought she could hear sheets rustling. Then came an impatient grumbling sound with an all-too familiar ring.

"Margaret who?"

"Oh for goodness— Sorry, Margaret, bear with us. I'm Cressida by the way. From the house next to Ursula's. I'm afraid your husband had a bit of a prang here this afternoon. All my fault, I should have said something, about my husband's prosthetic leg. And when he went through it with a saw, poor Victor! Fainted on the spot and took a nasty hit against our iron stove. The hospital checked him over and he's feeling a bit ropey, but basically fine. Only, the thing is, with any concussion they won't let you out on your own for the first twenty-four hours. So we've got him staying with us here for the night, bless him. While I keep an eye from the chair. He's been well out of it since we got back, and I was just nodding myself, to be honest. But let me just pass you over, he's right here."

In an ideal world Margaret would have put the phone to her sympathetic ear. Alas, it was all clogged up with this barrage of detail, which she was in no hurry to process. The fact that Victor was there in this woman's bed, or one of them, at such an unearthly hour, and in goodness knows what state of undress, was quite enough for starters.

"Margaret? Ohhhh God. Sorry, I think I've had a bit of a ... ohhh dear. I should've rung you, but ... hallo? Are you still there?"

A good question. She was still there, but for how much longer?

"So you've been in the wars then, I hear."

"Hohhh, don't. I can barely lift my neck off the pillow. And now it's gone all stiff into the bargain."

"I'll bet."

"Sorry, Margaret, I feel like I'm ... I'm ..." Whatever he felt like was left to the imagination, as his voice began to tail off into a dreamy distance. "I think, if you don't mind, I just need to get my head down! Cressida?"

Margaret didn't wait to hear if he got his head down Cressida or not, as it wasn't her place. Instead she just said she was sorry for disturbing them both at this late hour and she'd try again in the morning when she hoped he was feeling better.

The laser-sharp withering gaze once again went for nothing.

It's fair to say that Victor's nice relaxing break in Yorkshire had not been quite as nice or relaxing as he'd hoped.

After a week of turmoil that involved chasing giant spiders and coping with knife-wielding maniacs, and keeling over sideways after watching a man pick up his severed foot and head it into a bucket, he was more than ready to call time on the whole experience. There was, however, one unfortunate coda to his trip that cannot go unreported.

And as they say in the current parlance, you couldn't make it up.

Picture the scene. It was Friday lunchtime, and Victor was sitting in Ursula's front room with a tray on his lap, tucking into his final tin of baked beans on toast with two poached eggs on top. The news was on TV, with three very loud members of the public at a market stall spouting uninformed gobshite to a sagely nodding reporter. Victor studied their arguments carefully, and was just about to plunge a fork through his eyes when he received a phone call from Cressida.

"Sorry! Are you on your way back, or have I just caught you in time?"

"Oh! No, no," Victor hastily dealt with his mouthful and muted the TV. "No, Margaret's not arrived yet, I expect she'll be here shortly. Are you well."

"I'm fine, we're both fine. How's the head now? You've not been falling over or talking in Swahili? No, I just rang, Victor, to say I've printed up a copy of our own property plans, which I thought might be helpful on that boundary issue. I can put it in the post, but I don't have your address."

"Oh, well no, that's OK. Why don't you just bring it round if you've got a second. I'll be here for a while yet."

"Perfect. I'll call by and drop it in your box. And have a safe trip home both of you, and give my love to Margaret."

"Yes, will do. Bye Cressida. Regards to Roger."

Victor hung up and finished his food. Then he went back upstairs to pack his bags, and then he went round every room checking that all the windows and doors were locked. A text came through from Margaret saying she was just five minutes away, so he went into the hall and pressed a button on the console to open the front gate.

And of course that's when he realised.

"I'll call by and drop it in your box."

When he told her about those wasp stings the other day, had he actually thought to mention where the nest was? On deep reflection, he couldn't swear to it.

"Bugger it."

Glancing out of the window he could just make out a graceful head of auburn hair approaching his gate on the other side of the shrubbery.

"Ohhhh my God …"

In a flash, Victor was out through the front door and flying down the drive.

Time was of the essence. With any luck she'd spot the danger and back off. But with all that lilac in the way it was none too obvious, and heaven forbid she'd reach straight in and end up covered in the bloody things, as he had on Monday.

"Cressida??? Stay away from that post b— !!"

But no, it was too late.

"Shittt!"

Not more than a quarter of a mile down the road a dark blue Honda Ballade was just appearing round the bend.

Considering she'd been at the wheel all morning Margaret was feeling improbably buoyant. The drive had been a smooth one, with a nice little stop-off at a village pub for some coffee and a home-made muffin. The sunlit uplands were at their most non-metaphorical, with vistas to die for. And Steve Wright's selection of TV themes from the seventies made for a diverting backdrop. From Khachaturian to Carl Davis, via *Kojak* and *Black Beauty*, what was not to like?

More importantly, she had spent the last three days in detox, purging her mind of all those venomous thoughts that had no business to be there in the first place. This time tomorrow the pair of them would be safely back home, where the events of the past week could be gently forgotten.

On the radio, the final bars of *Tales of the Unexpected* might have served to warn her that complacency was fatal.

"*Ron Grainer's classic there, with the time just coming up to 2.56. And to take us into the news – this was originally written by Jerry Leiber and Mike Stoller for The Coasters back in 1958, but may be more familiar to viewers of a certain age in its instrumental form.*"

And this is where the comic confluence must be taken on trust.

As Margaret slowed down in front of the gate she was obliged to bring the car to a sudden, screeching halt.

The vision before her was skin-crawling enough: did it really need that musical accompaniment to compound the felony?

In a routine that had no place, surely, in the twenty-first century, Cressida Sheldrake was bounding across the grass, unbuttoning her blouse and skirt as she went, and tossing them to the ground. As she continued to scamper among the trees in her underwear with Victor in hot pursuit, the air was filled with a rollicking saxophone riff to which fans of *The Benny Hill Show* would need no introduction.

A detailed account of all the mitigating claims and clarifications that followed this display would only spoil a good story. So let us move on.

Suffice to say that as Victor drove the two of them home that night, the layer of frost on the car roof appeared to be forming on the inside.

Of all the superfluous comments Victor had made in his life, "It's lucky no one was standing in the way when that lamp post came through the window" may be the most memorable.

The incident occurred the day after they got back from Ursula's. Margaret had not long left for work, and Victor was in the back garden attending the funeral of his latest sweet pea seedlings.

It was less than a week since a team of contractors arrived to install the new streetlights, causing death and destruction in the time-honoured fashion. Death to several trees along the route that were chopped down in error, and destruction to the power line when a man with a drill took his eye off the ball to download a Three Stooges video. Council surveyors later declared the work one hundred per cent safe, and within the hour a car being chased by police had ploughed into one of the posts, uprooting the concrete sleeve and sending the whole thing over with an explosive crash.

"*What in the name of bloody hell—???*"

Racing through the hall, Victor emerged from the front door to discover a giant tubular steel column now resting against his house with its top disappearing through the upstairs window.

"For the love of buggery!"

And while the police were rounding up their hooligans and half the street came out to blabber and gawp, Victor was left to pick up the phone and pursue his case with assorted machines and recordings and the occasional life-form at the public works department. From which he eventually secured a cast-iron assurance that his complaint regarding the damage to a public structure impacting upon his private dwelling would be passed on to the relevant body to be given all due consideration for such remedial action as might be deemed appropriate subject to the necessary channels of approval within the given time frame, and if he had any further questions he should not hesitate to contact them as they greatly valued his input.

"Useless bloody shower," grumbled Victor as he climbed into bed that night; a diatribe variously aimed at bureaucrats, workers and councils, and a population in general that turned a blind eye to their broken society.

Margaret lay beside him but offered no comment.

"And I suppose we're going to have to put up with *this* thing now, are we, for a month of Sundays? Before anyone can be bothered to come round and sort it out."

His glare was directed at the huge outreach arm that was now poking into the room, and on which he had already banged his head three times while pulling the curtains. Everything around them: the walls, floor, ceiling and bedding, was bathed in a fierce golden blaze from the sodium vapour lamp, and their faces glowed like Steven Spielberg characters gazing at an alien spacecraft.

"Still! Not to worry, we'll both feel better after a good night's sleep! Hang on a sec, while I just turn off this sodding great bedside lamp. Where's the little cord on the side that you have to pull? Oh! It doesn't appear to have one! Remind me to send it back first thing tomorrow, won't you … pardon?"

Margaret didn't move. Her gaze remained fixed on the ceiling. But her eyes were dead.

"I didn't say anything."

"Ah! Now hang on, where's that old Dan-Air mask? Sure I saw that knocking about here the other day."

Ducking his head he got up and crossed the room to begin searching through a small flight bag in the wardrobe. A minute later he was back in the bed with a piece of black felt on his face, adjusting the elastic behind his ears. Then followed a period of fiddling about to reduce the spill of light round his nose, while Margaret grew steadily twitchier.

"Hohhhh *Goddddd* spare us."

Her words might have been mined in the pits of Hell. Bereft of all life and hope and purpose. Somewhere, in some fathomless void, lay the ashes of her future.

"Surely to goodness, there has to be something better than this."

Victor punched his pillow and then nestled his head in the dent.

"Yes, well that's the way the world is today, Margaret. And I'm afraid you're stuck with it."

"Am I?"

It was fired back with such force that it took him by surprise. Lifting his mask he blinked through the amber glare and shot her a curious look.

"What do you mean, am I? What's that supposed to mean."

Margaret didn't blink. She just sighed and shook her head.

Perhaps she'd said too much.

"Honestly, Victor? I don't know. I don't know anything any more. I just know I need to go and tire my eyes for a bit, or I'm going to be awake in here the whole bloody night."

Victor watched as she slid back the sheet and left the room. Then with a grunt he replaced his mask and burrowed down the bed. His wife was in a sour old mood tonight, there was no question.

And who could blame her?

Downstairs, in the gloom of the kitchen, Margaret stood at the window and drew her dressing gown tightly about her.

Something better than this?

From the darkness it beckoned.

Sitting down quietly at the table she fired up the laptop and returned to her recent browsing history.

Her searches for Gregory Birchall had thrown up plenty of material that she'd not yet got round to reading. Essays and extracts from his work, and reviews of his books, and quite a few online articles spanning the last forty years.

And yes, it all looked quite daunting. For this was serious stuff. Nothing less than the *"latent suppression of the politically bankrupt by forces committed to the preservation of their own social hegemony; via cover-ups, corruption and corporate conspiracy, complicity in human rights abuse and concocted wars to shore up the arms industry."* Oh yes, that last bit she remembered from when they were standing at the bus stop. In fact wasn't he just getting into his stride when those two characters turned up?

Truth to tell, it was all still so hard to believe. That nice young man with the golden curls, standing by the record player: she could see him now. The soft, almost cherubic smile as she caught his eye across the room. Who would have thought his career could take such a turn? That he'd end up devoting his life to a cause he believed in, where the stakes were so high?

Who indeed?

It was muscular prose that pulled no punches. But at one-forty-five in the morning an hour of polemic was close to her limit.

And then, just as she was about to fold for the night, she suddenly remembered that video he'd mentioned on YouTube.

The shadowy "they", whoever they were, had somehow removed it – didn't he say?

But it turned out there were other clips attached to his name that were still intact. From conflicts in Central America and the mass graves of Srebrenica, to the Shatila and Scabra refugee camps, and through to more recent encounters with Hans Blix and Edward Snowden. Did the man never sleep?

It was fearfully late and her eyelids were drooping.

Just time, before she turned in, to dip into a brutal attack on a small Guatemalan village by US-trained government forces from 1982.

It made for pretty grim viewing. But there, in the thick of it, was Gregory Birchall. Young, hirsute, intractable. Squatting amid the screams and the mortar fire, bellowing into a microphone as state-of-the-art brooms from the West swept in to brush all before them under a carpet of lies. His eyes were ablaze with conviction. His voice almost hoarse yet resolute. It was a moment in time, long ago now. But its power to shock remained.

Margaret took in the footage with awed disbelief. And as she stared at the face on her screen she saw the kind of moral courage that had never been in such short supply as it was today.

She was prepared to be startled, but not like this. This was a revelation of a different order, and her eyes were suddenly opened, in every respect.

One thing she knew now, with blinding clarity.

This was not the time to dither.

If objects could object they would surely object to their objectification. Even the handle of a screwdriver has some dignity, and the way it was sticking out between Victor's legs, all bulbous and red while he snipped away at some electric wires, did nothing for its self-esteem.

Margaret paused to shoot a look at her husband, sprawled in his armchair, and clicked her handbag shut with a grimace. The power to convert an everyday act like changing a plug into hardcore pornography was given to few men, and in its own way impressive. But you wouldn't call it endearing. And trifles like this she would normally take in her stride only served to rattle her as she paused to depart for the evening.

"Do you have to sit like that?"

"Sorry?" Recrossing his legs he jammed the two halves back together and began tightening the screws. "Typical isn't it. Night of a crucial cup tie, the TV decides to conk out. I've tried everything else, just thought I'd check the fuse. To see if it made any difference."

It didn't.

"What a surprise. So that's that then. You off now, I take it?"

"Yes. And it might be a late one, so don't feel you need to stay up."

"Yes, I can't wait to get back up there. Another night of *that* to look forward to. Shame it wasn't a Belisha beacon that came through, at least it would be dark every other second. Is that a new dress?"

"What? Oh! Fairly, yes. And you'll be all right, will you, getting yourself some tea."

"Yesss."

"And *not* beans on toast again."

"Nohhh."

"There's a ravioli in the fridge that goes off at midnight."

"Yes I'll be fine. Who did you say you were meeting, I've forgotten."

"Oh, yes. An old friend. I mean, I didn't imagine you'd want to come. Once we get talking, you'd be bored stiff in five minutes. And besides which, I thought, you've got your football, so …"

"Huh!" Victor pulled a face as he tossed the remote control down on the sofa and then stomped off into the kitchen. "Suppose they'll have it on round the pub, but … I'll see how I feel. Anyway, have a good time. And be careful on the roads."

Margaret said she would, and collecting her keys promptly left the house before she thought better of it. No lies had been told as such. She was very careful about that. But nor did he know the whole story, which was of course – well, another story.

As the water simmered in Victor's pasta pan so did he. Why did everything happen at once? It wasn't enough their spare bed had spontaneously collapsed two weeks ago. (Unsurprising, as the bloody thing had never stood up straight since the day it arrived, bearing the most chilling three words in the English language: "Easy Home Assembly.") And now their TV had packed up on the day of the big match.

So the Goat and Compass it was: and he'd just have to pray that pair of twins who looked like Alfred E. Neuman from *Mad* magazine weren't propping up the bar. Whenever they jumped up to cheer all you could see was ears. And the last time he'd complained to one of them she'd told him to just piss off! People!

When he'd finished his meal and washed up Victor jammed on his cap and left through the back door to tramp round the corner.

He did not, as a result, see the ambulance pulling up out the front.

In the West End of London a certain aged, stately hotel looked down upon its neighbours with that air of patrician disdain peculiar to the late Victorians. Twin columns of Corinthian design framed the entrance beneath a mouldering grey entablature reputed to house the original pigeon latrine that inspired Hansard. And through its double doors at precisely seven-fifteen that evening stepped Margaret Meldrew, all crisply presented and scented, with a twinge in her heart and her heart in her mouth.

Gregory had come down to the lobby to meet her. He looked like he'd made the effort to look like he'd made no effort. Open-neck shirt, casual jacket and jeans. The generous mop of hair unruly as ever. Preppy at a push, still classy after all these years.

The kiss didn't quite go as planned, with lips and cheeks all adrift. But this allowed them at least a chuckle and a burble that broke through the tensions, as he led her away to the lift.

"I thought we could eat in my room. The Dover sole here's to die for. Only, as I say, if I'm out in the open too much … well, we've been through all this."

"Oh right. You think that man and that woman are still …"

"Yesterday morning, I went for a walk by the river. I'd barely been out ten minutes and there they were. On the other side of the road, coming towards me. If I hadn't managed to jump in a cab …"

"Oh Lordy. But you can't go on like this, Gregory? Clearly."

"Well, clearly. I know. Something's got to give. Anyway, listen. I don't want tonight to be morbid. After you've come all this way to see me. You know it means a lot."

They had reached the fifth floor, and there was a clatter as the old-fashioned latticed grille folded back to let them out.

"Yes, well. I may not have much to boast about, Gregory. But I'm good in a crisis. Married to Victor all these years, God knows I've had some practice."

There was something in the warmth of her smile that said more than he was hearing. And something in her presence from which he drew comfort. Of course he couldn't have known at this point how things would play out. Nor begun to guess the precise nature of her calculations in coming to see him.

Had he done so perhaps, he would never have let her into his room.

"Blimey O'Reilly, what the hell's happened here! Someone been playing ten-pin bowling with the lamp posts?"

"Must have been a very big bowling ball."

Del and Jacinta both managed a hollow chuckle, though the sight through their ambulance windscreen was clearly no laughing matter. As they drew up beside the half-toppled mast they could only grimace in disbelief. Through the dense bank of cloud an early dusk was descending, with none of the lamps yet lit. But it didn't exactly blend into the background. More Pythagoras than Pisa (as one local wag had remarked): a hypotenuse from Hell.

At the base of the post was affixed a sticker containing eight paragraphs of small print regarding the theft and defacement of council property. The gist of which was that anyone planning to shove it under their arm and do a runner could expect to face the full force of the law. This had not deterred the brats at Number Nine from scrambling to the top and sliding down on a cushion; or from appearing at the window just as Victor was contorting his body to apply some ointment to never you mind. (The latter's reaction to a camera flash having subsequently scored big on Twitter, via the hashtag #whatanarselookslike.)

Del and Jacinta carefully wheeled Mrs Staveacre down the ramp of their vehicle and up the front path to the door of Number Nineteen.

There had been some debate about the scrappy handwriting on the hospital discharge papers: whether the patient was named Kitty

Staveacre or Kent Shreveport, and did the address say Riverbank or Ravel's Bilko? In each case the former was confirmed by the lady in question, who was still very fuzzy and weak after her recent surgery. At the age of ninety, with just a thin cotton nightdress under her blanket, she was not best placed to linger in the open, especially now the temperature was starting to drop.

"Not much sign of life," said Jacinta, after trying the doorbell three times. "Do we know who's supposed to be looking after her? Her husband? Or family?"

"They wouldn't have signed her off unless they knew there was someone. Husband maybe. He might be a bit deaf. Perhaps I'll try round the back."

But there was no luck here either: no lights on, or sounds to suggest that anyone was in.

Fortunately breaking and entering was all part of Del's job description. When poor old souls like Mrs Staveacre had a fall inside a locked house there was no other way. On this occasion a bit of fiddling with a strip of plastic down the side of the door did the trick, and the bolt sprang back to release the latch.

On his way through the kitchen he found a short scribbled note on the table: "*In case you're back first, have gone round the pub.*" A rather cursory message, you'd have to say, under the circumstances. But there was no accounting for some men's priorities. In the meantime the best thing was to just get his wife upstairs and into bed.

Hopefully that monstrosity sticking through the window would be soon sorted out. But for now they could only try and make her comfortable.

"So there we go, Kitty?" said Jacinta, as they tucked her in tight. "You just take it easy now and get a good night's sleep, all right? And there's a glass of water here, and your slippers. And I'm sure Mr Staveacre will be back any second."

Kitty mumbled something or other, but was already fast nodding off again.

"Still heavily medicated," said Jacinta. "Hopefully her old man won't be long."

"Righty-ho then," said Del. "Let's make a move."

When Victor returned after seeing his team get thrashed 4-1, he was in no mood for bedtime chat. Which was just as well, as Margaret barely stirred in the bed when he entered the room. Invisibly swaddled with the duvet scrunched up round her ears, she was no more than a softly rising shape beneath the covers. The street lamp was now back on, and the room a wash of fiery incandescence.

Victor threw down his clothes on the chair and did what he had to do in the bathroom. Then he trudged back and pulled on his mask and lay down next to his wife. When he whispered goodnight and kissed her on the cheek she appeared to mutter something back. But it might well have been just a snore.

Gregory slid his knife into the sole just below its head and scored through the skin, working slowly down the spine in a sawing action. Cutting at a slight angle to expose the flesh he drew out the fillet from the bone and lay it among the sautéed broad beans and potatoes.

Margaret looked on with a warm rush inside as another sip of Malbec went down the hatch. Twenty minutes in, her nerves were rallying. All those nagging doubts she had now picked off one by one as her confidence grew. How easy it would be to go to pieces and duck the challenge! But this was real life and time to behave like a grown-up. Besides which, the two of them went back a long way. On one level she was starting to hate herself for what was to come. But that would pass. And no one could say she'd rushed into all this.

"Mmm. Yum. You're an artist," she said, as he passed her the plate. "I missed out on lunch today, so ... talk about ravenous!"

Gregory leaned in beside her and topped up her glass, then sat down. The setting was mellow, with puddles of light from two table lamps. The two of them faced each other across a crisp white tablecloth. Five floors below in a ballroom, couples were dancing to *Moonlight Serenade*.

"There we go then. *Bon appetit*."

"Yes! *Bon appetit*. What a treat."

Margaret dug into her fish while he broke off some bread and ran it around the lime and ginger sauce.

"So, then. You and Victor. Seem to have stood the test of time?"

"Oh! Well. We have our ups and downs – who doesn't? But …"

"I can't help noticing you've left him at home today."

Margaret chuckled.

"Yes, well. I also left the ironing board at home. Some things you know you're not going to need."

He gazed at her smokily through half-closed eyes. As if somehow trying to take her apart.

"No, it's funny, I just got the feeling the last time we spoke. That you were hedging, for some reason or other. About today. I wasn't sure I'd even hear from you. And then, this week suddenly, everything seemed to change. As if … I don't know, I was just curious, that's all."

"Mmm. Well, to tell you the truth, Gregory. A couple of nights ago I watched one of those videos on YouTube. Which was interesting to say the least."

"Oh right? OK?" There was a pause, as he took a sip of wine. "Which one?"

"Oh from way back. It was somewhere in Guatemala. There was a lot of smoke and gunfire. Lots of people killing each other. The way you do."

Gregory stared down at his plate, as if the potatoes had made a remark.

"Yes, one more sorry chapter, I'm afraid, in the history of democracy. Not that it matters of course. 'Cos we're the good guys, remember."

Margaret eyed him closely. Perhaps it was her turn to take *him* apart.

"What does it take, I wonder, to go out there and report on a thing like that."

At this he seemed to stall.

"Not sure that's for me to answer. My God, we're talking a hell of a while back now, with that one? Should think I was barely recognisable, was I? An awful lot of hair in those days and a serious beard."

"As was the fashion." She fingered the back of her neck teasingly. "You should have seen *me*, I bet I looked a fright."

"I'm sure I would have approved."

"Oh, go on."

Too early? They were still on their entrées.

Something was stirring beneath the table which could best be described as a cry for attention.

"You were right by the way. This fish is divine. A very good choice, if I may say."

"I know, and wait till you see the dessert."

And so they moved into a holding pattern that took them up to their coffees on the squashy settee.

By which time the topic had turned to sex.

Was there even such a thing any more? The world they grew up in would die with them soon. And the minefield of modern life was for others to navigate.

Margaret had just told the tale of Victor and the six-foot nurse with a beard, causing pain in her listener that mimicked the signs of a ruptured appendix. Dabbing his eyes with a napkin, he threw up his hands in surrender.

"No, no, please, Margaret, stop! I can't cope, I'm sorry."

"*You* can't cope! I've had forty years of it, Gregory! And counting."

"I mean, it's just that picture, isn't it? Of him sitting there in the van— ... and that big yellow bucket with a slit in the top."

The laughter, in time, died a natural death.

But then nothing came along to take its place.

Margaret glanced at her watch.

It would soon be nine o'clock, and outside the window a light rain was falling.

Two people, physically close. And on the verge of something: they could both sense it. Perhaps the time for talking was past. One of them, certainly, felt that way. As for the other ...

It was a moment that begged to be resolved. But the resolution, when it came, was not pretty.

A rasping buzzer signalled someone at the door. And Margaret, who was sitting closer, rose immediately to open it.

The man in the long black coat was the first to step past her. His tall blonde companion two seconds behind.

Gregory seemed to melt away backwards. As if he had nothing left to give.

*

It's a sobering thought that for nigh on a third of our lives – as near as dammit – we dwell on a plane of surreal un-existence, where Freudian fears and suppressed paranoia take control of our minds. For Victor Meldrew, of course, this was also true of the other two-thirds. But tonight, for a change, he was in quite a good place.

The part of his brain designed to ensure he woke up a gibbering wreck every day appeared to have suffered a synaptic failure. And for the last ninety minutes his dreams had been restful and sweet. Serenity reigned, as in some parallel state of being he lay beside his wife, with one arm draped round her neck, the pair of them bathed in sunshine. As the bell rang out from the tower of a Spanish mission it seemed to seal the bond of their marriage in a way that was quite spiritual. And he found himself squeezing her closer while running his fingers through her thin wispy hair. It's true the hair felt a good deal thinner and more wispy than it should have done – but what of it? This was a dream, not a documentary. In fact, even that mission bell, once you began to study it, sounded more like—

"Oh, what in the name of— !"

— not a mission bell at all, but …

"For goodness' sake, whatever time is it?"

Jerking to life in the bed, he detached his arm from the slumbering form beside him and sat upright. Downstairs, those chimes at the door were growing more insistent. But still it was several seconds before he came to.

"Unbelievable! If this is those kids down the road again after more snapshots there'll be hell to pay. You stay where you are, Margaret, and let me deal with it. I'll give them something to tweet about, little buggers."

Having pulled off his mask he clambered out under the lamp and began to hunt for his dressing gown.

Downstairs the hall was in darkness and rain was beating on the windows. Victor appeared, still grumbling, and reached for the light switch. Then he flipped up the catch and opened the door.

If looks could kill Margaret would be lucky to cop for manslaughter.

"What the hell was *that* all about? How am I supposed to get back in with you sticking the ruddy lock on?"

Having just come through one major drama she didn't need another right now. Standing on the doorstep of her own house getting soaked to the skin she could well have done without. Chivalry be damned: she looked a wreck. Frazzled from the inside out, what she most needed now was a sensitive ear and a kindly word.

What she got was a volley of consonants from a man who appeared to have lost control of his musculoskeletal system.

"W— b— y— m— j— !!"

Margaret stepped into the dry and slammed the door. Then followed a passable impression of a dog that's just been for a swim as she shook herself down.

"Now all right, I know I'm much later than I said. So don't start. I was hoping not to wake you and just leave it till morning, but ... hohhh God, I don't know where to start. And you won't believe me when I t— what?"

Frazzled as she was, it was nothing to the discombobulation of the man before her. Even the consonants were now dead on arrival. Shooting baffled looks from his wife to the top of the stairs he could only stand there, hunched and goggling, with his sanity in shreds.

"Anyway. If you don't mind, I'm not sure I'm up to it tonight, so ..."

With which she was half way up the stairs, looking as if her legs would barely carry her.

In the bedroom she peeled off her jacket and gave it a shake. Perhaps if she hung it over that lamp it might help to dry it out.

Or more likely burn a hole in the back.

As she stood by the bed and began to unbutton her blouse she noticed that Victor had already turned back the covers on her side. Which was uncommonly thoughtful of him; not to say downright strange. There was even a glass of water and a couple of biscuits waiting on her table. And when did she ever eat biscuits in bed?

Stranger still was the way her husband continued to behave as if some kind of explosive device had been planted in the house which he was desperate to locate. Staring at the empty bed, he began to circle it slowly, like one of those apes in 2001 when it first sets eyes on the alien monolith. What on earth had come over him?

She did not have to wait long for an answer.

In the bathroom the sound of a lavatory was heard flushing, followed by the click of a light cord. And into the room from the landing came a diminutive, stooped figure, shuffling along with a gait much in vogue on the Galapagos Islands. There was something of the Old Testament about her longevity: did anyone live that long any more? In her shrunken flesh and the vacancy that hung upon her soul was the vision of a wraith. Through dull, sunken eyes she appeared to see little more than a route back to bed; pausing only to nibble at a wholemeal digestive, which she washed down with a sip from the glass before tunnelling back under the duvet.

Margaret and Victor both stood rooted to the spot. Perhaps they felt if they stared at this long enough the delirium would pass.

Alas, no. There she lay between their sheets, exhaling through a toothless maw, going nowhere. If we may return to Kubrick's masterwork and those final scenes beyond the star gate, she was a dead ringer for that shrivelled spaceman lying in the bed. But how they had got to this place was the mother of all conundrums.

If there was such a thing as a bellowing whisper Margaret had it nailed. Her sibilant outburst almost knocked Victor sideways.

"Wh— in the name of— who the hell is *this*???"

"Well I was— I mean I didn't— ... hmm?"

"Yyy— you – you— you—"

It was a truth that dare not speak its name.

"You haven't been *sleeping* with this person???"

"Ihhh— m— sorry?"

"For God's *sake*, Victor!! Who the bloody hell *is* she??"

"Well I just – I mean— I thought it was *you*."

"You th— !!" Collapsing backward, she clung to the wardrobe for support. "Well, thank you *very* much!! So I might as well just kill myself then? You think I look like *that*! Where did she come from?? And how on God's earth did she g— And why the HELL am I trying to keep my voice down!! This is MY BLOODY BEDROOM!!"

Victor had nothing. The thin ice of logic upon which he galumphed around every day could no longer support him. Compared with this, Josef K had it easy.

"I mean this is the end of a perfect day isn't it? To come home and find my husband's taken up necrophilia!"

Striding forward she grabbed hold of the covers and whipped them right back.

"*Excuse me!!? Do you mind awfully if I ask what you're doing in our bed??*"

And there perhaps we should take a small break from proceedings and catch our breath. On the grounds that:

i) It would be cruel to dwell on the fright of a harmless old lady, whose role in this whole charade was not of her making.

ii) The train of events in which the error was rumbled and arrangements made for her safe return to the care home are not especially thrilling.

And iii) We should not postpone any longer an account of what happened in the hotel room when Margaret opened the door.

By the time they were done with the phone calls and ambulance men, and their unscheduled guest had departed the house, Victor and Margaret both found themselves wide awake.

Downstairs in the sitting room, nursing mugs of hot cocoa, they sank back in their chairs. And having finally dialled down the squabbling it was Margaret's turn to come clean.

"So, yes. It's a rather long story, I'm afraid. This last couple of days, there's been a lot I haven't told you about. And I'm sorry about that, but this was something I had to do on my own. And I couldn't be sure, when I went there tonight, how the whole thing would turn out."

Victor watched as she took another sip of her drink. From the tremor in her voice he could tell he was in for a bumpy ride.

"You remember Gregory Birchall. From way back. Who we met that day at the bus stop. How he told us about this amazing career of his, travelling the world as this hot-shot reporter. Always on the wrong side of the powers that be. And then when that couple turned up, it was like something in a film. He couldn't get away quick enough. And it didn't half put the wind up us both at the time. You could just imagine him being found one day, in a wood or something. Like that weapons inspector. Or hearing he'd just mysteriously disappeared.

"Anyway, it began to prey on my mind. And when I started looking up all the stuff he'd done – God, talk about living dangerously. And then the other night I found this old video, from 1982. *Gregory Birchall reports from the conflict in Guatemala*. Where he's caught in the middle of these rocket attacks, and there's people all covered in blood. Women and children screaming and bodies everywhere. Sorry, it was just—"

A long, deep breath was required. And more nerve than you could shake a stick at. For none of this was easy.

"Then right at the end, when the whole thing was over, the screen just went completely black. And after a second this message came up …

"*Posted in admiration of Gregory Birchall, who died on the Gaza Strip. July 17th 2014.*"

Victor twitched slightly behind his mug but said nothing. This was all very baffling. But then so was most of his life. And something told him this wasn't the point to jump in.

There was no sense of her playing the moment. Just a steady resolve, as her focus held firm.

"But of course by that time I'd realised. The whole thing was wrong. From the minute that video started. Even with all that eighties hair and the beard. I didn't know this man on the screen from Adam. So what the hell was he playing at?

"And then I remembered that young man of yours with the razor. Who started shaving your bits in the hospital. And I just thought – what if he believed it all? In his own head somehow, he'd become this other person? Things like that, when the mind goes off on its own, I don't know how you cope with it. And here you'd got this other man with the same name – he must have looked at him and thought— I don't know, maybe it just made him feel inadequate. And at some point something happened … where he just took on that whole personality.

"So that set me wondering. About that man and woman who kept coming after him. And when I did a quick search under missing persons, it led me straight to his nephew and his wife. They said they'd been at their wits' end now for three weeks, trying to find him. Said he'd been like that for a year, ever since the accident. One day he'd gone out, apparently, with their three children on a quad bike, and it went over on some rough ground. The kids were fine, but he caught his head on a rock, and spent two weeks in a coma. Which exactly tied in with something he'd said to me on the phone. About crashing his jeep with a three-man film crew in Iraq. That's how his brain was rewriting it all.

"So we came up with this plan. That I'd keep him occupied in the hotel, and they'd get there for nine o'clock. And obviously I felt awful, but ... you know, the second he took the knife to that Dover sole I knew. This was a man who'd never left the fishmonger's.

"Nine o'clock, I let them both in. And when he saw them it was like he just seemed to crumble. Like a child. As if he recognised them without knowing why.

"But they were so good with him, Katy and Geoff, thank God. All they wanted was to get him back home, safe and sound with his family. And so I said my goodbyes and they said they'd keep in touch. And I felt I'd left him in good hands. And I just came away ... hoping I suppose, that somewhere, underneath it all, he understood."

Best to stop there? Before it broke her entirely. There was so much that still haunted her, on so many levels. And her voice had begun to catch several times.

Call it an intervention? Call it a benign betrayal. He had taken her at face value. And in the end neither had been what they claimed.

The death of truth.

For a while, early on, she'd almost imagined herself and Gregory—but of course that was all nonsense, and now best forgotten. Though a good legal team might have claimed mitigating circumstances.

As she dabbed at the cocoa round her lips, with a handkerchief that already felt strangely moist, those mitigating circumstances got up and came to sit next to her, and gently took her hand.

No words were exchanged, but none were needed.

He knew how she felt. And she knew that he knew.

Which was all that mattered.

Chapter Five
The Man in the Cube

Now and again, in one of his more fanciful moods, Victor wondered how the conversation must have gone:

"Oh wow, Tracey? Aren't you getting to be a big girl now! Five years old and just started school. And are you enjoying it?"

"Yes thank you."

"Making lots of new friends?"

"Yes thank you."

"And what do you want to be when you grow up?"

"I'd like to be an odious, condescending poser with no redeeming features, who gets off on spewing out bile and pretentious drivel to the masses."

"How exciting! And will you have to study really hard for that and pass all your exams and get lots of qualifications?"

"Not necessary. They just give you a weekly column and a byline and it's a piece of piss."

Ah, but wasn't that just descending to their level? And it gave no credit, surely, to all those in the media who approached their job with the utmost respect for artistic endeavour in all its complexity from a wholly benign and balanced perspective.

"Unbelievable! D'you see this?? In today's local? Unbelievable, the things people write."

The eruption came during a mid-morning tea break in the Meldrews' sitting room, as with an angry flourish Victor flapped his newspaper in the air, forgetting it was full of crumbs and globs of marmalade from a recently consumed slice of toast.

"How can I have seen it, when you only pulled it out of the letter box five minutes ago?" snapped Margaret. "And will you look what you're doing on that carpet? It's like living with Billy Bunter."

"That comedian with the big teeth. D'you remember? Used to do the rounds of the working men's clubs with a Cardew Robinson tribute act. They gave him such a terrible write-up, he went out and jumped off the roof of a car park. And d'you know what they've d— ... they've only got a *review* of it in here! Underneath the report of his death – can you believe that? Listen to this.

"*Arts critic Marjorie Quail is unimpressed by comic's final caper! Though undoubtedly funnier than any of his jokes, the sudden death last night of orthodontically challenged Larry Hackett by plummeting from a six-storey building fell as flat on its face as the man himself. Even at the moment of truth, buck-toothed Hackett couldn't hack it. Ranked against the self-destruction of other famous funsters, this creaky* cri de coeur *lacked the vintage martyrdom of a Hancock or Fatty Arbuckle, and was about as emotionally affecting as a bag of winkles.*

"I mean the poor bloke was only trying to earn a living! And they wonder why people commit suicide! I've a ruddy good mind to join them sometimes. Given it one star, look, for *'Don't Bother'*. What's *that* all about."

"So you don't think you would then, Mr Meldrew."

"What?"

Victor threw a hasty look past his wife to the far end of the sofa, as if surprised to find there was a third party in the room. If he had a tendency, in any given situation, to overlook Mrs Warboys' presence it was down to years of practice. And on this occasion, since he didn't have the faintest idea what she was talking about he felt obliged to add:

"Don't think I would what?"

"You don't think you'd be interested. In having Mr Burkett's dog."

"Oh."

Had she already mentioned this? It was ringing vague bells.

"Jean, you might as well just talk to yourself!" said Margaret. "I've told you before, once he gets his nose stuck in that paper we've all had it. He won't take a blind bit of notice."

"*Who* won't take notice? I was taking notice."

"What did she just say then?"

" Well, I j— when?"

"A few minutes ago. What did she say to you about Mr Burkett?"

"I heard her! Plainly enough. She was just saying about … when she was talking to him the other day …"

"Mr Burkett died six months ago, Mr Meldrew."

"Well that's right."

"And unfortunately his wife's not so good these days. What with being on her own now and everything. She's been finding it more difficult to cope. Ever since the laryngectomy she can only communicate like Lionel Blair in *Give Us A Clue*. Says her prayers in church like that and everything. Anyway, the other day she happened to mention, she was looking for a home for that border collie of theirs. Such a sweet little thing, you must remember it? I mean, obviously I'd take it myself like a shot, but with Oscar so particular about other dogs round the house, I don't think it would work. So then I thought of you and Margaret. And I mean, it's not like she'd want any money for it."

"Yyy— errm! No I don't think so, Mrs Warboys. If you don't mind. Got quite enough to worry about round here as it is at the moment. Thank you all the same."

"Yes well. Perhaps I'll just leave it with you, anyway. You never can tell, you might just suddenly change your mind and—"

"No, I really don't think I will, Mrs Warboys. I have no desire whatsoever to own a dog. Definitely *not*."

"Ah. Right. Oh well. Erm, is there any more tea in that pot, Mr Meldrew? I wouldn't mind another if it's going? Though it looks like we might need a fresh brew. It doesn't go far does it, in these big cups."

Not the way you keep guzzling them back, Victor thought. But he got the message and rose from his chair.

"I'll put the kettle on."

Once the tap was heard running Mrs Warboys reached for her bag and drew out a sheet of folded paper. Having not very subtly got Victor out of the room she lowered her voice, which took on a sombre tone.

"Now Margaret. While I've got you to myself. I thought you'd want to see this email I've just had from Chesney."

"Ohhh ... really?"

"Yes, well. As I'm sure you must be feeling a close connection with him by this time."

Close connection? What twaddle was she talking now?

"Jean, just because a convicted axe murderer's got a photo of me eating a mince pie on his wall doesn't make us the best of friends."

"Oh, well! I know, I know, but ... don't let's go over all that again, please? Especially as he's being executed next week."

"What?"

"Well, you remember they were lodging a last-minute appeal to try and corroborate his version of events. That the man down the road had done it, and Chesney just happened to be walking past and picked up the axe to have a look. Which of course was his story all through the trial. I mean, obviously it's never a good sign when the jury bursts out laughing, but ... now the governor's ruled the sentence has to be carried out within seven days. As they desperately need his cell. I mean how can that be justice? It breaks your heart."

Margaret sighed. This whole sorry saga was one she would gladly have put behind her. But she could see her friend was taking it badly. Those were real tears landing on the forkful of chocolate gateau.

"And yet, in spite of it all, Margaret, he still somehow manages to be philosophical, it's incredible. Let me just read you this bit here.

"*And so, Jean, after all the false alarms it seems like now's the time and this will be the last you hear from me. They say I've got five days left in here. Inside this ten-foot cube, before they take me away down that corridor. Meantime I want to thank you for all you've done and all you've been to me. You sent me hope when that's what I needed most. You sent me belief, and you sent me respect. It seems I don't have too much to send you in return. Only my heart I guess, that's a part of me* when I'm gone, won't belong to no one but you. And when I go next Wednesday at two o'clock I'll go with your kind eyes right there in front of me. And I want you to know you'll be with me on that final journey. Which way I'm headed, that's in the Almighty's hands.

"Ohhhh God. Sorry, Margaret, sorry, I shouldn't but ... it's just really upset me. The way he talks about it and everything. I've just got to put it behind me, I suppose. And try and move on."

"Well I'm afraid, Jean. It's the only way. You did a good thing. But let's be honest, you never really knew this person. Or knew the truth of what he did. And let's not forget the poor victims of that horrib— Ohhhh for heaven's sake ... ohhhh heavens *above*!"

"What is it, Margaret? What have you found?"

"Oh I can't believe this. Please!"

Now, it would help the reader at this point to know that for the last three minutes Margaret had been crawling around the floor collecting bits of her husband's toast from the carpet. And having just shaken them all off his newspaper onto a plate she found herself staring at the back page in disbelief.

"No, it's this piece in here, about those riots the other week in the town centre."

"Oh don't remind me. What was it, ten million pounds' worth of damage?"

Margaret nodded.

"Three days of arson and looting after someone missed a late penalty. And now they've got some pictures from the CCTV cameras. Released by police to try and track down offenders."

"Let me see? Oh, what is it with these people! Especially *this* one here, you'd think he was old enough to know better. At his age, ransacking a shop like that? What on earth does that say about you – honestly? Actually, is it me, or does he look a bit like Victor?"

Margaret snatched back the paper with a hiss.

"It *is* Victor! That was the night he'd gone in to have his ear syringed. Got off the bus and found all *that* going on! He was just going past Currys and came across this young boy, waltzing out with a DVD player. And of course being Victor he had to wade in, and after a lot of kerfuffle managed to grab it off him and scare him away. But now look at this. They've got a shot of him here, putting it back on the shelf."

"Well ... yes, but you can't really tell from this, can you? That he's putting it back? It looks just like he's stealing it."

"I *know*!!! God spare us! The times I tell him, to leave well alone. Does he ever listen?"

"And you see? This is just what happened to Chesney! This is how you end up with a miscarriage of justice."

"Miscarriage of j— it's hardly the same, Jean, is it? As hacking someone to death in cold blood. Anyway, for God's sake don't say anything. With a bit of luck he'll never see it."

"Bit of luck I'll never see what? What are you doing with my paper? I haven't read that bit yet."

"What?"

Margaret spun round as Victor returned from the kitchen clutching his teapot. By which time she had already crumpled the page into a ball.

"Oh, it's just some stupid article that would only get you going. And anyway it's all full of your crumbs and marmalade now. I don't know why you bother in the first place. You only moan about everything you read in it. "

Victor grunted and sat down. There was some truth in this. And yet a suspicion remained, based largely on Mrs Warboys' next remark, that something fishy was going on.

"Don't worry, Mr Meldrew. There's nothing fishy going on. Shall I pour?"

And then again, what if there was? People banged on about transparency but he could see through all that. If his wife chose to wrap him in cotton wool that was fine by him. He was only just getting over all that ruckus upstairs with workmen sorting out the lamp post. Two solid days of noise and non-stop banter: if he'd had to listen to one more crack about George Formby needing to cut down on the pies he would have screamed.

But at least it was done with now, and once he'd finished his tea there was a nice relaxing afternoon to look forward to, pottering about in the back garden.

How could anything upset him out there?

*

When he was at school Victor had never seen the point of studying History, and would have much preferred to study the Future.

He realised, of course, that since this comprised an infinite number of possible outcomes it would put quite a strain on the syllabus. But then as with History, you could always specialise – like choosing the Tudors or Ancient Rome – and just go for a future that held the most appeal. Like, say, the future where most of our world leaders fall prey to a flesh-eating virus. Or one where dodos survive, and Cadbury's Tiffins turn out to be vital to a healthy diet.

Or indeed any future in which he didn't find a grubby-looking tramp in his shed, knocking back meths.

"What in the name of all that's holy—"

At first he just took it for an optical trick. The bewhiskered round face with its glowing red cheeks, grinning through the window as Victor stepped onto his patio, was surely some form of reflection? But when the "reflection" began swigging from a bottle of purple fluid, and a quick glance behind confirmed that his garden gnome had performed no such deed, the truth was apparent. This vagrant, whoever he was, appeared to have just parked himself – without so much as a by-your-leave – in Victor's potting shed, where the absence of an en-suite shower was not likely to bother him deeply.

"Where the hell did he come from??"

Victor jumped at the sudden presence of his wife, peering over his shoulder. Somewhere in the background was the sound of Mrs Warboys starting her car and driving home. But no joy lasts forever.

"I have no idea! I just came out here, and there he was, as large as life! Could have sworn I put that padlock back on the other day. I mean, he didn't even move when he saw me. The cheek of it!"

"Well how long d'you think he's *been* in there??"

"You tell me. Coming to something when every Tom, Dick and Harry thinks they can just plonk themselves down on your property. Like a cross between Howard Hughes and Fagin, look. And now he's waving at us!"

"Well don't bloody well wave back!! Just get rid of him!"

"What do you mean."

"Tell him to get out! And sling his hook! He can't stay in there, can he, for goodness' sake. Go and have a word with him."

"Oh here we go again! Funny how it's always me that gets these jobs."

"Well what do you suggest? That *I* go down there? And get a garden fork through the ribs for my trouble? We don't know *what* he's capable of, do we?"

"Garden fork through the r—!??"

"Just do it! While I go and make the bed!"

Margaret was still fuming ten minutes later when she came back in the kitchen to find her husband fishing out a packet of biscuits from the top cupboard.

"What's happening now?"

"What do you mean?"

"And what are you doing with that?"

"Oh! Nothing."

Victor was wearing that look of complete and utter innocence that only comes with true guilt. And his attempt to render the object invisible by casually tapping it against his hand was frankly a non-starter.

"So what happened? You went down there. And is he gone now?"

"Erm! Not exactly, no. He's … still in there. For the moment."

"What do you mean still in there? But you told him he couldn't stay?"

"Yyyyes. Well. I tried to. But he said to be honest he was quite comfortable where he was. And then he invited me to sit down and have a little chat."

"*He* – invited *you* to sit down??"

"He said he hasn't eaten for three days, Margaret. Since they turfed him out of his cardboard box under the railway bridge. I mean, what are we supposed to do? The poor bloke's got nowhere. I said he could at least stay there for a bit, till – well, till the morning anyway. And then I don't know, perhaps we can get on to one of those homeless charities and try and sort something out."

"Stay there till the mor—"

Lifting the net curtain she cast a glance through the window. Down in the shed the shabby figure looked out and gave her a thumbs-up sign. Still fuming, she let the curtain drop and made a grab towards her husband.

"He's not having my Boasters!"

Back went the packet into the cupboard, and out came a box of strange German cookies Mrs Warboys had given them three Christmases ago. As she slammed it down on the worktop Victor imagined the contents crumbling to powder.

"And first thing tomorrow, I'm telling you. He's out! And you can make sure he understands, or else! I'm calling the police."

A question not many people will be asking at this point is – whatever became of Mr and Mrs McVitie? It might naturally be assumed that after their clash with the cow they'd settled down in their new home next to the Meldrews, where they could expect to live happily ever after.

So let's unpack that narrative.

What with waiting around for builders and decorators to get their act together, and all the fun of solicitors, Tony and Betty McVitie had only moved in ten days ago.

And it just so happened that this very evening they'd invited Victor and Margaret round for a meal to establish what they hoped would be a lasting neighbourly rapport.

"Oh now! I love what you've done in this room," said Margaret as she gazed around at the hideous primary colours and clashing fabrics. "Really stamped your personality on the place." It was the same line she'd used with Patrick and Pippa when they first arrived and many times since. But you had to know when to hold back. Victor had tried it once and come a cropper in a friend's new holiday home, after some locals had just broken in and daubed graffiti all over the walls. They had not been invited back.

"Well that's all down to Betty, I have to say," said Tony. "She's the one with the magic touch."

"Oh go on with you." Betty waved her hand airily and proffered some more nibbles. "Victor, can I interest you in some cheesy snaps."

"He didn't know you'd posed for any," said Josh.

"I *beg* your pardon?" said Betty.

"Ha! Ha! Ha!" laughed Victor. "Very funny. Very quick."

"Now don't encourage him," said Tony. "Mr and Mrs Meldrew haven't come here to listen to all that silliness. Just ignore him, he's only after attention."

"Oh no, no," said Margaret. "I think it's wonderful that children are allowed to express themselves these days." (While mentally adding: "Express *this*.")

"Yes, you must let us know when your next gig is, Josh," said Victor. "We'd love to come and see you, wouldn't we?"

Would we? Margaret made a private note to have her husband sectioned the minute they got home. He was already wearing that gormless Stan Laurel grin which always appeared half way through the third glass of wine. After which normal brain function invariably ceased.

The McVities were a pleasant enough couple: in that slightly dull, dim sum dumpling sort of way. Soft and doughy with a few too many grams of fat about them. If Betty had a generous bosom it was not so generous as to grant men more than a hint of cleavage, and what was unremarkable about her face would have filled volumes. Tony was all pullover and varifocals, with the sort of hair that remained perfectly groomed even when it was lying on a barber's floor. If his voice had been put through a trouser press it would explain everything. But the one thing that was interesting about him was – no, you've got me there.

"So anyway, yes, it's been quite an exciting time for us, coming here," said Betty. "After the last ten years, in that rented flat. It's fair to say we've had our ups and downs. Haven't we darling."

Tony reached for another crisp but then thought better of it.

"Oh yes. Well of course, after my first marriage went south. It was all erm … well, let's say, a pain in the A-R-S-E, if I'm honest. I'm afraid she was a bit of a money-grabbing S-O-D. Took me to the cleaner's in the end, and left me … well …"

"Without a P-O-T to piss in," said Josh.

"Ha! Ha! Ha!" laughed Victor.

"Excuse me!" said Tony.

"I *can* spell," said Josh.

"I don't care," said Betty. "Just watch your language."

"And anyway, spelling's not like that any more, is it. Have you noticed. It's like, when you ring someone up and say you're from Kent they go 'Kent? Is that Kilo Echo November Tango?' Or you go 'Hallo, I'm calling from Rhyl' – 'You mean Romeo Hotel Yankee Lima?'"

"Oh I know what you mean!" laughed Victor. "Drives you right up the wall!"

"And they're like, 'What name is it please?' I go 'Josh McVitie. That's Jimmy Oboe Ski Haddock ... Mississippi Cha-cha Vomit iPad Tizer iPad Earwig.'"

"Ha! Ha! Ha!"

"All right I think that's enough, Josh. He's doing his act now."

"And that's Earwig spelt Earwig Archimedes Ratatouille Wackadoodle iPad Glassblower ... usually shuts them up."

"Ha! Ha! Ha! Oh he's very good, isn't he! Very good," said Victor, clapping his hands. "He could be another Ned Metcalf."

"Who?" said Margaret.

"Yes but I think it's time you went to bed now, don't you," said Betty.

"That's right, so come on, say goodnight to our guests," said Tony.

Josh drank in the applause along with his Sprite and turned his baseball cap round the right way.

Always leave them wanting more.

"Night night then, Victor. Night night, Margaret."

"Night night, Josh," said Margaret.

"Yes, sweet dreams," giggled Victor.

And away the infant toddled upstairs.

Margaret held her sickly smile for exactly three seconds, then attempted to re-engage with the other two adults in the room.

"So it sounds like it's been a bit of a struggle for you then, Betty, in the past? From what you were saying."

"Oh! Yes, well. When I first met Tony the poor man was in a dreadful state, weren't you? He'd already got two nervous breakdowns under his belt."

"And then when I found out my wife had been 'doing it' with a windscreen wiper! That was too weird for words. Sent me right over the edge I'm afraid."

"Doing it with a w—"

Margaret looked at Victor and Victor looked at his shoes.

"You know, those annoying young men?" said Betty. "Used to jump out and start cleaning your car at traffic lights?"

"Oh! Right, OK."

"Yes, it turned out they'd been at it for months, behind my back. Getting up to all kinds of strange games and I never had a clue. Even the squeegee ruts in her bottom I just took for cellulite. And with all the strain of the divorce, on top of everything else, I came out in this horrible rash. You know that thing, where you're losing so much body heat, they have to completely wrap you up in metal foil."

"Talk about oven-ready when we first got together!" Betty squeezed her husband's knee with a chuckle. "Oh God, we wouldn't go through all that again, would we!"

For a second or two the man beside her seemed to exit the room without physically leaving his chair. The traumas of the past had summoned him back for one last look. And it was all he could do to shake himself free with a shiver.

"Yes, I was a basket case if you want the truth. And no two ways about it. But thank the Lord, those days are behind me. It's all about mindfulness now, and living in the moment. And just learning how to de-stress. And since I've got rid of all the grief in my life, and all the things that might upset me or disturb me … well, touch wood, you know, I've never felt better."

For such moments the words "hostage to fortune" were surely invented.

There were no stars in the sky that night, and no moon. The universe and its infinite mysteries were beyond the sight, and reach, of Man. And Man, who was perilously close to understanding an infinity of nothing, was nowhere near an understanding of himself.

As Margaret stood at the window of the spare bedroom peering down into the gloom she found herself struggling to make sense of a world that made precious little concession to logic. A world where the dying of the light seemed to throw all your fears into frightening focus; and co-morbidities sprang from the darkness to vie for attention.

"He's reading one of your old *Private Eyes* in there now by a citronella candle! You can't tell me that's not a fire risk!"

In the other room Victor switched off his light and slid down the bed.

"Are you going to come away from there? That's twenty-five minutes now. I told you, the poor sod's harmless enough. I'll go down tomorrow and have another go. And I'm sure he'll listen to reason, just come back to bed."

"Listen to reason? He was trimming his beard with my secateurs a few minutes ago! Can't believe the nerve of these people! Anyone else would have booted him out by now – but not us! We're too soft by half."

With a final shake of her head she flicked down the blinds and tramped back through to rejoin her husband.

That little soirée next door had been a welcome distraction from the problem at hand, but it still needed sorting. The man was a health hazard apart from anything else. And there was no point being soggy about it: the full force of the law was required and nothing less. You had to move decisively or a situation like this could lead to all sorts of nightmares.

Margaret was spot on there. Though she could hardly have guessed how bizarre those nightmares would be; or that, sadly, it was already too late to stop them.

Well it seemed like a good idea at the time. But when Margaret suggested a nice crystal whiskey decanter as a housewarming gift for their new neighbours she forgot to factor in the "Victor Meldrew effect".

Inspired by the musings of Heisenberg, this essentially concerned events one could never predict, so it was a waste of time trying. The only certainty was that taking him to their local department store to make a purchase in Household Goods was unlikely to end well.

"Is it me or is it freezing in this place?" grumbled Victor, as his wife picked her way through the Waterford range. "No need for their air conditioning to be on this high, surely to goodness? This middle finger's gone completely numb now! Look at that! I can't even feel it! Look at that!"

Margaret immediately smacked down his hand in a panic.

"*Will you*—!! Not do that in a public place! For heaven's sake, I can't take you anywhere!"

"What?"

"It *would* help if you didn't appear to be making rude signs at the security staff while we're in here! God spare us."

"What security staff where? Oh."

Sure enough, a glance across the hall revealed a rather beady-looking man in uniform, who didn't look too thrilled at being given the finger for no apparent reason. His job was hard enough as it was, standing stock still all day long with his hands loosely clasped across his testicles. He didn't need this elderly twerp giving him grief.

"And I've told you before, it's always like this in here." Margaret tugged at the sides of her jacket with a shiver. "You get a couple of cold days outside, everyone comes in wrapped up to the nines, so they turn all the heating right down to compensate. And then when it warms up again it takes another two days to get back to normal. That's why I always put two tops on when I come in, because I know it'll be like a fridge. Now look, which one of these d'you think? The square or the round? *Think* she said the one that got broken in the move had a square base to it. Or do we think they'd prefer a change?"

"Yyyy— stick with the square, I imagine. If that's what they had before. I know one thing, all this cold's not good for my bladder. I shall have to go and find somewhere in a minute. Before I burst at the seams."

"No, I think you're right." Margaret took out the stopper and held it to the light. "This one's definitely got more sparkle. Okey-doke then, let's go for that. You want to take it over there and pay? While I pop downstairs to see if that blouse has come in."

"Ye-es, OK then. I suppose."

"You know where the clothing department is? On the second floor? And I'll see you down there in a bit."

"Right, yes. See you there."

So far so good. As Margaret scurried off toward the lifts Victor crossed to the till to settle up, then made a beeline for the toilets at the far end of the room.

"*Brilliant!*" he said when he got there. Though many other words would have done nicely. "Absolutely *brilliant*."

He was sorely tempted to tear off the sign that said "*Out of order. Sorry*" and change it to "*Right out of order! Not as sorry as I am!*", but the eyes of that security man were still on him, and why play into his hands?

"Ohhhh for heaven's— wwwwyyy ffff!!"

Drawing in air, he wriggled about on the spot and tried to compose himself. Which was not easy. His sphincter, now primed for action, was suddenly forced to row back. And if the train hadn't quite left the station it was certainly close to dribbling off the end of the platform.

Why did this always happen when you were desperate?

But no, the trick was to not *think* you were desperate. The trick was to just calm down and take it easy. There was nothing to be gained by hopping about from one foot to the other like a Morris dancer. It was all about willpower, and mind over matter.

Victor took a long, deep breath, and told himself his bladder was in actual fact not very full at all. It was really quite empty. And nowhere near ready, as yet, to discharge its contents.

Sadly his bladder didn't believe him.

Two floors down, it was all go in Separates. With the summer sale in full swing Margaret had to wait a good five minutes for one of the changing cubicles. And even as she stepped inside and closed the door she could feel all the usual misgivings about her choice. She'd been after this blouse for weeks. But was she pushing it with such a modern style? It was a fine line between embracing a young look and *Whatever Happened to Baby Jane?*

Only one way to tell.

Having hooked up the hanger on the wall she slipped off her jacket. Then she slipped off her top. Then she slipped off the other top that was under the first top, and immediately remembered why she'd put them both on in the first place. It really was like a meat locker in there today.

Strangely, as she buttoned herself up in front of the mirror she was pleasantly surprised. Nice line and length, and not too snug; and those fine blue stripes didn't make her look that much like a packet of ballpoint pens after all.

Decision made, she returned the blouse to its hanger and got ready to leave.

"All right, cubicle number nine!" said the voice. "Just hold it right there!"

Why oh why oh why had he ever got into the lift?

It was the worst thing you could do when you needed the toilet! As he stood there with his legs pressed together, watching that flashing downward arrow take its time to reach the next floor, Victor knew – beyond a shadow of a doubt – that his goose was cooked. Any second now it was going to jerk to a halt, and that would be that. Trapped between floors with no hope of escape for the next five hours! Without question this was the worst decision he'd made in his entire—

Ping!

The lift came to rest on the second floor and the doors slid open.

It was a miracle! And if further proof were required for the creed of Intelligent Design there it was before him, in large black lettering …

GENTLEMEN.

With one bound Victor was out of the lift and through the door.

"Good morning, sir."

But of course, he'd forgotten. This was no ordinary freezing cold department store: it was a very posh, upmarket, freezing cold department store. With the sort of high-class washroom in which an everyday oik like Victor could never feel comfortable.

Not that he had a problem with the chandeliers and the rich oak paneling; or the classic Edwardian taps and the marbled porcelain. But wasn't there something creepy about this stiff little man in the waistcoat and white gloves? What was his story? Standing there in the corner like a snooker referee, watching your every move. If anything was designed to put you off your stride!

Even as he dug into his flies Victor knew it was futile. Only a second ago he'd been dying for this moment. Yet psychologically now he was scuppered. The wretched man might as well have been standing on the end of it: for now his whole system had gone into lockdown.

Ask not why Victor remained at the bowl for the next thirty seconds miming the act of urination. He just did. Right down to the final shake-off, the tuck-back and the zip-up. All bogus. All for the benefit of not quite the elephant in the room, but a small unwelcome lizard.

"Towel, sir?"

No sooner had Victor finished at the basin than a white starched roll was plucked from the pile and placed in his hands.

"Oh. Erm. Thanks."

The centre parting was the worst of it. But those tight weasel eyes came a close second, along with the thin crooked smile that was more like an incision in his face.

And then, the final piece of pointlessness: as Victor allowed his raincoat to be brushed down, before fumbling in his pockets for a pound coin; and finding nothing smaller was forced to leave a ten-pound note in the gentleman's saucer before departing the room.

His insides were still as tight as a drum, and now close to elastic limit.

"Ohhhhh *myyyy Goddddd*."

And then, in a flash, the solution was right there in front of him.

The object in his hand.

The sign on the wall that said *Menswear*.

All right, it was a long way from ideal.

But these were desperate times, weren't they?

"Just take a seat please, madam. I need to ask a few questions. And it *would* help matters if you tried to co-operate."

The manager of the clothing department gestured to Margaret from behind his desk and prepared to take notes.

"*Co-operate?*"

The word came back as a snarl.

"Yes, it doesn't help when you behave like that to a member of my staff, who was merely trying to escort you from the cubicle to my office. I can see the teeth marks in her wrist from here."

Mr Killick threw a glance towards the beady-looking woman in uniform, who was standing stock still with her hands loosely clasped across her testicles.

"Yes, well she's lucky I didn't do something far worse!" said Margaret, who was clearly having a bit of a Victor moment. (Having learned from the master.) "For a start, I take a dim view of being spied on by your security cameras when I'm half naked! And then having my clothes snatched away and being told I'm a criminal! If you don't mind, I'd quite like that back please."

Margaret made a grab for the cream cotton top that lay on Killick's desk. But Killick was there first, stashing it safely away in his drawer. The desk was vast, the room was a mausoleum, and that high domed head would have given Dan Dare the shivers. Hilary Killick was monarch of all he surveyed.

"All in good time, madam. When we've established who it belongs to."

"It belongs to *me*!"

"That may be for a court to decide, so let's not prejudge the issue. Now then, name."

"What?"

"May I have your name please, madam."

Margaret took a deep breath. Sardonic enunciation was her only recourse.

"*Margaret Meldrew.*"

"Meldrew … mmm." Killick ran this round his mouth and found it sticking to his teeth. "Why does that sound familiar."

Margaret shuddered to think.

"OK then. Mrs Meldrew. You don't deny the garment we're discussing is a brand new product, sold exclusively in this store? And that you were caught just now trying to smuggle it out of the building underneath a top of your own."

"Don't be so bloody ridiculous!"

"Is that your answer?"

"You say brand new, I bought it here last month, and this was the first time I'd worn it. The reason I'd got two tops on was to try and avoid freezing to death out there."

"You seem to be sweating now, Mrs Meldrew?"

"Well, in here, yes? It's like an oven. And besides which, what am I supposed to have done with the ticket and the price tag? I suppose I cut them all up into little bits and ate them?"

Killick's left eyebrow shot up.

"Interesting."

"Don't write that down!"

"You'd be amazed, Mrs Meldrew. The lengths some people go to. Juanita here could tell us a few tales, couldn't you, Neet? And if anyone has a talent for winkling these things out …"

"Yes, you can spare me the details. For goodness' sake, if you check your recording back you'll see I was wearing that top when I first went in."

Killick shifted slightly in his seat.

"As it happens we've only just begun trialling this new system, following a recent spate of offences. And sadly we're still getting a lot of pixellation on playback. Modern technology, eh! Now of course, if you were able to produce a receipt for this item – which you claim to have purchased – we could tie up the whole thing in a jiffy. But I'll take that groan as a no. In which case, I'm afraid, I've no alternative but to refer the matter t— ah, the very person!"

There was a brief tap on the door and a uniformed policewoman stepped into the room.

"Constable Briggs. Thanks very much for coming."

Margaret turned towards Constable Briggs. And Constable Briggs turned towards Margaret.

And here's a most interesting thing.

Before their departure that morning Victor and Margaret had finally got their act together and rung up the police about the man in the shed. Two officers turned up to see him off the premises, and afterwards Margaret had got chatting to one of them, a nice young WPC, about their trip into town. When she'd mentioned the store and made a joke about being warmer in a morgue the latter had chuckled and said she knew just what Margaret meant; and she'd remember that tip about wearing an extra top the next time she went in there.

And what were the chances that very same WPC would now appear in Killick's office – just when Margaret had given up all hope of a fair hearing?

The chances were zero.

And from the look on this woman's face she'd never chuckled in her life.

Sinking back in her chair, Margaret felt the world slowly crumbling beneath her.

At a time like this the support of your loved ones was everything.

However bloody long did it take to go to the toilet?

It was lucky for Victor they weren't trialling any new systems in the men's department that day. Or goodness knows where we'd be.

Some things are best left to the imagination. All we need know is that after five minutes in the changing room "to try on this pair of trousers and see if they suit me" (they didn't) he came out looking a lot more relaxed than when he went in.

It was easy to beat yourself up, but what other choice did he have? In any case, those decanters could soon be washed out and sterilised: he'd see to that the minute he got home. Once he'd restored it to full sparkling health who would be any the wiser?

By the time he got an urgent text from Margaret the manager's office had turned into a regular Old Bailey. Under forensic cross-examination the case for the defence was in tatters, and Margaret half-expected a black cap to come out of that drawer any second.

In a last desperate throw of the dice she suggested they send for the young lady who had sold her the original top in the hope she might remember the sale. Unfortunately Margaret had no idea of her name. In her mid-twenties maybe? Medium height. Medium build. No particular accent. Lime green hair.

But when Courtney was called to the stand she simply looked blank.

"Mmmmm, sorry, Mr Killick. Can't say as I remember this lady's face. You see so many customers in a day. And we're talking six weeks ago now?"

"Oh now please just think, Courtney?" said Margaret. "I asked if you'd got a size eight, and you went off to look, and it took you ages.

And when you came back you said it was the very last one you had in stock?"

Courtney thought for a minute then shook her head.

"No, you *must* remember. It was bucketing down that day, I came in looking like a drowned rat. And I showed you my red umbrella, which had just been blown inside out"

Courtney bit her lip and frowned. Nothing was coming.

"Oh and yes! Don't you remember? I also bought that orange cashmere scarf to go with the top. And on the label it said *Colour, pumpkin. Reduced to £31.10.* And you said how weird was that, being thirty-one ten, the date of Halloween, and this was a pumpkin, and we both had a good laugh about it – you must remember?"

Courtney frowned.

"Sorry ..."

There was a knock on the door and Victor looked in.

"Excuse me, I'm looking for my wife ..."

"Oh God – now! I remember *him*! He was having a right old go at someone on the phone! About his broadband speed? Saying that 'cos it was six times slower than advertised he was gonna be six times slower paying the bill! Ohhhh yeh, yeh, sorry. Him and this lady here? Definitely, that's coming back to me now, how funny. The cream broderie top and the pumpkin scarf. Yeh, no, I think that's right to be honest. Pretty sure now actually. She *is* telling the truth."

Margaret closed her eyes and breathed freely again.

Mr Killick threw a look at Juanita, who shrugged her shoulders, then put down his pen and slapped his book shut.

Policewoman Briggs, meanwhile, was giving Victor a very deep, thoughtful look. And having muttered something quietly into her radio she took him to one side and asked if he'd mind accompanying her down to the station.

Behind the glass partition Witness X could hear her heart thumping loudly as she polished her spectacles.

Detective McFarlane urged her to calm down and take her time, and assured her that no one on the other side would be able to see them.

The Man in the Cube

Witness X was not her real name. But in the sensitive matter of an identity parade we are bound to respect the victim's privacy.

After a moment six gentlemen filed into the room and turned to face the window. A seventh was then invited to choose where he wished to stand among them and the other men shuffled along to accommodate him.

All seven men were in their late sixties, wearing flat caps and light-coloured raincoats.

On the other side of the glass the woman studied each man in turn, scanning the line from left to right and then back again.

The men all remained perfectly still and expressionless through this, although one of them began to wonder if he needed the toilet.

After much consideration the woman said something to the detective, and the detective flicked a switch on his intercom and said something to the uniformed officer in the room.

The uniformed officer relayed this to the seven men, who all unbuttoned their raincoats and held them wide open.

"Try and keep still please, Number Five!"

Number Five was beginning to quiver slightly.

He had just remembered something really alarming.

The woman continued to ponder. Then finally had to concede: she couldn't swear to any of them. It was just one of those things.

Detective McFarlane said not to worry, she'd done her best. And the seven men were allowed to leave the room.

"OK then Mr Meldrew, you're all done," said the desk sergeant, as he signed the men off, one by one. "And thank you for agreeing to take part at the last minute. I gather you came here in a squad car."

"Yes, and she said you'd be able to take me back afterwards."

"Did she now?" said the desk sergeant, in a voice that caused the colour to drain from Victor's face. "Not sure what she was thinking there, I'm afraid. We're a bit strapped for manpower right now. Isn't there someone who can pick you up?"

"Well, my wife will have gone home by this time. And I really need to get back to the store unfortunately. There's erm, something I may have left behind. What with all this cropping up. Only I believe they close at six."

"Five o'clock on a Sunday, I think you'll find."

"Oh God, really?"

"Your best bet now'll be the bus station just round the corner. There's one leaves on the half hour, if memory serves. If you hurry you might just make it."

And in the modern vernacular, he probably would of.

If the young people of today hadn't been so bloody public-spirited.

In fairness to Bob and Doug they thought they were doing a good thing. From where they were sitting, in a truck parked opposite the nick, the sight of a man suddenly bursting through the front door, casting frantic glances this way and that before dashing off down the road, did look decidedly dodgy.

Couple this with Doug's astonishing memory for faces and you had the perfect recipe for yet another hilarious mishap.

"Now where've we seen *that* geezer before?"

"Can't say I know him."

"Yeh you do. Give me that paper."

Sure enough, a quick glance through the local, which by happy co-incidence was lying stuffed against their windscreen, confirmed the fact.

"Yeh, see this, it's gotta be! Half-inching a video! All day long, the same bloke, look – one of those rioters they said to look out for."

"Wow."

"Looks like they pulled him in, and now he's doing a runner! Come on!"

Well of course, youth and fitness were always going to tell in a case like this. And before he knew what hit him Victor was being floored by a flying rugby tackle – slap bang outside the entrance to Harrison Spratley's Specialist Angling Supplies.

As a knot of bystanders turned up to applaud the have-a-go heroes, no less a person than Harrison Spratley himself stepped out to observe the proceedings, and declared he'd the very thing for restraining runaway villains like this one.

There was little joy for Victor when he tottered back into town at 5.02, looking like something no cat would have bothered to drag in.

As he approached the big glass double doors at the front of the store, who should he see but our old friend the beady-looking security man, driving home the last bolt in the floor as the lights dimmed behind him. Whatever remark he made when he spotted Victor outside was inaudible, but we get the drift. And recalling a certain gesture the latter had made upstairs he was more than happy to return the compliment.

Victor's spirits sank.

There was nothing for it but to ring home and come clean.

"Oh! Hallo! I wondered where you'd got to. How did it all go down the police station?"

"Terrible! Since you ask. I wish I'd never agreed to the damned thing. Some bloke up for indecent exposure, I don't know where they thought *I'd* fit in. And then afterwards, when I was running down the road to catch a bus these two yobs came after me, and started wrestling me to the ground! Said they were performing a citizen's arrest if you please!"

"A citizen's arrest?"

"Turns out they'd seen some photo in the local paper this week. You remember that night with all the riots? When I caught that young kid coming out with a DVD player, and I managed t—"

"Yes! Yes, but – so what happened, were you hurt or what?"

"So then some idiot came out of an angling shop and started poking his nose in. Next thing I'm being dumped in front of the police desk, all trussed up in a fisherman's net like a haul of cod! Tied up so tight I could hardly breathe. The way that twine cut into my skin I'll have marks there now for ever more. And they only had the nerve to ask if there was a reward!"

"But you got it all sorted eventually?"

"Eventually! Then by the time I got back to the store it was closed."

"Back to the store? Why would you go back to the store?"

"Yes, well. That's what I was coming to. When you left me and I went off looking for a toilet … I did find one in the end, but what with that weird little creep in there I couldn't go for love nor money. I mean, I was so desperate by that stage, Margaret? I couldn't have lasted another second. And at that point, of course, I was still carrying the decanter, which … only the thing is—"

"Oh yes, you don't have to say! You'd forget your own head if it wasn't screwed on. Thankfully I spotted the bag, where you'd left it on the table, just as I was leaving. So it didn't get left behind, you can stop fretting."

"Oh really? Oh thank goodness. I mean you know what it's like, you put something down, then forget all about it."

"And obviously I saw what you'd done."

"You did?"

"As soon as I picked it up, I could tell it felt heavier."

"Yyyyes."

"And what a lovely thought. You didn't say you'd been down to wines and spirits? No wonder you were a while. And as it happened I was just coming in as their car pulled up next door. So I did a quick gift wrap and popped it straight round. They both seemed thrilled, I just hope it's to their taste when they open it, but … hallo? Victor?? Sorry, it sounded like you just dropped the phone on the ground?"

"D'you know one thing I really hate? Is them fucking stand-up comedians!"

"Ha! Ha! Ha! Ha!"

"Them fucking stand-up comedians, right, they're fucking everywhere! It's like a plague! With their fucking little clever insights and their fucking witty life lessons and their personal journeys, why can't they all just fuck off!"

"Ha! Ha! Ha! Ha!"

"Oo! Have you noticed how people put milk on their cornflakes? Haven't they ever heard of a knife and fork?"

"Ha! Ha! Ha! Ha!"

"Ooo! Has anyone noticed Prince Michael of Kent's got his fucking head on upside down!"

"Ha! Ha! Ha! Ha!"

"Here, that politician's a bit of a nob-end isn't he! And that bloke on the radio's shite! And Dads, eh? *They're* all fucking stupid twats! And don't get me started on audiences! Fucking crowd of uncritical cackling wankers, they'll laugh at anything if you say it fast enough!"

"Ha! Ha! Ha! Ha! Ha! Ha!"

"Yeh, fucking stand-up comedians, I fucking hate them! Oh hang on a sec …"

"Josh? What on *earth* are you watching in there? Switch that off now!"

"It's OK Mum, he's nearly finished. What does anarchic mean?"

"It means give me that phone and get back to your homework! *Now!* This second! I've never heard such vile talk, whatever next."

"Is everything all right up there?"

Betty McVitie closed the door of her son's bedroom and came downstairs.

Her husband was waiting at the bottom, fiddling with a scrap of sparkly wrapping paper.

The pair of them looked queasy.

"Honestly, you start to wonder sometimes. If it's a good idea, all this comedy business. When you look at what's out there."

Tony grimaced.

"Yes, and never mind what's out *there*. It's when it turns up on your own doorstep! I still can't believe they would do a thing like that."

"Well you'd never imagine it. Even as a joke."

"I was on the verge of pouring myself a drop as well."

"And what did she write on that gift tag? *Have a wee drink on us?*"

"If that's meant to be humour, I'm sorry."

"You checked it was OK to go in the dishwasher?"

"Thankfully, yes, but … it's just the thought of what was in there …"

"And we did wonder after last night? If there was something a bit odd going on. With *him* especially. The way he kept laughing in all the wrong places."

"I know. I saw him just now through the front window coming home. He'd got like these strange diamond patterns all over his face. Like some kind of Batman villain."

Betty sat down with a shudder.

"And you hear such things in the Co-op. I mean, there was that awful story about the old people's home."

"You said they weren't sure that was him?"

"Well no, they reckon the addresses got mixed up. But why would he be ordering frozen urine to be delivered in the first place? If you're planning a trick like this, why would you need someone else's? The whole thing just freaks you out. And then I heard something else today that— oh I don't know *what* to believe any more. You wonder where people get all this stuff."

"Oh what you going to tell me now?"

"Well no, it doesn't bear thinking about. Let's just say, instead of a decanter it was a big plastic bucket. And he was— well, something else I can't even mention."

"Really?"

"In a hospital car park of all places."

Tony took off his glasses and pinched the top of his nose. Then he put them back on and tried to rise above it.

"Look we've got to be sensible. Instead of just jumping to conclusions. We don't know there aren't all sorts of rational explanations, if you look for them. Remember what the Trenches said. They'd not had one moment of trouble with them in all the time they were living here. And what reason would they possibly have to lie to us?"

The next day, across the country it was all kicking off. The usual stuff and nonsense with assorted do-gooders and people on a mission trying to upset the applecart.

Massive demonstrations were staged that were too big to ignore, but no one noticed. And sensible people were arguing about which one of them was more sensible, so no one noticed them either.

Somewhere in the south-east RAF fighter jets were scrambled, while the prime minister chaired an emergency meeting of the COBRA committee.

And once again the nation rejoiced.

Victor Meldrew, by the time he got back from next door, was just about done in.

Having set out to make amends for the day before he'd merely tied himself up in knots. Sometimes more is less, and by piling on the detail to shore up his case he may have made matters worse. Tony and Betty had tried to keep up, but still couldn't fathom how he'd lost ten pounds without spending a penny; or what that strange little man in white gloves – who he kept referring to as Urinal Heep – had to do with anything. Had he, perhaps, been watching too much David Lynch?

Still, an understanding was reached of sorts. There was only so much Tony wished to hear about the joys that lay in store for his prostate as the years rolled by. And Josh, who was always in the market for new material, was much amused by the whole account, and wondered if there was a sitcom idea in a man who was a walking disaster area.

"Anyway ... yes, once again, I'm terribly, terribly sorry," burbled Victor, deciding the best thing now was to scarper. "It was just one of those unfortunate things, and erm ..."

Not since the last G20 communiqué had so much waffle been issued to paper over the cracks.

As he tramped back into the kitchen and threw down his cap Victor could imagine how John Hurt felt with that thing about to burst from his chest. His heart was going full throttle, and he badly needed something to calm down.

All roads led to the bathroom cabinet, where a small brown bottle held the key. In the fifteen months since it was issued that Diazepam supply had been a lifeline; stepping into the breach when it was needed most.

Today a single yellow pill remained.

But not for long.

Victor lay across the bed and let his body go limp. In a minute or so a blissful serenity would begin to wash over him: erasing all the ills of the world and affording him perfect peace of mind. As he lay there gazing at the ceiling through drooping eyes, what could possibly rile him or ruffle him on his way to a mellow oblivion?

The ceiling!

Those bloody workmen had left a right old mess behind, he knew that much. You could still see every dent and scuff mark where that lamp post had come to rest. He'd said as much at the time and got nothing but cheek for his trouble. "Who's doing this job, you or us?" was not the most gracious reply but his comeback may not have helped either. You didn't win these people over suggesting a new place to stick their chisel.

Some restoration was needed: he'd get straight on to it in the morning ...

Must pop down to the hardware shop first thing. Paint required, obviously. Polyfilla probably. Sandpaper definitely. More turps? Would need to check.

Best to jot it all down ... before he nodded off completely ...

And how appropriate was it, that a certain piece of paper was still lying in the drawer of his bedside table, having made its way there two weeks ago when they were still making plans for the hall.

Some things in life are just too predictable.

For all her faults, Victor would never have claimed Mrs Warboys made him sick. But that was because she'd never tried hard enough.

Never one to shirk a challenge, she immediately found there was nothing to it. Prescription emetics were all very well, but for instant results you couldn't beat a good firm finger down the back of the throat; forcefully driven as far as it would go.

Who would have thought she had it in her? To take on the stomach of a man who famously could keep things down that a waste disposal would have thought twice about.

And all because ...

When she called round to pick up her reading glasses (carelessly left behind on Saturday) the house had appeared to be empty. Margaret of course was still at work; but why would the back door be unlocked unless Victor was home?

Calling his name was met with silence. And so with a shrug she collected her glasses from the sideboard and turned to leave.

But then came a sound from upstairs which caused her to pause.

It was the sound of a dull clunk, like a shoe hitting the floor.

"Hallo? Is anyone up there?"

Still no answer. Which was distinctly odd and worthy of investigation.

A moment later she was there in the room, unable to believe her eyes.

On the bed lay a figure in a posture that could best be described as random. As if it had been dropped there from a great height and landed any old how: legs splayed; one foot, shoeless, jutting over the edge; head to one side, in a state of lifeless collapse.

"Mr Meldrew??"

Mr Meldrew did not stir. Nor did he when lightly prodded or gently poked or briskly shaken.

And the reason was frighteningly clear.

Still resting in his hand was a ballpoint pen. And close by lay The Note:

"By the time you read this I will be dead. My life has become such a gutted shell, I have decided to snuff out my worthless existence once and for all. Farewell sweet love, I go now to my grave."

"Ohhhh … merciful saints preserve us!"

A few inches from The Note was The Bottle: on its side, on Margaret's bedside table. Empty, of course. The whereabouts of its contents only too obvious.

"Ohhhh Mr Meldrew!! Mr Meldrew! What have you *done*?"

But of course she should have seen it coming! What had he said to them both, only forty-eight hours before: *"And they wonder why people commit suicide! I've a ruddy good mind to join them sometimes."*

"Oh dear God, dear God, dear God."

Seconds were precious, and she had to act fast.

From Victor's perspective what followed was the very definition of a surprise attack; as he woke to find his head being viciously smacked about from side to side, while Mrs Warboys' face blurred backwards and forwards through his field of vision. Seconds later, she had dragged him off the bed with his head over a waste bin, to begin forcing out everything he had eaten in the past seven hours.

Among the contraindications for the benzodiazepine drug group "being made to spew your guts up when someone thinks you've topped yourself" is sadly not listed. And it's fair to say that whatever stage of sedation Victor had reached was no match for this sudden assault on his tonsils. Finally winded beyond measure, and with nothing left to bring up, he could do no more than lean back against the bed gasping for air.

"Mr Meldrew? Are you all right? Mr Meldrew, talk to me!"

Mr Meldrew would have loved to talk to her, though it's doubtful she'd have liked what he had to say. And dialogue would have to wait till his vocal cords were back on speaking terms.

"I still can't believe it! That you could even *think* of such a thing! And to leave a note like that for poor Margaret to find—"

Note?

Victor's eyes flared sharply as the reason for this madness came rudely into focus.

Fumbling for the piece of paper that had fallen to the floor he thrust it under his visitor's nose, tapping furiously at one side, then the other.

"Wh— sorry, what's this? What are you trying to s— ... *Dulux satin eggshell, twenty-one pounds f—* ... *Sandpaper* ... *Polyfilla* ... *Turps* ..."

By this time, even Mrs Warboys was starting to see. That maybe, just maybe, she'd been a little hasty.

The fact that half the writing was in black? And Victor's pen was blue?

"But if you— oh now I'm really confused. You mean, you d— ohhhh my God, what have I done?"

It would be another twenty-four hours before Victor could face the sight of food. And the best part of a week before the back of his tongue began to heal. (Ironically, Mrs Warboys had been due for a manicure that very afternoon, but forgot to put it in her diary!) And when Margaret had suggested some nice pea and lentil soup the very thought had propelled him straight into the downstairs toilet with a cold flannel on the back of his neck.

"Ruddy woman, she must have seen I was just lying there asleep for goodness' sake? Didn't need that today, on top of everything else."

Margaret glanced up from the table as her husband entered. A moment later he was flaked out on the settee, still grumbling to the heavens.

"Had no business coming up to our bedroom in the first place. What if I was lying there completely naked?"

There was an easy ad lib about which one of them might have been sick, but Margaret didn't lower herself, and continued with her tuna salad.

"No I definitely didn't need *that* today. On top of everything else."

"So you said. And what's the latest with our new neighbours by the way. Are they still talking to us? Or can we expect another For Sale sign going up tomorrow."

"Yessss. I told them the whole story and said I was very sorry. I think they understood. I asked them if they'd like another one, and Josh said that was very kind, he'd get me a funnel. He's very sharp isn't he. For his age. Pair of *them* didn't crack a smile of course."

"I wonder why."

"Ohhhh God! Never retched up so much in my life! And I was just having an interesting dream as I remember – Gladys Knight and the Pips were living in the potting shed. Then to wake up and find *her* fizzog in front of me! Slapping me about to kingdom come, I didn't know where I was."

"I can't believe you'd been hanging on to that thing all this while? Any normal person would have thrown it in the bin."

"Well I thought it might come in useful."

"Oh yes! Many's the time I've wondered where to lay my hands on a decent suicide note! God spare us."

"But it had the price of all those paints on."

"I mean we all know she's irritating. She's always been the same and she's never going to change. But just try and let it drop, can't you? In any case she might have had other things on her mind today, so …"

"Like what."

"Nothing."

"Like what?"

"Never mind. It doesn't matter. Are you just going to lie there all night moaning and groaning about being sick? It's not exactly helping my digestion."

Victor gave a grunt and hauled himself to his feet.

"Perhaps I'll have a bath. See if that settles me."

"And remember to rinse it out afterwards."

Margaret watched him plod off upstairs and waited till the footsteps had died.

Then she put down her fork and sat gazing ahead.

Her eyes were on the clock beside the door.

The thin rhythmic click had seized control of the silence, and in less than a minute it would be eight o'clock.

Or not.

For of course there was no such thing as eight o'clock. Nor any other time by which we measure out our lives to give the illusion of purpose.

In time there would be no time.

No sense of time.

No sense of sense.

Only seconds were left.

For some of us those seconds would be weeks. Or months. For some they would be years. But they would go all the same.

In time.

Eight o'clock precisely.

Chesney Dubois Pinkerton III was gone now, and would never return. He had gone taking with him the kind eyes of one he never knew; who had never sought to know him; and from this moment on would know him ever less.

There was only so much pain on this earth you could bear to absorb. And a grisly double axe murder in the Deep South was more horror than anyone had a right to. Yet thanks to Mrs Warboys she'd somehow found her way into this killer's life as the face of empathy from which he'd drawn such strength.

Her photo on the wall of his cell no less.

And worst of all, if we bought that final message, there in his mind's eye, smiling sweetly at the very end.

It was enough to give you the willies.

Would she have felt better if she'd shared her friend's conviction? Hardly so. It was tragic enough that two innocent lives had been lost let alone a third. She had to believe, for her own sanity, that justice had been served.

Of course there was justice and justice.

And both were a myth.

In another reality Victor had been looting that store and she had tried to steal that blouse. And that was a reality too close for comfort.

As Gregory had shown: when it pays to lie the truth always goes to the highest bidder.

Upstairs there was a loud gurgling sound as a bath tap was turned on. Followed by an angry voice demanding to know why soap always got stuck to the dish.

Margaret closed her eyes. And muttered a brief something to Someone somewhere, hoping it would pass muster.

Then she picked up her fork and went back to her salad.

Chapter Six
The Suburban Spaceman

Summer had passed away and would not be mourned. Victor and the planet were still standing but not for long. After all their recent scrapes, and the driest spell since records began to get on your nerves in the seventies, autumn came as a blessed relief.

There was an early morning nip to the air as Victor arrived downstairs and stepped into the kitchen. That last banana in the bowl was in a sorry state, but portions are portions and Victor forced it down with a mug of coffee to take the taste away. On the radio a man from Wigan was insisting all those doctors should stop dithering about and just cure his cancer like he'd asked them to. Or something of the sort: Victor had stopped listening to the voice of the people since it brought him out in hives. Besides which he was keen to get outside and work on his kennel for an hour before starting on the window-cleaning round.

A haze of gossamer delicacy had draped the land and was taking a while to burn off. It seemed to hang from the rooftops and trees, applying a ghostly varnish to the day and softening the glare of a golden—

But hang on, you say, what was that about a window-cleaning round?

And kennel?

Well as we know, if there was one thing Victor had set his sights on it was early retirement from early retirement. And if full-time employment was now a distant memory it would be nice to feel his working days were not quite numbered. From his last field of endeavour in a field of manure the only way was up. And when Haziz who'd been doing their windows for the past three years announced he was going back to Kabul for a better life the opportunity was there on a plate. How would Victor like to take over his franchise and earn a few pennies? The roster of clients was already in place, and he'd even thrown in his bucket and ladder.

Meanwhile there'd been no let-up from Mrs Warboys in her efforts to find a new home for that border collie. And at what point Victor changed his mind we can't be sure, though it seems to have been after he started his new job. Having made friends with a miniature Schnauzer who followed him round every room licking the other side of the glass even Victor had begun to soften. Perhaps there was, after all, something to be said for a new friendly presence around the house, as an antidote to the human race.

Margaret was all for it of course. Anything that got her husband outside on a lead twice a day couldn't be bad. (Yes, in theory it was the other way round; but who was going to tell him?)

And so here he was now, putting the finishing touches to a piece of work that had kept him out of mischief for the past six days. Like a miniature version of the potting shed it had taken shape nicely outside the back door, and now required only a coat of epoxy sealant to be ready for business. Victor was well pleased with his handiwork. And even Mrs Bithery, who peered into their garden every day through her telescope, had given it the thumbs-up.

"Morning, Mr Meldrew!"

If the words had been played on a flute they could not have sounded more jaunty. Simultaneously the slats in the fence behind him slid open like a vertical blind to reveal a face that in times past would be rarely seen outside a circus tent. Wreathed in a grin for which no natural cause could be found, with its wide dancing eyes and big dimpled cheeks it was a face that Terry Gilliam might have sketched in an idle moment. Bizarrely it seemed to glow from some inner light source, which Victor found deeply unsettling.

Still less impressed was he by the manner of his neighbour's appearance as he stared several daggers across the garden.

"Erm. Yes, morning, Mr Swainey. What's all this in aid of then, when it's at home?"

"Oh yes! Just a little idea I came up with!" trilled the other. "To get a bit more sun on my sweet williams. I didn't think you'd have any objections."

"*Didn't* you … right …"

Victor's scowl went for nothing as the entire fence panel now swung back into Mr Swainey's garden, where the owner was discovered in the middle of the lawn, directing a watering can at some daisies. He was wearing blue wellington boots and a balaclava.

"No I just thought I'd pop out and nuke a few weeds while it's fine. I don't know if it's me but it feels a bit chillier today."

"Well. Perhaps just a bit."

"And it looks like you're expecting a new arrival then? Unless I'm mistaken. When's it due."

"Sorry?"

"Yes, many's the time I've heard you banging away with that hammer just lately. I said to mother, he's up to something out there! He's either getting a dog, or a very large hamster!"

This being the cue for a violent shaking fit in which his face turned the colour of a beetroot, Victor was obliged to wait for several seconds before replying:

"Erm, yes, tomorrow morning, she's supposed to be bringing it round. Little border collie, that a friend of ours erm—"

"Oh yes? Border collie? Very nice too."

"And so, how is your mother now."

"Ah well. Not making a lot of sense these days, I'm afraid. She's got it into her head she's being kidnapped by aliens every night and taken to the planet Neptune."

"Oh dear. Aliens."

"Yes, she says they come down about half past two in the morning in this great big spacecraft and just whisk her off. She says three of them are just huge protoplasmic blobs with a kind of pulsating nucleus inside and the other two look like Eamonn Andrews. I had to laugh. I said, but mother, surely there isn't any atmosphere on the planet Neptune? She said there will be once they've put the jukebox in!" At this, he turned to shout up at the bedroom window as if someone was watching though Victor had always had his doubts. "I'm just telling Mr Meldrew, mother! What you said about the jukebox! He's laughing his socks off down here!"

Victor peered hard in search of a movement in the curtains. But could see nothing, as Nick Swainey turned back to him still chortling away.

"I mean what can you do. Still, the main thing is how much it's perked her up. Is the way I look at it. Put a real fresh glow in her eyes. And what with the way things are these days. Perhaps we could all do with a trip up there, what d'you reckon."

"Yes, probably be an idea," said Victor. Little knowing how oddly this theme would pan out. "Well anyway. Give her my best, won't you, and erm …"

"Oh thank you, Mr Meldrew, yes. I will do."

For one joyous second it appeared the exchange was over. But no. The buffoon had now put down his watering can and crossed into Victor's garden, while fiddling with something in his back pocket.

"Now actually I'm glad I've just caught you today as it happens."

Victor wasn't.

"Because you remember that thing we discussed the other week?"

Victor didn't. As a rule he tried to avoid things wherever possible.

"Yyy …"

"Action for the Elderly? You very kindly offered your services to do a bit of driving for us. If the need arose. And I'm hoping you're still up for it?"

"Oh. Yes. Well, if you're erm …"

"Only there's an old lady we'd love you to pick up from the airport this afternoon. She's not entirely with it I'm afraid. It's a Mrs Akhani, she's been over in Bangladesh for a family funeral, poor soul, and the flight gets in at five, so … that's her address and our set of keys to her flat. If you could just settle her back in and make sure she's nice and secure."

Victor glanced at the envelope that had been pressed into his hand and nodded. In truth it was not a big deal. He'd be done with his round by three-thirty at the latest, and let's face it, these little good deeds were surely what life was all about.

"Yes OK then. I'll try and see to that."

"Oh lovely, and she'll be ever so grateful, I promise you."

In a perfect world that might have been true. But guess what.

Victor stood behind the cordon in the terminal building and waited. This was a skill he'd perfected after many years on the phone to the man at the bank. And so far he'd been waiting for fifty-two minutes and counting. (To be clear, we're not suggesting the man at the bank had actually kept him on hold, waiting, for many years, as that would be frankly outrageous, and a slap in the face for the very customers upon whom their business depends.)

The flight from Dhaka, needless to say, was delayed. During boarding, a middle-aged couple from Essex hadn't liked the look of another passenger and had asked to see the pilot. When they saw the pilot they hadn't liked the look of him either and complained to a national newspaper. By the time they'd been finally restrained, somewhere over Kazakhstan, the video of their shouting match was trending on Instagram.

When eventually the first stream of arrivals appeared through the doors there was a sudden surge of interest with everyone jockeying for position.

As per the protocol Victor was holding a big white card to attract the attention of his fare. It said simply AKHANI in bold black capitals. And it wasn't long before a small, trim lady in her seventies spotted the name and broke from the flow to join him. In her bright orange handloom sari she cut a more elegant figure than he was expecting. Her hair, which was tightly drawn back beneath a broad silk band, was still sleek for her age, and there was a crisp, rather fruity tilt to her voice as she introduced herself and apologised for keeping him waiting.

Victor responded with various pleasantries. But since he spoke no Bengali and she spoke no English this was all conducted with a lot of nods and smiles, as he took the trolley and led her outside to the short-stay car park.

All of which was unfortunate, as but for the language barrier he might have discovered her name was in fact Mrs Khan; and whoever was meant to be picking her up had somehow got lost in the crowd. Rule one, you would think, when you're holding up one of those cards: to make sure your fingers aren't covering the first and last letters? But don't forget Victor was new to this game.

And it's not for us to speculate that a woman who was subsequently rushed out to a waiting ambulance in a diabetic coma may have been the very same Mrs Akhani that Victor wasn't about to drive home all nicely safe and sound.

Inkerman Terrace lay in a corner of society we'd rather not own up to. As part and parcel of "the burning injustice I came into politics to stamp out" it had its uses but let's not get carried away. Ignorance and want, after all, are the stuff of diversity: the glue that holds our country together, by sniffing it till we cease to care.

Or in layman's terms it was a bit of a dump. Joined-up houses that long ago should have been put out of their misery and were now inflicting it on their tenants. At one end of the cul-de-sac was the rusting hulk of a burnt-out van, home to a cadre of rodent warlords. In this part of the world litter was king; and who's to say it didn't sugar the pill? With gaily coloured Skittles bags that skipped along the gutters and grease-encrusted fast food cartons that shimmered in the blush of a setting sun.

The drive from the airport had taken longer than expected, and by the time they arrived Mrs Khan was fast asleep on the back seat.

Victor switched off the engine and checked his notes to make sure he'd got the right address. Yes, this was the place – 17b Basement Flat, lurking behind a drab iron railing that appeared to be shedding its skin like a snake. Two windows on the ground floor were boarded up, and if the building had ever known a stucco finish it was unlikely to remember it now.

There were three big cases and a holdall in the boot, so it took a couple of trips to cart them all down and deposit them in the hall. Then it was back to the car to collect his passenger.

On the seat beside her lay a raincoat and a folded umbrella. Victor picked them both up and gave her a light shake on the shoulder.

"Mrs Akhani? You can wake up now, we're here."

"Uhhh??"

Mrs Khan jerked sharply to life and opened her eyes.

Then she let out a startled cry.

She could no longer see!

A man was talking to her in his native tongue. The same one who had taken her to his car? With this blindfold on she couldn't be sure.

"Hang on! Hang on a second, I see what's happened here. Your hair band's slipped over your eyes. Let me just sort that out for you. Therrrre we go. And if you want to get out now, Mrs Akhani? Then we can get you inside."

As her sight was restored she blinked in the light and gazed through the windows. My God, what manner of place had he brought her to! This wasn't where she lived! What on earth was happening?

One thing she knew: this was not the moment to get hysterical. You read about these monsters in the papers, and there was no telling what he might do. That gun he was holding under the raincoat would surely be used if she stepped out of line. (OK, *we* know it was an umbrella but she wasn't thinking straight.) For now it made sense to co-operate. Just do what he said and try not to get him angry. And do *not* be fooled by that big dopey smile. She'd seen enough Robert de Niro films to know that was all part of the technique.

And so she was led down to her place of confinement. To meet what unspeakable fate? Would there be others of his kind there waiting? A cabal of old men in flat caps all bent on some heinous misdeed? What did that word "*Mindyourstep!*" mean? It sounded horrible, she knew that much. A threat of some kind not to try anything silly? It was certainly having the desired effect.

Inside, the flat was a spartan affair: starved of light in morbid monochrome. An unkind observer might have taken the cobwebs for curtains. And whatever is the next level down from "not much cop" would describe all the furnishings ("former special constable"?), while the mustiness in the air seemed to enfold you like a chrysalis.

"OK then? I think you're all set now. I'll double lock the doors when I go just to make sure. And you've got your own keys haven't you. These are the ones *we* hang on to just so we can keep an eye on you. Perhaps you'll settle down now, will you, and make yourself a cup of tea or something."

Mrs Khan backed off meekly and tried to ask how long she was going to be kept there. Whereupon the man just grinned and mimed the turning of his key in an imaginary lock, to make it clear she was going nowhere in a hurry and she'd better get used to it. With her voice beginning to fail she asked if he was planning to kill her. Again, he just grinned and nodded happily before giving her a thumbs-up sign. It was heartlessness off the scale.

Finally she put her hands together to plead for mercy. But any hope of leniency was dashed. His response was simply to taunt her by mimicking the action, and then turning to leave.

Mrs Khan collapsed back onto one of the kitchen chairs and wondered if she would live to see another dawn.

As Victor locked up and left he felt he'd done the best he could. The old dear was back now in her own surroundings, all nice and secure, which was the main thing. And from the look of this neighbourhood you couldn't be too careful. She seemed more than grateful at any rate. With that gesture of peace and light, or whatever it meant. But living on her own like that, you had to feel sorry for the poor soul.

Perhaps he'd pop back in a day or two, to make sure she was OK.

"Mrs Swainey's mother's being kidnapped by aliens every night from the planet Neptune," said Victor. "Must be good for a few air miles."

"Yes, I daresay. Tchohhh! Will you watch where you're stepping on that floor! I've just mopped it." Margaret shot her husband a testy look from the hall as he stepped in through the back door. "And what have *you* been up to out there with an extension lead? You've not been using my new Dyson in that kennel I hope? Or there'll be merry hell to pay."

Victor unplugged the cable he'd just brought in, then grudgingly wiped his feet on the doormat.

"I was just getting some bits out with the old one, that's all. Before madam arrives. And what's *that* supposed to mean anyway?"

"What?"

"'Yes, I daresay'."

"Oh. Well. I mean *we* don't know, do we. What's out there and what isn't? It stands to reason, we can't just be totally alone in the universe. It wouldn't make sense."

Victor paused as he stowed away his reel under the sink.

"Yes, it's hard to imagine a race of super-intelligent beings hurtling across the solar system every night to get a batty old woman out of bed. Though you can hardly blame her wanting to get away from everything down here. Now where the hell's she got to, d'you think? It's nearly half past, and she said ten o'clock."

"Well, she'll get here when she gets here. You know what she's like. God, it's worse than a child. Couple of weeks ago you wouldn't have one in the house for love nor money and now look at you. Couldn't believe how many bags of kibbles I found stashed away in that stair cupboard. It's a border collie she's bringing, not a hundred and one Dalmatians."

"*And* I notice that dog basket's still not come. Promise you next-day delivery these people, it's a joke. I was thinking perhaps for now it could sleep on one of Ronnie and Mildred's Christmas presents."

"Which one?"

"I thought maybe that big flat one from six years ago. With the green wrapping paper and red ribbons. It was quite soft and squashy as I recall."

"You don't think we should open it?"

"Why?"

Margaret nodded.

"I suppose. Well whatever you think. If you want to go up the loft later and I'll give you a h— ah! Now. Talk of the devil."

At the sound of the doorbell they both snapped into action. While Margaret hurried off to let in their visitor Victor reached for a plastic bowl and tore into a 15kg pack of Chicken And Rice Canine Diet With Multivitamins.

"Morning, Margaret! Sorry I'm a bit later than I said."

In the hall Mrs Warboys huffed and puffed as she squeezed her way through the front door with a big wicker basket.

"I'm afraid a few tears were shed at the last minute, when it came to saying goodbye. You know what it's like. After all the time they'd been together."

"Oh dear, was she upset. Erm – you want to just pop him through then, Jean? Into the sitting room. And I'll close this door."

"Righty-ho. Oh, good morning, Mr Meldrew. Are you well."

"Yes, morning, Mrs Warboys. You managing all right there?"

"I think so, yes. If I just put him down here on the floor. Then it'll be easier to get him out."

Having unlatched the lid she reached inside, and gently cradling and stroking the animal set it down on the carpet.

It was, by any measure, the cutest creature. Its coat was golden-red with a sheen that picked up the sun from the back window. And its long floppy ears framed a face that was primed for love. Standing there, in the middle of the room, it gazed back at Victor, tongue unfurled, with bold, playful eyes; as if in supplication to its new owner with one of its paws in the air and its head cocked slightly to one side.

"Therrrre we are then, at long last. As I say, it's been quite a journey for the little soul. We were starting to think nobody wanted him!"

Victor did not immediately respond.

As he stood there clutching his bowl of dog biscuits, eye to eye finally with his new best friend, he was seized with a sudden paralysis that rendered him mute.

He was not the only one.

Margaret, also, appeared to have turned to stone; while Mrs Warboys stepped back with a wide, fixed grin of expectation that could have passed for a freeze-frame.

And as for the dog ...

It was, as previously noted, a cute little thing, with a mischievous nature that was there for all to see in its bright, sparkling eyes and its lively posture.

The taxidermist had made sure of that.

"So where do you want me to put him?

"What?"

"Where do you think he should go? I thought over there might be best, on that table in front of the curtains. You'll be able to see him looking out at you then, when you're in the garden."

"Please tell me this is a joke!?"

"In what way?"

"Hohhhh, Jean … Jean …" Margaret screwed up her eyes and turned away as all her insides seemed to collapse.

"I mean, obviously you'll want to have a play around, both of you, before you decide."

"*Have a play around???* Have you taken leave of your senses?"

"Sorry, Mr Meldrew?"

"What in heaven's name's it supposed to *be*?"

"What do you m— well, it's Mr Burkett's dog. Nippy."

"*Nippy???*" There were times when Victor seriously imagined Mrs Warboys must have a team of malevolent goblins in a writers' room somewhere, punching up her dialogue for these occasions. "He doesn't look very nippy from where I'm standing! You never told me it was stuffed!"

"Didn't I?"

"No you didn't!"

"Are you sure?"

"I think I'd have remembered!"

"But – why would you want a dead dog that hadn't been stuffed? It would look dreadful."

"W— y—!!" It was back to that Groucho Marx logic again that drove you up the wall. "I *do not* want a dead dog! Why in the name of sanity would I want a dead dog? So I can throw it across the room on elastic and shout 'Here boy!'?? I've just spent six days out there building a kennel! Why didn't you tell me it was dead?"

"Well ... I thought everyone knew about Nippy. He was Mr Burkett's pride and joy. And when he died he couldn't bear to part with him, so he had him mounted. Everyone in the street knew that."

"Well I didn't!!"

"Well I'm very sorry. But I'm not psychic am I?"

In desperation she turned to Margaret for support.

"*Donnn't* bring me into the discussion! You two can sort it out for yourselves!"

"I mean how am I supposed to take it for walks! Glue his feet to a skateboard? I have never in my life heard of anything so utterly ridiculous—"

It was not in Margaret's nature to run from a fight. But this one was already setting new standards of lunacy. And when she heard the doorbell go for the second time she was only too glad of an excuse to leave them to it.

Outside was a figure she barely recognised.

"Mrs Meldrew? Oh God, I'm sorry."

"Mr Swainey! What is it?"

A good question. The infectious glee, for which Victor prayed a vaccine might one day be found, had vanished. His eyes looked dull and sore; the impish dimples more like puncture marks where some cruel blow had hit him hard. And his voice was disintegrating. Only rarely had Margaret seen him like this but she could guess what lay behind it. And closing the door on all the kerfuffle behind her she stepped outside.

"Is it your mother? What's happened?"

"No, I'm sorry, I shouldn't be bothering you like this, it's just that— she's gone."

"Gone? Where?"

"In the night. I don't know. Just vanished. I've looked everywhere. The whole thing's just— I mean, there's no sense to it. And I didn't suppose, that by any chance you or Mr Meldrew might have—"

"Well, no, no. We've not seen anything of her. Have you been to the police?"

"I mean obviously I'll have to now, but ... something else that's weird. You see just there? On the front lawn."

"Oh, heavens."

It was certainly no trick of the light. Five circular patches in the grass outside her neighbour's house, all smoky brown in colour, in the shape of a near-perfect ellipse. We could call them strange geometric scorch-marks that were not of this earth; or not, depending on our taste for adventure. What's certain is they weren't there twenty-four hours before.

The two of them looked at each other. And then with no words spoken both looked up at the sky.

They saw nothing of course.

But did anything see them?

Alan Radlett took three steps back from the big Ralph Lauren dining table and decided the microphones were still too subtle.

The sound recordist assured him a couple of shotgun mikes were well up to the task, but he'd happily stick a few large condensers in for that vintage look if more gravitas were needed.

The detective said that would be good. To stand any chance of finding Mrs Khan alive they had to make this TV appeal count, and impact was everything.

Like most of his breed, Radlett could have doubled as an East End gangster. Clean-shaven, with a bullet head and a neck that had no beginning and no end. An easy, laconic stillness defined him, and gave the listener a sense that he knew what he was about. But warmth and forbearance were not part of his box of tricks. He was a professional with a job to do.

It was his idea to broadcast from the victim's house. It lent a personal touch and gave you more to play with. The giant portrait of Mrs Khan on the wall was nicely balanced on the left of frame by the window on the right, down which rain was now pouring. Nothing wrong with a bit of pathetic fallacy: the water on the glass would chime rather well with the tears of the family all weeping hysterically in the background.

As Mrs Khan's son took his place at the table he was immediately set upon by the make-up and wardrobe departments, intending to take down his hot spots and tidy his clothes. Radlett sent them away. The more harassed and crumpled his man looked the better. The name of the game here was audience empathy.

A producer who had been to a rather good school signalled they were ready to go, and someone clicked a stopwatch.

"OK very quiet then everyone please! Sound's running and camera's set. Whenever you're ready, Mr Khan, in your own time."

Sajib Khan took a sip of water and gripped the hand of his wife who sat next to him. His tone and diction were controlled, as he was used to public speaking. But his nerves were frayed and his senses raw.

"As a man of faith, I believe there is ultimately goodness to be found in every heart. And so I say now to whoever is out there watching, that has done this cruel thing and taken my mother, please show compassion. To her, and to the family for whom she is everything. In the name of our God we beg you – just return her to us safe and sound. Any amount I will pay. Just get in touch, to let us know she is still alive. Please, *please* do not harm my mother!"

"Indeed …"

There was a flicker in Radlett's eye at the mention of limitless cash changing hands this early in the game. It was his belief they were dealing with a highly sophisticated operator here, a Napoleon of crime if you will, to whom no quarter should be given. And at this stage they had to tread cannily.

"We are, obviously, treating the disappearance of Mrs Khan as a malicious act. And we can't rule out the possibility that she's been abducted, only minutes after arriving in the country, for the purpose of extortion. As yet we've received no ransom note or demand from those responsible. But in view of the fact that her son is one of the wealthiest businessmen in Britain I'd imagine they'll be looking for a seven-figure sum. In particular we're appealing to anyone who was at the airport that day to get in touch immediately if they saw something suspicious. And if you do see anyone you think was involved, on no account approach them, as we believe these people to be *highly* dangerous."

Victor groaned as he got out of the car and hauled down his ladder from the roof rack. The rain was now falling heavily after a nervous start, though most of the day had been dry. But it wasn't the weather that was giving him grief. Dark forces were out there, plotting to sabotage his new window-cleaning round. And he'd just about had a bellyful of it.

How else to explain the fact that four of his six clients that morning had suddenly cancelled without rhyme or reason? Two of them saying they'd changed their minds; one rubbing his finger through the grime to declare they didn't really need doing; and another couple pretending they weren't in, even though Victor had peered into the front room and could see their feet poking out from under a curtain.

To cap it all he'd had five texts from other customers saying they no longer required his services. With excuses that ranged from "we've found someone a bit cheaper" to the charge that on reflection he was not sufficiently BAME.

What the hell was going on?

As he stomped back into the kitchen and threw off his coat he was still trying to get his head round it. Coincidence be buggered, he knew a conspiracy when he saw one.

"Well that was a fun day at the office! If ever there was one. Can you believe what's been happening, Margaret? I shan't have a customer left if this carries on. Everyone dropping out left, right and centre suddenly! What's *that* all about, I got the plague now or something? Margaret?? Are you back yet, or— oh."

Having slipped off his boots and stepped into the sitting room he could almost feel the temperature drop by several degrees.

Margaret was sitting in the far armchair, directly facing him with her hands resting on the arms. For the moment she did not move or speak. But the death stare she fired across the room was bang on target, and caused her husband to flinch. He knew these looks of old and they always spelt trouble.

"Sorry, I wasn't sure if you were erm ... I thought you might not be back from work yet."

"*Ohhhh* yes. I'm back. I've been back half an hour now."

Not good. She was using *that* voice.

And now a thin sickly smile had crossed her face.

He was as good as dead.

"Oh. OK."

Then came the pause.

Anything but the pause.

"So is everything all right?"

His wife did not so much speak the words as pronounce them: much in the way a judge might pronounce sentence. And they came at Victor like bullets.

"You may like to know that I've just had Pippa on the phone."

"Oh yes? What's she got to say for herself. Is she OK?"

"Well. That depends what we mean by OK, doesn't it."

There was enough insinuation there to sink a battleship. And the molten look in her eyes would have spoken volumes if he knew how to decode it. That smooth, furry tone was fooling no one: she was softening him up for the kill.

"To say she was in a state of shock would be putting it mildly. The poor woman could barely string a sentence together."

"State of shock? Sorry, I don't understand."

"Oh you don't understand? Because you have no idea, I suppose? What could possibly have upset her like that?"

"Well, no? None at all. Why would I?"

"You don't imagine, for example, it might be in any way connected with you texting her an image of your private parts this morning? I gather some women can be funny about things like that."

"What?"

Flying out like the cork from a bottle it hit him smack in the face.

"Texting her an ima— of my private p—??"

Even by the measure of his own frequent lapses this one was a cracker. And it landed with such a thump as to leave him winded.

"Why in the name of all that's holy would I text her an image of my—"

"*You - tell - me, Victor*!! By all accounts it's lucky she hasn't got a weak heart! You hear a sudden ping in your pocket, you don't imagine something like *that's* going to come out and stare you in the face! And in the most graphic detail known to man, from the way she described it – she said it was like you'd used a telephoto lens!"

"Oh for goodness' sake! She's making the whole thing up! You surely don't believe that in a month of Sundays I w—"

"Something I've *never* understood! Why men want to boast about their 'equipment' like that! And flaunt it around for all the world to see?? What on earth was I supposed to say to her? There was nothing I *could* say!"

"Boast about their equipm—?? Has she gone stark raving mad?"

"God *spare* us, Victor! Isn't it bad enough to have *sent* the bloody thing, without making a big deal about the measurements!"

"Measurements?? What on earth are you talking ab—"

"She said you were holding a *ruler* next to it!!"

"A what??"

"Just to make sure she was in no doubt, was that? About the dimensions??"

"A *ruler*??? Oh for crying out lou— oh! Oh, hang on a sec." All in a flash his indignation stalled; as somewhere, in some deep mental recess, something began to stir. "Ah, now then, wait a second. Yes …"

"Ohhhh good! So it's all finally coming back to you now is it?"

"Erm … yes I think I might know what's happened here actually."

"I think we *all* know that!!"

"No, it's just … when you rang me up earlier on from work, and said could I do you a favour? And take a quick snap of that cactus to send to her. Because you'd just been telling her, on the phone, about how well it was doing and everything … since she brought it round that time …"

"Go on?"

"Only … I think I might have accidentally …"

"Might have what? For heaven's sake?"

"Well you know what it's like, with all those tiny thumbnails you have to scroll through. When you're looking for the one you want to send. They're not always easy to make out. I suppose if I'd had my glasses on … in hindsight it would have erm … I mean, it was a mistake anyone could have made?"

"A mistake anyone could have m—??? *No*, Victor!! I think you'll find it was a mistake only *you* could have made! What the *hell* was a photo like that doing on your phone in the first place, am I allowed to ask? God knows, I'm *praying* it was a selfie?"

Not for the first time her husband was on the back foot. And struggling to dig himself out of a hole that was a long way beneath the earth's crust.

"Yyy— well— it was that chap Huffenfeffer. You remember? I saw at the hospital. After he made a point of saying I should keep an eye on it, just to be sure. And to watch out for any change, or if it got bigger or anything. I just thought, the best way to keep an accurate record ... of the size and everything, was ..."

"Godddd give me strength! And that was your idea of a succulent was it? How many of these blessed things have you got, sitting on there? Like some hideous spot the difference competition? I mean, this is the image I've got to carry round with me now is it? Of you there fiddling about in your trousers every week, with a phone and a ruler? I wonder you didn't put a *compass* next to it, to show which way it was pointing! I mean— I just - *despair* sometimes, Victor! Utterly! The next time you're in one of those police line-ups, at this rate you'll be lucky if they don't lock you up! And throw away the key!"

"What the hell's that supposed to mean!?"

"Because you've just got a knack, haven't you! Of upsetting our neighbours! Past and present! It's a wonder there's any of them still talking to us!"

Having risen from the chair she threw a brief, sorry look at the cactus in the corner, as if to absolve it of any blame in the drama.

"And on which subject, as it happens, they're all off tomorrow next door for a week at her sister's. I said I'd pop round to go over what plants they need watering. So if you want to get your own tea I may be a while. And if you could *try* to avoid sending them a video of your foreskin while I'm there it would be greatly appreciated."

With which parting shot she left the room. Victor heard the back door slam and collapsed into his armchair. Then he let out a long sigh, and wondered how much more he could take of this thing called life.

That ruddy saguaro cactus. It was bad enough he kept jabbing his leg on it every time he pulled the curtains. And granted, it *was* more of a pale green colour, seen in the flesh. But then natural tones were always bleached out in those flash photos, so it was hard to tell. No, no, as he flicked back and forth on his Camera Reel he was even more convinced. In miniature, and without his reading glasses, the two pictures were not that dissimilar. The ruler and the door frame, for example, were in exactly the same position. And especially when you think it was all done at speed, as he was just about to go out on his round. Though as things turned out he needn't have hurried, but …

And that was *another* story. Who was it said, when one door closes they all bloody close?

Victor's gaze drifted away from the plant pot to a small plaintive object propped up against the sideboard. And once again he let out a long, dismal sigh.

Perhaps taxidermy was the way to go.

It always pays to think ahead. And if Mrs Khan had done that it's likely she would now be a free woman.

But Fate had other ideas.

Attempting to squeeze head first through a fanlight window was not the smartest of moves. As she dangled there, half in and half out, with a solid concrete surface rising to meet her, the Bengali for "arse about tit" sprang to mind and she was forced to retract her body and try again.

The worst thing so far about her imprisonment was the fear. Fear of where it was leading, and fear of every sound or movement that might signal the return of her captor. It was presumed that he wished to keep her alive for the time being as there were various cans and packets of food to be found in the cupboards. The only way out was through the front door and this had been double locked. Plus there were steel bars across all the windows. The exception was a narrow fanlight in the bathroom, which stubbornly refused to open, until on the third day she had found a rolling pin in the drawer and finally managed to budge the handle.

Climbing onto the toilet seat she had begun to effect her escape, till it dawned on her she was going the wrong way. Manoeuvring her feet and legs out first was a lot trickier and required some delicate acrobatics.

But by clinging on to the pipes and the overhead cistern she began to make progress.

Sadly, she had lost valuable minutes. And before she could wriggle to freedom there came the sound of a car pulling up nearby, and a familiar voice approaching down the steps.

"What on *earth* are y—! Oh don't tell me! You went out and forgot your keys? Don't worry, I know exactly what that's like, it's easily done."

As it happened, Victor had almost not made the effort this afternoon. All that business the day before had rather knocked the stuffing out of him. But then conscience had prevailed, as he recalled how the poor woman was positively shaking the last time he saw her. Imagine if she'd come back with some tropical infection and no one was there to help. He'd never have forgiven himself.

And from the looks of things he'd made the right call, as here she was in a right fix. Her bottom appeared to be firmly wedged in place, and where she'd hoisted up that lovely sari it was already getting torn to bits.

"Now hang on there just a second, Mrs Akhani! And I'll give you a hand."

Swiftly letting himself in, Victor dashed into the bathroom to set about easing her through from the other side, and with some firm but careful handling managed to pull her back indoors.

"Therrrre we are. How are you now, all right? And let me just shut that up again for you, nice and tight."

He pushed at the handle but it was mightily stiff. Was this why she kept a rolling pin handy on the edge of the bath? Well, two or three firm whacks should do the trick.

"Ah! Sorry about that …"

Victor picked up the broken handle from the floor with a rueful smile. At least no one could force it open now in a hurry.

"I'll have a word with the people who come round and see about getting that fixed."

Mrs Khan began to tremble again. Her one escape route had now been closed off: he'd made damn sure of that. And was he planning to use that thing on her now, to teach her a lesson? Instinctively she shrank back as he, and the rolling pin, came towards her. On a table by the door there was a notepad where she had earlier scribbled something down. It was a long shot but she grabbed at it now in desperation and thrust it towards him.

"Oh! What's this. A phone number. Sajib … Khan, does that say?"

Communication, as we know, is everything. But in this case it was nothing. Network coverage in that basement was a non-starter; as these villains well knew. And the handset in the hall, as expected, was dead. Those unpaid bills had a tale to tell, though not one she could ever have fathomed.

With tears in her eyes and a stream of words that meant nothing to him, she appeared to pour out her heart; frantically pointing and dialling with her finger. The message was clear enough: it was someone she'd like him to ring. A relative or friend perhaps. Something was troubling her, that much was evident. Some family problem, or health issue, or other pressing matter she wished to get off her chest.

"You want me to call this number for you? Yes, I can do that, Mrs Akhani. Of course. That's no problem at all."

It didn't help that he'd left his own phone at home. But hopefully she'd understand from all his nodding that she could safely leave it with him.

And so having confirmed that she was, at least, still safe and well, he wished her all the best and then locked up as before and went on his way.

Mrs Khan said a prayer, and hoped that when he spoke to her son they could sort all this out between them and very soon she'd be released.

There were, after all, only so many Pot Noodles you could eat in a week.

While one mystery was solved that night another seemed to deepen. And in neither event was there much room for hope.

The long-term effects of the first would sadly bring more ruin to others than to Victor himself, as we shall see. For it has to be said when considering the misfortunes that dogged him through life a holistic approach is always advised. Like cosmic ripples from the Big Bang that can be measured to this day, his every misstep seemed to reverberate exponentially. Which is another way of saying that given enough time he could bring misery to millions.

It was gone six-thirty when he stepped in through the front door on his return from Inkerman Terrace, and found the latest edition of the parish magazine lying on the floor. With a grunt he picked it up and flicked briefly through its pages before continuing into the front room to look for his phone. It was, of course, down the side of the armchair, as always after a night on the whiskey. But even as he fished it out a flash of something caught up with him. Something he'd just seen in that newsletter. Or had he? Or was this just sheer paranoia taking over?

Margaret was in the kitchen, doing whatever she was doing in readiness for their next meal. And it's lucky she'd just placed a delicate glass bowl on the table when the eruption occurred, or we don't like to think where it would have ended up, and in how many pieces.

"Un – be – lievable!!! Absolutely unbelievable!! If that isn't the bloody limit I don't know what is!! Will you *look – at – this*!!"

"Ohhhh for heaven's *sake*, what is it now?"

Striding into the room, Victor slapped the offending publication down on the worktop and jabbed a finger into the text as for two or three seconds he struggled to get his words out.

"This! Here, in that thing they stick through every month! Can you believe what they've printed? A *review* of my window cleaning!"

"What?"

"As large as life! Look at this! '*Asked to contribute a short piece on the role of casual labour in the community, local arts critic Marjorie Quail assesses the work of newcomer Victor Meldrew*' … I didn't even know she was one of my customers! Ruddy woman – just listen to what she says! '*The Afghan émigré Haziz Abiz, who has lately left our shores, was an artisan artist, with a genuine mastery of his craft. I never knew a window he had touched that did not move me to tears with its crystalline splendour and clarity of purpose. Meldrew has none of these skills. His squeegee action is limp and flaccid. His subtext mired in cliché. He appears to confuse transparency with translucency, and in so doing insults the glass. Where one longs for elegant strokes of pellucid coherence*

Meldrew has nothing to offer but a thoughtless residue of suds. As for his technique with a chamois leather, I have seen it more deftly employed on a goat's arse.'"

"Ooh dear, that *is* a stinker. No wonder your business has been dropping off."

"Got a picture here, of a man in a flat cap on top of a ladder, having an argument with the woman inside. *'Posed by models.'* I mean, what is wrong with these people? You think they get some sort of perverted pleasure from crushing your spirits like that."

"Oh I expect so."

"So that's that then! The rot'll have set in now. You know what people are like round here, who read these things. Suppose I may as well just jack it all in and be done with it."

And thus was Victor so consumed with a sense of injustice for the rest of the night that no other thoughts got a look in.

Margaret would have said all the right things, but quickly discovered there weren't any. And besides which she had quite enough on her mind with Mr Swainey's mother and her aliens.

Yes, she knew it was all barmy. And she hated herself for entertaining such thoughts. But the poor man was out of his mind now with worry, and so far there'd been no word of her whereabouts.

And of course it was all so much worse in the night.

In the thick unyielding silence of the night, when phantoms tricked the senses and fiction was made real.

As she lay there in the early hours, rolling and tossing, adrift among the stars, outside the window a sudden, blinding purity of white for several seconds lit up the room. And then just as suddenly expired.

Somewhere nearby a cat screamed.

Margaret awoke and was grateful for the darkness.

Thank goodness, it was just another dream. And in a minute or two she was back fast asleep.

Fenella Fortune's new summer house was a thing of beauty. With its multiple panels and planes and projections, and skylights to highlight the sparkling reflections, it stood as a monument to tin-eared lyrics everywhere. "A cathedral in glass" had been her brief to the builders. And a cathedral in glass it surely was. Plonk a few repressed natives among its soaring palms and wicker chairs and you might have been back in the Raj. As if, in a sense, the likes of Fenella Fortune had ever left it.

For there she was this morning, reclining on her cushions with not a little majesty. Imagine a loin-clothed eunuch rubbing oils in her back (which she frequently did), and we see how she viewed her station in life. An independent, professional woman, made more independent still after copping all the goodies in a divorce settlement, she knew how to work and play. And today she was looking forward to a bit of both.

In a leafy lane not more than a mile off, a Mazda Sedan was gingerly rounding the bends. Inside, the topic of conversation had already been well aired, but Patrick was never one to give it a rest. Especially when some fresh *aperçu* about the man in question had just popped into his head.

"So it looks like that prediction by the witch wasn't far off the mark then."

"What?"

"Meldrew. Wasn't it something about *coming* … to a sticky end?"

"Ohhh *please*! Stop making it worse than it was! And it was bad enough to start with." Pippa wobbled briefly at the wheel but managed to recover. "I wish I'd never shown you the ruddy thing. It's all been explained to us now, he got the pictures mixed up on his phone, so can't you just let it drop?"

"At first I thought it was that character Wilfred in the Bash Street Kids, wearing a red polo neck. You know the way his bald head sticks out the top of his—"

"Yes!! I get the reference! Thank you very much. How many more times do we have to go through this?"

"And you can't help feeling for all those old ladies. They must have wondered what hit them."

"Old ladies?"

"The word on the street is that he was hauled in by police the other week for flashing in the park. But then got off on a technicality."

"Yes? That he had nothing to do with it."

"Well that's as maybe. But I refer you to the curious incident of the van in the hospital car park. Which is another one that's doing the rounds. You're not telling me these things are all just coincidence."

Pippa took deep breaths and let it go. Life was too short.

"Now then. Is this it here? The Old Nunnery. Looks like it."

Patrick grimaced at the sight of a large brass plaque on a gatepost.

"Yes, and I wouldn't take *that* too literally. I wonder what merry japes we've got to look forward to this time. If she could keep her hands somewhere north of my bottom I'll be well pleased."

They had turned off down a long straight drive towards a house that was neither old nor monastic. If the grounds were historically hallowed the boxy brick and timber home that now sat squarely on the lawn did little to honour the fact. And we can assume its present occupant had dispensed with the vows of chastity.

"Listen, it's not every day your new boss invites you round for lunch. Is it too much to put up with the odd straying hand? You think of the power she has, over your prospects and future. A good personal relationship is everything."

"Yes, I'll try and remember that when I'm outlining the year's profit margins with her tongue in my ear. Just promise me, on no account will you leave us on our own together."

Pippa parked the car round the side of the house, and they were on their way to the front door when a voice called out from behind.

"Patrick! Over here! We're in the conservatory!"

Patrick turned round, and almost fainted. The woman who had spoken had no clothes on! But no, it was just some kind of leotard; in a fleshy tone that was too close for comfort. Had she been exercising or was this for show? And where would you put that body? Mid to late twentieth century at a guess, though these days it was hard to tell. Most likely she'd had the workmen in for one or two refurbishments. Her hair and her skin were both golden, to add to the leonine air, and with all that make-up she could have been a nurse in a private healthcare brochure. Indeed, with a little more blusher she might have been a patient.

"Ooh! Love this to bits," cooed Pippa, as they all stepped into the vast glassy sanctum. "It's the size of our *house*! But great for all your plants and your fruits and everything. Is that a grapefruit tree over there?"

"I know, isn't it a dream? It's something I've always promised myself. And took a year to put up. Now, of course, I practically live in here." She nodded across to an exercise bike and a rowing machine in the corner. "I work out in here, take meetings in here, and in a bit we'll have our lunch in here. So are you both well? I just thought it would be nice to leave the office behind for a change. So we can get more familiar with each other."

"Yes," was all Patrick could manage without calling for assistance. That word 'familiar' was giving him trouble. Meanwhile, Pippa pressed doggedly on.

"So how long you lived here then, Fenella? Must be a lot of upkeep."

"Yes, since my ex-husband did the dirty. But that's all history. There's a lot to be done in the grounds of course and … oh! Which was something I wanted to ask. You don't know of anyone, I suppose, who might be looking for that kind of part-time work? Someone who's retired maybe, who could do with a little extra pocket money coming in."

"Unfortunately not!" said Patrick. "Erm … no. No, we don't, sadly. Can't think of anyone like that, can we, darling."

"Well not really, no."

"Ah. That's a shame. Only I can't expect Mr Meldrew to do it all on his own."

It was a long while since Patrick had had one of his asthma attacks. And in truth he'd come to regard them as a thing of the past. Luckily his inhaler was still up to the task and he quickly settled. But for a moment it was touch and go.

"Goodness, are you all right now, Patrick?"

"Yes … yes … no, I'm … OK thanks. Really."

"You don't want me to call an ambulance or anything."

"No, no, Fenella, I think he's fine, I think he's fine. It was just erm … sorry, did you say something just then about a Mr Meldrew?"

"Oh, do you know him? Yes, he rang up this morning in fact. After seeing my ad in the parish magazine. I think some other job had just fallen through, and he was glad of the opportunity. It's really a two-man operation at the moment, with all the stuff that needs clearing in the wood. But for now I've just said he can see to the lawns and the flower beds. Anyway, before we eat, did you bring along those spreadsheets, Patrick?"

"Oh yes. They're right here."

"And I'm sure Pippa won't want to be bored to death by all our sales talk, so … why don't you take a stroll off down to the lake for half an hour, Pippa? There's a lovely little brood of goslings just hatched, and they're awfully cute. You might want to take some photos."

"Oh. Really? Yes, OK then."

"And shall we say come back at one?"

"One o'clock … right."

"Erm!" Patrick had just flicked open his briefcase, but found he was fresh out of distress flares.

Fenella snugly lowered her bottom onto a two-seater chair and patted the cushion beside her.

"And now why don't you come and park yourself over here, Patrick? Then we can both see what we're doing."

With his wife gone she had him in the crosshairs of her long black eyelashes. And that lioness purr meant she was ready to pounce. Her claws, though strictly figurative, could still do a lot of damage.

Patrick crumbled. The #MeToo movement should have something to say about this. But he wasn't taking bets on it.

"Ruddy landline's off again. That's the third time, since they went through those cables putting the lamp post back up."

With these words Victor ensured that his next-door neighbour would shortly be bundled into a van and then sheathed from top to bottom in tin foil.

"Oh, you're joking!" said Margaret as she trotted downstairs. "And my mobile's flat as a pancake this morning. After I asked you to put it on charge last night? Well I'm not going out without a phone, I'll have to take yours. And I'll try and get in touch with BT later."

"I'll lend you a ouija board."

Having scooped up all her bits for the day his wife threw a bag over her shoulder and opened the front door.

"And you won't forget to water their plants, like I told you? Remember to leave the weeping fig, but make sure the geraniums get plenty."

"Yessss. And give them all my love in the call centre."

"And I'll see you when I see you. Bye."

"Bye."

And thus was the scene set for a turn of events that can only be described as indescribable. Oh, if only the McVities had come back two days early because the weather was so awful. But no, they were having a rare old time, basking in the sun; and thus was their fate sadly sealed.

Victor let himself into their house and began to set about his duties with the Baby Bio and the watering can.

His mood, for a change, was quite chipper after talking to that Fenella Fortune woman first thing. By the sound of it this new job would be right up his street. Nice big house in the country, left to his own devices, what could be more pleasant? And he certainly wouldn't miss all that slopping about up and down ladders from now on.

"Oh damn."

Had it not been for Marjorie Quail he would surely have made that phone call for Mrs Akhani last night as promised. Since when it had utterly slipped his mind. Until now, when a small piece of paper fell from his pocket as he fished for his keys.

Yes, there was the number she'd asked him to ring. But how urgent was it? She'd sounded quite desperate, and that was a good twenty hours ago. It was typical of course that technology was collapsing all around him today. But in the meantime …

Having completed his tasks he lifted the phone from the McVities' kitchen wall and began to dial.

The conversation, when he got through, did not go well.

"Hallo? Is there somebody there called … Sajib Khan? Oh, there is. That's you. Yes, you don't know me, I carried out a little job the other day, collecting a lady I think you might know from the airport. And she's perfectly safe and secure now, I made sure of that, but … that's right, her name is Mrs Akha— what? I *beg* your pardon?? Well I don't know why you have to take *that* attitude! I rang you up because she asked m— Oh will you indeed!! Is that right? Look I don't have to listen to this! And if you're going to be like that, next time I won't bloody bother! Good-*bye*!"

Victor slammed down the phone feeling quite badly bruised. What the hell what this person's problem, whoever he was? If anyone had got out of the wrong side of bed that morning! He sounded like one of those posh young city types as well, who couldn't be doing with mere plebs like himself.

"Spread *his* ruddy entrails all over the floor! Never heard anything like it."

At the other end, in the posh young city type's London townhouse passions were riding high. Shouting and swearing at the speaker-phone had just become a family affair, with brothers and sisters and uncles and aunts all joining in the melée. Sajib, who had taken the call, was still shaking with anger as he fell back into a chair and loosened his tie. At a table in the corner Detective Inspector Radlett and two colleagues were tracking a stream of data that was dancing across their computer screens.

"Ohhh look – I am sorry, I am so sorry, it was just the sound of the man's voice. You know? It was like he was *gloating*, about what he had done, and I just – lost control."

With a flick of his hand Radlett had sprung from the chair.

"Don't worry, Mr Khan, that's not a problem. Gentleman was on plenty long enough, and we've got all we need. That's it, guys – I think we're in business!"

If you'd asked Margaret Meldrew to name the moment her husband began acting strangely the answer would likely have been "Oh come *on*!"

But judge for yourselves.

It was to be expected that his first day at the Old Nunnery would have fazed him a little. But not at all. When he got back he was as happy as a sand boy, declaring the day had been "a real blast". This might in itself have set alarm bells ringing; but not nearly as much as his remark about how much he'd missed his wife while he was there, and how much had she missed him? And though it wasn't unusual to see him dig into a packet of peanuts with his beer after tea, that trick of tossing each one in the air and catching it in his mouth was most certainly new.

To say the new job agreed with him was to state the obvious. And when she happened to remark on a "fresh light in his eyes" he replied that was just what Mr Swainey had said about his mother after her extra-terrestrial excursions. Indeed, he was so chuffed at being able to say the words "extra-terrestrial excursions" that he said them again with even greater relish and a roll of his eyes that could not be described as normal.

All of which was still festering at the back of Margaret's mind the next morning when she heard a tap on the back door and Mr Swainey made an appearance.

"Sorry to butt in, Mrs Meldrew. Were you just about to go out?"

"No, no, I'm in plenty of time. Victor's already left, but ... how are things, dare I ask? There's still been no news, I suppose."

"Well! No, that's just it, she's back! I came downstairs this morning and there she was. At the kitchen table sipping a cup of tea as large as life."

"Are you serious? Well, that's absolu— but, I mean ... did she say where she'd been all this time?"

"Jupiter. Well, to be accurate, one of its twelve moons, Ganymede. Said she liked it up there so much she decided to stay on for a couple of days. And I mean ... obviously you don't want to rock the boat, so I left it at that. But no, she's had a huge great smile on her face ever since, so ..." Here he paused, with a curious look, as his neighbour seemed to lose her focus. There was something else there beyond empathy, that was dragging her down. "And what about you, is everything all right? I haven't come at a bad moment or anything."

"Ohhh, no, no, no, it's just ... oh I don't know, Mr Swainey. What to think about anything right now. Obviously there's been all this upset with your mother. And now ... well, Victor's been behaving rather oddly."

"How d'you mean, oddly."

"Well, I don't know really, how you'd describe it. More cheerful."

"Oh crikey."

"And it's just since he gave up his window cleaning, and started at this other place, doing some gardening. It's like he's got, I don't know, more energy from somewhere. Like a second lease of life almost. Three times I woke up in the night, he was just lying there staring at me, grinning. And ever since I had that dream, that there were these blinding lights outside the window, just above all those marks on the grass, it's like … I don't know, I can't get that film out of my head. Where all those old people got suddenly younger when they— Oh, for heaven's sake! Listen to me, I think I'm going off my rocker. And look, I couldn't be more thrilled to hear the good news, so … you both take care won't you, and thanks for letting me know."

"Yes, bubb-bye to you then, Mrs Meldrew."

And her neighbour departed. Leaving Margaret to plunder her imagination in search of the truth.

As usual, it was a truth that was better left alone.

In the big wide world, things were moving swiftly to a grisly conclusion. This was apparent to anyone who could be bothered to look out of a window. But such people were few. For the old order was in good heart and good voice, and would ever more prevail. Sanity was denounced as lunacy, and life was a crucible of Crucibles.

There was nothing left to believe in now but fear.

Somewhere in the south-east RAF fighter jets were scrambled, while the prime minister chaired an emergency meeting of the COBRA committee.

And the nation rejoiced.

For Tony McVitie, like the rest of us, the writing was on the wall, though his personal apocalypse did have some novelty value.

Returning from their much-needed break, the family were in fine fettle as they stepped into the house at the end of a ripe autumn day. And when Josh, who was first in, popped his head round the door of the sitting room and asked what three men with guns would be doing behind the settee his parents naturally took it for some new piece of shtick.

"Three men with guns."

"Behind the settee. Erm …"

"Waiting for Simon Cowell to come on the box."

"Yes, that's good. Using the coal scuttle for target practice?"

"Oh, I know – something to do with open fire."

"How about, Anthony James McVitie, I'm arresting you for the abduction of Mrs Sunitri Khan on the 18th of this month. You do not have to say anything, but it may harm your defence if you do not mention when questioned something that you later rely on in court. Anything you do say may be given in evidence."

"*What??*"

This last voice had come from the kitchen, where Radlett had rather cheekily made himself a pot of Earl Grey while awaiting the return of his prey. And if the man under caution had harboured any thought of escape, those three gorillas in stab vests would have given him pause.

"What on *earth* are you talking about? What in God's name's going on?"

"And how did you get into our house?"

"Now we can do this one of two ways, Mr McVitie. Either you come quietly or I let the lads take over. Which is it to be, are you going to co-operate?"

"W—"

Taking this as a no, the lads snapped into action. And a second later Tony was being cuffed and propelled through the front door like a battering ram. Protestations of innocence were all very well, but didn't count for much when your face was compacted into a man's armpit. And whatever directives he issued to his wife about seeking legal counsel can only be imagined as he was tossed head first into the back of a police van parked outside.

As Kafka-esque nightmares go this was right up there, and no amount of pleading by Betty or Josh could shake the detective's resolve. He'd got his man and there was an end of it. And at this stage he couldn't rule out the pair of them as accessories after the fact. That youngster's face seemed vaguely familiar: whether from some comedy club handbill or a wanted poster he couldn't be sure. But at this stage he was taking no chances.

"Let's have these two in as well, sergeant, they might be able to tell us something. I think we can let the SOCO boys loose in here now. It wouldn't surprise me if we find her in a dozen different places. There was a very handy-looking carving knife in the kitchen drawer. Mark my words, they'll be making BAFTA-winning dramas about this case a year from now."

And mentally polishing his nails on a lapel, Radlett left the building.

That night there was no mistaking it. Margaret had never heard a cat scream so loud. And this time there was an odd vibrating energy to the light that tore into her sleep and cast her out into the world of nightmares. Even for one who had known the joys of a live street lamp poking through the curtains it was a shock to the system. And such was the intensity as she scrambled out to investigate that she could barely find her way to the window.

When she got there it was all over.

Like the momentary brightness in death we call life it had gone, and returned her to the night. Her eyes took a moment to adjust. When they did she found she was alone in the room. If Victor was in the toilet he had not bothered to turn the light on. (And the less said about that scenario the better.) In fact there was no hint of light, so far as she could tell, in any corner of the house.

"Victor???"

Calling from the landing she paused to listen. But there was not so much as a scuffle or murmur. Why did this send an uneasy ripple through her insides? Because it was not yet three-thirty: a good four hours before her husband could normally be crowbarred off the mattress. Unless she'd missed something at the top end of the Richter scale it was hard to think what might have roused him, let alone caused him to disappear like this.

Downstairs as she wandered from room to room a chill took hold, though the night was warm. There was too much to think about that was simply unthinkable. Mr Swainey's mother, for one. And those ghostly white figures in the garden next door for another …

Had she seen these before or after she'd woken up? She couldn't believe she had to ask herself that question. But it was hard to stay tuned to reality with all that was going on.

Then came a scratching at the door that was drawn-out and purposeful, like someone trying to pick the lock with a key. The door fell open and Victor stood in silhouette against the moon. Stepping forward he stepped back in time: to a party at Carol Hawksworth's house and some bushes outside the window. The years had peeled away and here he was, oddly rejuvenated, with a spirit to his eyes that had burned out long ago.

"Where the hell have *you* been?"

"Mmm?"

"What was that big flash of light all about? You must have seen it?"

She almost added "and people in strange white suits" but didn't want to sound like an imbecile.

"Light? Oh! Yes, I did see something. But I couldn't tell you what it was." Couldn't, or wouldn't? "Yes … no, sorry, it was just one of those nights, I'm afraid. When I couldn't get to sleep for love nor money. So I thought I'd go for a walk."

"A *walk*? At twenty-five past three in the morning? Where to?"

"I don't know, here, there and everywhere. Across the park and the playing fields. Up by the canal to the Frog and Lettuce. I know one thing, it's the most beautiful night out there, Margaret. I've never seen the stars so bright. It makes you realise what we are in the scheme of things. Compared with what's out there, in the furthest reaches of the universe. We should go up there together some time, the two of us."

"To the furthest reaches of the universe?"

"To the Frog and Lettuce. Hooh dear. Actually, I think it might have done the trick, you know, and tired me out. I'm definitely feeling a bit drowsy now. And I suppose I ought to get a couple of hours in while I can. I've got another long day ahead of me, and I need to be at my best."

That yawn seemed to come from nowhere, as if someone had just pulled a plug. And as she watched him totter off slowly up the stairs Margaret was still none the wiser.

Tomorrow, of course, was another day.

But there was today to get through first.

Tony McVitie could feel his skin starting to itch, and that was not a good sign. It took him back to the dark days of his first marriage; a place he did not care to revisit. To a wife with the allure of an H. R. Giger creation he had given everything: his home, his health, his manhood, his livelihood. And it was only through Betty and certain advances in modern dermatology that he'd eventually got back on his feet.

But that night in the police cells had done him no favours. He had formed the impression early on, based on several "conversations" with an officer's elbow, that he was not among friends. And by the time he was being marched down to the interview room at 7.30 am, after throwing up three cups of tea and a bowl of porridge, he was definitely running on empty.

Protocols were observed, and as befits all the best police dramas the room was filled with smoke and all the lights turned off, so that proceedings could take place in conditions of strict chiaroscuro.

Radlett, as ever, appeared coolly composed. But then he wasn't the one who'd spent the last twelve hours expecting a reality show host to jump out and tell him it was all a bit of fun; just as the defibrillator was being wheeled in. Plus he'd been too long in this game to be impressed by that sweaty palms routine. Someone's life was at stake here, and he'd cracked tougher nuts than Tony McVitie in his time.

"OK, so listen, Mr McVitie, or whatever your real name is. I'm a relatively young man. And I'll sit here for as long it takes till you tell me where you've hidden that young gentleman's mother."

"Is it cold in here?"

"I *repeat*—"

"No, no! Look, look. I've got no idea, honestly, what on earth you're talking about, inspector. I don't know who this person is even. I've never heard of him or his mother. This is all the most dreadful mistake, you've got to believe me, you've got the wrong man."

"Oh ah? In that case you can explain why a call made by the kidnapper, who was almost certainly about to hit Mr Khan with a ransom demand, was traced back to a telephone in *your* house? A rather careless mistake I'd venture? And one that will cost you dear. So I ask you again, Mr McVitie. What have you done with this gentleman's mother?"

"Yes, well … I don't think I need to say anything, do I, until my solicitor arrives? In the meantime I'd like to assert my right to a large tube of hydrocortisone cream."

To Patrick's mind, there were two types of moment in life upon which the future invariably hinged. There was the "uh-oh!" moment, when it suddenly dawned on you things were about to get a bit shit. And there was the other moment, traditionally marked by the words "so that's that then!", when you knew that all hope was lost, and you had to resign yourself to some awful, predestined calamity; the discovery that Victor Meldrew was now working for your boss falling squarely into the second category.

"So that's that then!" said Patrick as he prepared to leave the house for another session at the Old Nunnery. "It was bad enough trying to talk monthly cash flows all day with her head in my lap. I didn't need *that* on top of everything. I can only assume the Pentagon must have used him as some sort of prototype for the Patriot missile. The man's tracking ability is deadly."

"Are you ever going to give it a rest?" Pippa threw her dishcloth into the bowl with feeling as she finished the washing-up. "You go on about him like he's the Terminator or something. As if he's on some personal mission, to make your life a misery in every way possible."

"And your point is?"

"He's just there to do a bit of gardening! How on earth is that a problem?"

"My dear, living on the same planet as Victor Meldrew is a problem. Like playing chess with Death. I may as well just hand in my notice now and have done with it. You just know that in some weirdly ingenious way we can't begin to predict the man is going to kill off my career. And there's not a thing I can do to stop it. No doubt I'll have more to report when I get back tonight. God willing."

"And good luck with the Americans."

Ah yes, it was the one saving grace today for Patrick that four senior partners from the States with IMCD would be there? To like, spitball a few visionary concepts? Which would at least mean there was safety in numbers. In fact, by the time the whole bunch of them were gathered together in the summer house an hour later, sipping cocktails and shooting the breeze, he was teetering on the brink of equilibrium.

It didn't last.

Outside the window, in the distance, appeared a man with a wheelbarrow. Arriving at a flower bed he emptied out some compost and began raking it in. When he had finished he turned to leave, and catching sight of Patrick behind the glass raised his hand in a friendly wave.

"Are you all right, Patrick?"

"Sorry, Fenella?"

"I thought I saw you crying."

"Oh! Ha ha. Yes, pollen I think. Starting to get to me."

"OK. So anyway, gentlemen. I hate to be boring, but we're here today to take some very tough decisions, about staffing levels and the future of the company. And I think, André, you had some thoughts you wanted to kick off with."

"Right, but I think we need firstly to dialogue specifics? On how to strategise best for the future?"

"Also to evidence the methodology?"

"I think the methodology's been well conversationed, Ted?"

"Agreed, but I'd like if we instanced one or two contradicts?"

And so on, and so on.

It should have been a day like any other with Mrs Warboys taking Oscar for his run in the park. Rather than, say, a string of unalloyed horrors that would haunt her for years to come.

But such is life.

The run in the park bit had gone well, as it happens. Oscar was on lively form, chasing his plastic bone into the lake and emerging with only three twisted Miller Lite cans this time. The sun was shining, with barely a drone in the sky, and among the sea of bodies that lay sprawled on the grass at least ninety per cent had homes to go to.

And how much was Mrs Warboys looking forward to her coffee at the Meldrews'? Victor would be working but Margaret was off today, and would be at a loose end and keen for some company. Of course she'd insisted on the phone there was no need to go making a special effort – but didn't she always? It was all part and parcel of her selfless nature.

And talking of parcels, there was that package they tried to deliver the other day which she'd still got to pick up from the depot. Happily it was directly en route, and this time she'd brought along three forms of identification, to avoid another scene with the man at the desk who insisted the face on her bus pass was a still from *Bugsy Malone*.

Having signed for the item and taken it back to the car she sat there for a while wondering what on earth it could be. A pointless exercise that most of us go through when we can't place the handwriting. Here's an idea, why not just open the thing and find out?

The packet was barely six inches across and could not have weighed more than twelve ounces. But although her own name was clear enough the lettering on the sender's details was quite badly smudged. And it was only after several minutes staring at what appeared to be the names *HITLER* & *CARUSO* that she finally fathomed it.

But then her thoughts were interrupted by a figure in the rear-view mirror. No time to hang around on that double yellow with a warden on his way, so she put down the parcel and swiftly moved off.

Twenty minutes later when Margaret opened her front door it was hard to tell which of the two women looked more befuddled. And even Mrs Warboys, whose world view tended mostly to begin and end with Mrs Warboys, could see that her friend was not herself today.

"Are you all right, Margaret? You look as if you've not had much sleep."

"Ohhhh, what with one thing and another, Jean! Come on through, the coffee's ready."

As they settled in the front room Margaret filled her in on Victor's travels in the night. And then went on to say this wasn't the half of it.

"And whether it's connected or not, I don't see how it can be, but … first thing this morning, I was up at six with my mind turning everything over. And I thought I'd make myself a cup of tea. Now earlier on I wasn't sure if I'd seen them or not, because I was still half asleep. But this time there was no doubt about it … I was wide awake, and they were definitely there."

"No doubt about what? Who was where?"

"All these people in white suits and hoods. Coming and going next door. I mean, the things that go through your mind at three in the morning, but now it's obvious. They were police officers searching the premises. Like on one of those crime scenes you see on TV."

"Crime scenes? What crime?"

"Well I know! And they seemed to be just leaving, so your guess is as good as mine. If I'd gone out and asked they'd never have told me. I mean, they've been away there for the past few days, at her sister's. So the house is still empty, but … God only knows what's happening round here. You start to wonder if you're going doolally. But anyway, what have you got there?"

"Sorry? Oh! Yes." Mrs Warboys had forgotten the object on her lap, but returned to it now. "Yes, I've just come from the post office. And that's another mystery. I'm not even expecting anything. It looks like someone's spilt red wine over this bit on the back, so it took me a while to make out all the fuzzy letters, which I finally realised spelt LITTLE ROCK AR USA. Though who'd be sending me something now from Arkansas I can't imagine. Now that poor Chesney's gone."

"Well don't you think you should open it, Jean? And find out?"

"Well yes, of course. Could I borrow those scissors?"

Getting through all the brown paper and tape took a minute or two. And what emerged was a small plastic container resembling a lunch box. This, too, appeared discoloured round the edges; as did the short printed note that lay on top.

Mrs Warboys read it and frowned.

"What does it say?"

"It's from the funeral home by the looks of things. It must be the people who— oh dear. It just says *'Dear Jean Warboys. We have been instructed by the estate of the late Chesney Pinkerton to forward the enclosed, in accordance with instructions he left shortly before his passing earlier this month. We trust you will find it in order.'* What in heaven's name?"

With trembling fingers she prised off the lid and nearly passed out. And when Margaret looked in something nasty began to rise in her throat. Both turned away at the same moment, to spare their eyes and their senses the ghastly reality that had been uncovered. And it was a long moment before either could find a way to speak.

"Is that ... really—"

"Don't say it, Margaret! Please don't say it?"

"I mean— it can't be? Surely it can't."

But sad to say, it was. To the untrained eye just a sticky crimson mass with a few hollow bits poking out here and there, like miniature bagpipes.

To a cardiologist something rather more vital.

And though attempts had been made to seal and insulate the organ for transit, a certain seepage, it seemed, was inevitable. As attested by all that "red wine" across the label outside.

"B— what in the name of— !!" Margaret was having serious trouble keeping it together, as a recent mouthful of coffee prepared to set off on a return journey. "What the hell are they talking about? Instructions he left?? Has everyone gone mad?"

"Well don't ask me! Oh God, oh God, oh God! Whatever it is I can't look at it! Take it away from me, Margaret – please!"

"But – we've got to get to the bottom of this for God's sake?? Let me get the laptop. The whole thing's too ghastly for words."

But of course it was all there in the email, for anyone who cared to look.

"Ohhh Margaret, this is just ... I don't know what to say."

The words on the screen seemed to quiver as Mrs Warboys read them aloud.

"I suppose ... it must be this bit here? *'Meantime I want to thank you, for all you've done and all you've been to me. You sent me hope when that's what I needed most. You sent me belief, and you sent me respect. It seems I don't have too much to send you in return. Only—'* Oh dear. *'—only my heart I guess. That's a part of me when I'm gone, won't belong to no one but you.'*" Oh God, I feel sick. I mean – what do we think? He actually left some sort of special request to these people, when they were dealing with his remains, to—"

"Yes!!! Thank you, Jean, I'd rather *not* think about it! If you don't mind? Can we just put the ruddy thing outside or something, and try and forget about it? You see, you write to these people, there's no telling *what* they're capable of! Even after they're dead! It's obvious there was something seriously wrong there from the word go. Oh please give it here. For the love of Mike."

It was as much as Margaret could do without retching to ferry the object, at arm's length, through the back door and down to the end of the garden where she could place it by the bin for now, and try to pretend it didn't exist.

For several seconds she stood there taking deep breaths.

As she did so there came a tap on the high gate behind her, which was opened by a smooth-looking man in a suit and tie. He was dark and trim and not long in his forties with a face that spoke of aftershave.

"Good morning. Is it Mrs Meldrew?"

"Oh! Yes? Can I help?"

"Sorry to trouble you. DC Frank Millichope, CID. I wonder if I could have a quick word?"

"Oh gosh, is it about next door? Tony and Betty – are they all right? What's happened, I saw all those people earlier on."

"Excuse me? Oh! No, no, no, I've not come about that. This is another matter. Entirely unrelated. If you could spare me a couple of minutes?"

Margaret took a step backwards and almost lost her footing. A sudden visit from the law will do that to you, especially when you're disposing of human body parts. The trick was to make her guilty smile look innocent as she led him away into the house and as far from that plastic box as possible. But for some reason he was in no rush to follow, and remained by the fence looking pensive. The forensic eye and procedural tone that we've come to expect from these cocky young detective types were more than enough to test her nerve. And on this of all days she could have done without more drama.

"I understand from one of my colleagues, Mrs Meldrew, that a few weeks ago you found a man sleeping rough in this shed."

"Oh. Yes, and two of your officers came round and got him to move on. He was only there for the one night I think."

"Mmm." Millichope fingered the padlock on the door. "And would it be possible for me to …?"

"Oh. Yes. Hang on, I'll go and get the key."

When she returned to open the door her visitor stepped inside, and taking out a slender pocket torch began inspecting the shelves. Then squatting right down he studied the floor from one end to the other, running his finger through some dust which he tapped onto a piece of paper and examined carefully by the window. Margaret watched all this from the doorway looking puzzled.

"I'm sorry, constable. Do you mind me asking what this is about? What exactly are you looking for?"

Millichope paused for a second, as if to centre his thoughts. Then clicked his tongue with a grunt of frustration.

"I gather he'd passed himself off to your husband as some sort of vagrant? With nowhere else to live."

"Yyyes. Why?"

"Hah. Well that wasn't the whole story, I'm afraid. This man is well known to us, Mrs Meldrew. He's got a list of convictions as long as my arm. And two weeks ago we almost had him, round the back of the Beech Hill shopping centre, but he managed to slip away. And that was that, we couldn't trace him for love nor money. Reason being, he'd gone to ground in *this* little hidey-hole. Spinning you that hard luck tale, he thought he'd be safe for a few days till it all blew over. Of course those two officers, who escorted him off the premises, didn't realise. Just put him in the cells to cool off, then let him go. It was only yesterday we put two and two together. This is where he must have stashed the merchandise, planning to come back for it later on. Though if he did I'm not seeing any evidence. And he's not been back since as far as you're aware? There's been no sign of forced entry?"

"Nnno, not that I know of. But … when you say stashed the merchandise. What type of merchandise are we talking about? Something valuable?"

Millichope let out a thin, sardonic chuckle.

"Well it's certainly not what you'd call *cheap*, Mrs Meldrew? We're talking a street value of two hundred grand a kilo."

*

Victor had stuffed all his pockets with tissues before he went out, and already used the whole lot up. It was always the same when you were adding that plant food to a watering can: half the powder went straight up your nose. And after two hours of sneezing he was reduced to tearing out pages from an old paperback that was lying in the glove compartment; which was far from ideal and *Far From the Madding Crowd*.

All in all though, he was pleased with his efforts so far. The beds and the borders were looking a lot more tidy, and the roses that were dying of thirst two days ago had already begun to perk up. Of course a functioning hosepipe would have made life easier. But the owner wasn't kidding when she said he might find they were "short of one or two things". Almost every tool so far he'd had to bring there himself, though even he couldn't run to a fifty-metre hose. Perhaps if she was serious about looking after the place she might try stocking up on a few basics? But he got the sense that, like most of her kind who thought nothing of splashing out on a bloody great summer house, she was careful with her money elsewhere. She'd even queried the charge for those two packets of Phostrogen he'd brought along from home. Wouldn't one be enough if he used it sparingly?

It was the kind of quibble that would normally have sparked one of his tart rejoinders. But here's the strange thing: he not only let it go but let it go with a merry philosophical chuckle. And bear in mind that for Victor Meldrew to emit a merry philosophical chuckle would either involve some rogue mutation in his genetic code, or else—

Well, whatever it was had put a great big smile on his face. And not for the first time of late. So enough with this sparing use of plant food. Some of those wilting specimens needed all the help they could get. It was time to be generous.

Victor flapped away the clouds of white dust as he emptied the last of his Phostrogen packet into the can. Then he sneezed three more times and pinched his nose and began gaily snapping his fingers. Then he left the outbuilding and filled the can from the tap on the wall. And then off he went on his merry philosophical way.

When he got back after dousing the asters and the agapanthus he decided it was time to move on, and put that big ride-on lawnmower through its paces. It was a hefty old beast to be sure, that had likely been gathering dust in the barn for years. But beneath all the cobwebs and spiders, you could see, was a pretty cool piece of kit. And the fuel gauge was still showing half full, so plenty of juice there still for a good old thrash around the grass. Of course he'd never actually driven a machine like this before. But hey, life was meant to be lived.

And it would be really neat to see how fast it could go.

"So Mrs Meldrew, if you could just try and think back for a second? Were there any large packets or boxes in here, can you remember, that might have gone missing in the last week or two? About so big?"

Margaret studied the space between Millichope's hands and frowned.

"Nnno, only a few bits and pieces from that shelf, that we use on the roses and the pots outside the back. I think Victor's had most of those for his new gardening job, so I don't imagi— oh! Ohhhhh Goddd ... *nohhhh*??"

"Gardening job?"

That clatter in her head was the sound of countless pieces falling into place and knocking her sideways. What else but a dose of happy powder would account for her husband's new turbo-charged conduct this week? From the strange midnight rambles to the way he'd begun snoring in 5/4 time, all was made suddenly clear. While as usual the man in question was the last to notice.

Millichope let out a long cool whistle as he took this in.

"Well if that's right, the sooner I get round there the better. You wouldn't have an address handy for this lady at all?"

"Erm – yes! I'm sure he must have jotted it down somewhere. Let me see if I can dig it out."

"I'll be in my car round the front."

But when Margaret emerged with her piece of paper Millichope and his car were both sounding the worse for wear. Nothing beyond a series of clicks was coming from under the bonnet. And inside the car the detective groaned as he wound down the window.

"Looks like the battery's packed up on me. It was making some very strange sounds earlier on."

"Oh dear. Well I've just tried to call him and it keeps going to voicemail. Lord only knows what state he's in there by now."

"I could try and radio for help, but we're a bit screwed for manpower. You ever feel like you're having one of those days?"

"Is there anything *I* can do to help?"

"Excuse me?"

Now at this point we may all have forgotten about Mrs Warboys. But Mrs Warboys hadn't. Having earwigged enough to know the score – so to speak – she was ready and primed for a piece of the action. Or perhaps, on some deeper level, she could feel the symmetry of history beckoning? For the events that followed had a curiously familiar ring.

"I've got to pop Oscar in for his booster jab at the vet's by three, which is just out of town. And from the looks of this place it's more or less on the way. So why don't I give you a lift?"

"Oh – really?"

Millichope loosened his tie and weighed up the person who had just opened his passenger door to poke her head inside. He got the feeling she was not averse to poking it more or less anywhere if the occasion arose. But this was no time to be choosy.

"Well, OK. If you're sure, madam. That would be a big help."

"I'm parked just across there. And it's Jean, by the way."

"I'm much obliged. It shouldn't take us more than twenty minutes."

Margaret stood at the kerb to see them both off and took another long breath. Was it too much to hope that her life could run smoothly for one day at least?

Well not this particular day, it would seem.

When she stepped back indoors the phone was ringing. Please God it was Victor at last? So she could explain what was happening to him.

"Hallo? Oh! Yes, speaking. Sorry – Detective Inspector who?"

As if she'd not had her fill of police officers here was another.

"Oh yes? The man in the shed. Yes, I've just had one of your constables here, not more than a minute ago. And he told me all about it. He had a good search but couldn't find anything. And then of course it suddenly struck me that my husband would have taken those p— what??"

It was at this point she had to sit down on the stairs; as not for the first time that day she was put through the wringer and hung out to dry.

"You can't be serious!?? *Escaped?* When? Well— no, he just appeared, out of nowhere, down at the back gate. And said he was a detective. Frank Millichope? I think was the name he g— I mean, without all that hair and the beard and everything, he looked a completely different man! And then his car wouldn't start so a friend of mine said she'd give him a lift. To this woman Fenella Fortune's house, and I mean— so … what are you telling me, inspector? When you say 'dangerous' … how dangerous are we talking about?"

"Well for me this was a play about missed opportunities. Comedy of manners it may have been but where was the ambition? The author is plainly too starved of insight to offer an effective metaphor for the human condition. She has nothing original to say about death for example. Now Beckett, of course, was a one-trick pony, but one can never come away from his work feeling less than suicidal …"

"Yes, excuse me! Would you mind erm—"

"Oh sorry, constable! Is Radio Four not really your thing? I should have asked."

Mrs Warboys threw a look at the face in her rear-view mirror and reached for the tuning button.

"Well many thanks there to our special guest Marjorie Qu—"

"I mean, we can see what Ken Bruce is up to, if you'd rather listen t—"

"I'd rather not listen to anything! If you don't mind? And is there any chance of you driving a bit faster? So we get there before Christmas?"

Now was it her imagination or had a certain testiness crept in since they set off? Like one of her previous passengers he'd seemed less than thrilled to be offered the back seat; this time between twelve bags of bottles, an old busted microwave and a kitchen mangle. Perhaps she'd forgotten to mention she was calling in later at the tidy tip? Even so, he might have been more gracious. What was she supposed to do, just dump them in a lay-by? If it came to that she could have asked *him* to pipe down with all that shifting about and clanking when Oscar was trying to get some sleep on the front seat. How would he feel if that was one of his police dogs?

"The thing is, I don't like to go too fast down these country lanes. There's no telling when you're going to meet some Stirling Moss coming round the bend. I always think it's better to get there late and safe than not at all, don't you agree?"

"Stirling who?"

"That was something my old grandad always drummed into me. And of course he'd just come through the war, so he was grateful to still be with us. When you think what a hard life he'd had. When he was eighteen, lost both his testicles in a poker game. Now that's what you call a rough neighbourhood! Of course he told us a lot of these stories, you never knew how many were true. I mean, he'd have you believe he was fluent in Serbo-Croat when it was really just dialogue from *The Flowerpot Men* ..."

"All right, shut up and stop the car."

"Sorry?"

"I'm not telling you twice."

"Is it the ventilation? I can turn up the cold air if you're too warm."

"Maybe *you'd* like some ventilation? Through the back of your head! Now pull over!!"

"Sorry? I d— ohhhh myyyy Godddd!!"

Peripheral vision is a welcome tool, though not so much when it reveals a 9mm Glock pistol at your ear. And as a test for glaucoma you couldn't see it catching on.

What happened next was that she reviewed the accuracy of his aim and felt he was unlikely to miss, then pondered whether to draw him out on the reasons for his action to see if he might be persuaded to change his mind before deciding he most likely wouldn't. This took her less than a second, then she jammed on her brakes and brought the vehicle to a halt.

"OK, now get the fuck out. No ifs or buts, just do as you're told."

Mrs Warboys got the fuck out. Other options were available but most of them involved dying. So "get the fuck out" was the one she went for; along with a silent prayer that any second now her bedside alarm would do the decent thing and wake her up.

Millichope also got out, and looked the better for it. There was only so long you could sit with your knees splayed apart and your nose in a headrest, with three months' worth of Evian bottles for back support. With respiration restored he threw open the passenger door to let the dog out and grabbed up an old hessian sack from the seat.

"Maybe I'll just walk from here? It'll be a damn sight quicker!"

"Well it's still quite a way, but if you really—"

"God help us, she thinks I'm serious! Get in the sack."

"Excuse me?"

"Inside the sack. And I'm not hanging about." Having tossed the article to her feet he sealed the instruction with a flick of his gun.

(Any resemblance here to a man named Melvin is purely deliberate, and the product of social Darwinism.)

"That's an old potato sack, that Oscar likes to sleep on. I'm not sure it's even big enough for me t—"

"Well let's give it a try, shall we? Move!"

Mrs Warboys moved. Opening out the top on the ground she stepped inside and wriggled the sides up as far as her neck.

"I think that's about the full extent I can get it to without g—"

"Squat down more! Come on, all the way! Get your head in!"

Once he'd secured the neck of the sack with rope he dragged his victim away and sent her rolling into the hedgerow.

From inside came a muffled squeal and a voice that was tearfully pleading.

"Does this mean I'm under arrest, constable!? Can't you even tell me what I'm supposed to have done wrong?"

"What you've done wrong?? Apart from shoving me into that bloody awful seat with a shitload of household waste, then boring my arse off with all those dopey stories?? Hasn't anyone ever told you? Your conversation is really, really tedious!"

Mrs Warboys could have replied "To the best of my knowledge you're the first", but was not sure it would help her case. Blinded and breathless, with just nettles and thorns for company, she could scarce believe this was happening. How could an act of kindness be so harshly repaid? Though not by nature a sceptical person she was beginning to wonder if this man was a real policeman at all.

"Sorry and all that, but this is where we part company!"

Mrs Warboys squirmed and struggled to no avail, as through the hessian blackness came the sound of boots tramping back to the car and the driver's door opening.

This was followed by another sound that caused her to jump. Which given her predicament was no easy task.

It was a sound she'd been taught to recognise, and strongly advised to heed.

Somewhere between a yap and a whimper it managed to be earnest yet sensitive. A kind of diagnostic bark if you will, wherein the dog, with its singular power to sniff these things out, had gone all Lassie in a bid to convey some urgent information. This was followed by a series of delicate snuffles designed, perhaps, to introduce a positive note to its findings; though sadly as a bedside manner it cut little ice with the patient.

"Get away from me! Go on! Get!"

Millichope was about to close his door on the animal when a voice on the air, which might have come from some guardian angel, but was actually from a woman in a sack, called out to him.

"Oh my goodness – before you go! Oscar, that's enough now! Oscar!? Please! It's just, I think he may be trying to tell us something! Don't ask me how, he just seems to have this thing, when it comes to certain medical conditions! I don't know if you've ever heard of it but—"

Millichope, for all his desire to be off, held back to stare at the wriggling heap by the roadside.

"Medical conditions, what are you on about."

"I don't suppose you'd let me out? To try and explain?"

"You suppose right!"

"Well, it's more in the way of a colorectal matter – you might want to look into. Which of course may be nothing at all, but … if you'd only untie me? Please? I mean you can't just go off and *leave* me like this?? At least let me out before you go?"

"Sorry, the pair of you can sort yourselves out! Good luck!"

It would be flippant to suggest that Oscar's parting growls were cocker spaniel for "Well, it's your funeral"; besides which that wasn't his style. As Millichope restarted the car and roared off down the road, like any loyal pet he was more concerned with the welfare of his owner. And waddling across to give her a comforting nuzzle he was delayed only by several rather interesting smells at the base of a footpath sign, which required at least half a minute to check out.

Something was telling Patrick Armageddon was at hand. Call it intuition, call it fatalism, call it the scriptures of St John the Divine. Or call it a man in the garden going apeshit on a lawnmower: any way you sliced it the omens were grim.

As it happens, no one else in the summer house was taking much notice. Assembled in the tall, vaulted atrium, beneath an archway of palm fronds, the top team were all more than fully occupied. André and Ted were busy counterpointing each other's interjects, while Trevor and Seth, having been warned to watch out for their employer's straying hands, had failed to prepare for her straying feet, now in active service beneath the table. Only Patrick, having shifted his chair beyond the reach of those sinuous legs, had attention to spare. And for the last ten minutes his eyes had been glued to the figure outside, as it charged around all over the shop like a dodgem car at the fair. What in hell's name was the man up to?

A second later the spirit of the rodeo was in play, as the rider began twirling his cap in the air and slapping it against the sides of the vehicle. And was that really a "Yee-haw!" he just heard waft across or his imagination filling in gaps? The occasional burst of maniacal laughter, rising above the birdsong, suggested otherwise. What was that old saying? People in glass houses shouldn't employ a lunatic as a part-time gardener? And it was as true today as ever.

For the moment, the lady in question was unaware of the antics behind her. And best that it stayed that way. With a bit of luck, and fingers firmly crossed, this madness would pass. And as long as he kept his distance all would be well.

It was a nice thought.

But here he was now, having swung round on the spot, heading up onto the high grassy bank that led directly towards the conservatory.

Patrick forced himself to look away and get his head back into the meeting. Something of vital importance was being discussed, and it was vitally important that he had the faintest idea what it was. A stream of what sounded like words was flying past, which so long as he took the time to slow them all down and examine each one carefully made no sense whatsoever.

"... 'cos I think once we 360-review where our leverage lies we could likely move the needle back to these hot-button issues, which would counter-impact all the negative bandwidth into something more customer-centric ..."

"I agree," Patrick heard himself say, while praying no one asked why.

Meanwhile, in the world of recreational chemicals, all was good.

From Victor's viewpoint Armageddon was nowhere to be seen. But what Elysian Fields there were to mow! On a day like today, in this best of all possible worlds, there was nothing he couldn't do if he set his mind to it. He was as free as a bird and the sky was his oyster – wasn't it? Or if not an oyster then some form of edible crustacean. Or was it a mollusc? And was that the same as a gastropod? Or was a gastropod one of those bars where they served fancy grub.

"C'mon, let's crawl, gotta crawl, gotta crawl ..."

No, no, the Ugly Bug Ball was the last place they'd serve a fancy grub. They'd just throw it out for being too fancy and not ugly enough. That much stood to reason.

Talking of fancy grub made him suddenly feel hungry. And there were still a few hours to go before tea. But if he got his skates on and put his foot down perhaps he could get away early.

So far it had been a pretty good session, if he did say so himself. On the big central lawn he'd gone with a kind of freeform technique; much in the style of that American artist who slopped paint around the floor from a bucket. A bold approach was the key: just cut the steering wheel some slack and let the mower suggest its own organic patterns in the grass. This had thrown up some interesting results that overturned centuries of classical garden maintenance. And yet the main thing, surely, was to stimulate debate. One man's pig's breakfast was another man's self-expression. And a certain critic, he felt, would have hugely approved.

This thin stretch along the bank gave him less to play with. So maybe just stick with convention, and straight, regular ribbons each way. It would allow him to get some speed up and see how much poke there was left in the engine.

It was a funny old brute, this mower: quite cumbersome in its way, but once you'd got used to the smell of burning rubber under the cutting deck it was fine. The biggest surprise was the fact there were no brakes. The trick being presumably to come off the gas pretty smartish and hit the reverse pedal to kill your speed.

It was a trick he'd not quite fully mastered as yet. But give it time.

Mrs Warboys' car was really not used to not being driven by Mrs Warboys. After many long years on the road it was suddenly having to cope with something called fourth gear. And once this man Millichope got going that dog bowl full of water under the passenger seat had no chance.

After a breakneck journey round the highways and byways of rural England the driver reached his destination and paused by the gates. Yes, the name tallied with the one he'd been given. And from the look of those cars parked outside there seemed to be a lot going on here today. All the better from his point of view: once he'd tracked down this Meldrew person and got his goods back he could leave them in peace. And if anyone asked, he was DC Frank Millichope on the trail of a ruthless drugs baron.

What could go wrong?

Well for starters, that long straight driveway was too long and straight for its own good. And the sign on the wall that said "*10 MPH*" had to be a joke. This was a man on a mission, with no time to hang about.

As he flew towards the house an imposing glass structure was revealed at the back, within which half a dozen folk were busy yapping round a table. Beyond this point, where the drive narrowed by the foot of a grass bank was a track that took you to an old wooden outhouse with its doors open. Here was parked a slightly dodgy looking Honda with a bag of soil on the roof and a garden rake sticking out the back window. There was no one down there so far as he could tell, but it seemed like a good place to start looking.

Except of course he never got that far.

We've seen how fish fingers did for Margaret at the wheel, but this was much worse. And quite why those three words should have popped back into his head at that minute we can't know. But pop back they did with a vengeance.

A colorectal matter.

Easily dismissed at the time as a ploy to distract him; but what if all that doggy stuff were no quackery? And those twinges of late that he'd just put down to a tight pair of trousers—

In such nanoseconds of panic does our focus dull and we lose our grip …

… enough to be taken aback by a whacking great shape that seemed to fly from the sky, like some *deus ex machina*, to crash his ambitions in the most literal fashion.

Questioned afterwards, neither party would have much of a clue what had happened.

Victor, for one, was in no fit state to account for the near-collision. If pressed he might have hazily recalled mixing up his forward and reverse pedals for the umpteenth time as he went to swing the machine round. But how he came to be careering down the slope at that point was a mystery. Or as he later said in his police statement: "The thing just had a mind of its own."

Millichope took what evasive action he could, and immediately wished he hadn't. It wasn't so much the speed with which he swerved across the grass and smack into the summer house as the angle that he hit it. By ploughing headlong into the south-facing wall he managed to take out three corners of the octagon at a stroke.

The panic this caused inside can be well imagined, with grown men leaping from their chairs and texting in terror. The sudden appearance of Mrs Warboys' headlights coming at them through a shower of glass was enough to bring the meeting to a close, with no motion for adjournment required, and send them racing outside.

You'd think this would be enough of a shock for all concerned, as Fenella and Patrick and the rest of them stood on the grass gawping at the section of building now shattered beyond repair.

But more was to come.

That faint, ominous creaking noise reminded Patrick of something though he couldn't immediately say what.

It started low, then gradually rose in volume and pitch in a way that was all too familiar.

If he could just put his finger on where he'd heard it before—

SMAAASSSSHHH!!!!

Ah yes, that was it.

The sound a tree makes when it's just been chopped down.

Where this maniac had bulldozed his way in, two giant palms, imported from Spain as a centrepiece to the grand vaulted atrium, had just gone the way of Victor's lamp post. Though without Victor's house to break their fall the result was horrendous. The weight of the stems was too much for the delicate matrix of windows and walls, which proceeded to cave in, one after the other like a house of cards, until the whole thing was no more than a sea of splinters buried among the ruins of an indoor garden.

The air was filled with bits of stuff: mostly soil and dust and the words "shitting hellfire". A daintier woman than Fenella Fortune would have passed out on the spot. And let's not pretend she wasn't tempted. One of her colleagues had gone down that route and the concrete flagstone had the better of it. For the moment there was only numbness. Real time in her head had ceased to be, as if the events around her were now moving frame by frame, at the only speed by which she could process them.

Deep within the wreckage of her dream house a battered Opel Corsa was sputtering its last. In the driving seat a man was bleeding into an airbag, but that was about all he was doing. Whatever had driven him to this act could only be guessed at for now. But it's fair to say he'd done a thorough job. Some radical nihilist, drunk on the politics of envy? The fingerprints of the left were clearly all over this.

In those formative seconds just after the crash Patrick wasn't so sure. While everyone's eyes were on the attacker, back on the big lawn a second vehicle was just pulling up. For a few seconds it juddered and spat before convulsing in a long drawn-out death rattle, then appeared to expire. Then the man in the seat, who had his back to them, took a moment to recover his breath and having slipped off his cap began flapping it in front of his face.

Climbing down from the mower Victor screwed up his eyes with relief as he called out to no one in particular:

"Myyyy giddy aunt! Got away with that one then – just!"

Not everyone there would agree.

"So how you feeling now? Still a bit woozy?"

"Woozy! Is that a joke?"

With a glare that would prepare a surface for painting Victor swung his legs off the hospital bed and attempted to fall over. Since he did not, at this minute, trust any part of his body to respond as it was meant to he figured this was the best way of making it stand up.

He immediately fell over.

Margaret helped him to a chair and poured some water from a jug one of the nurses had brought in.

"Come on, I don't think you've drunk enough, still. You know what they said about keeping hydrated. After what your body's had to cope with this past few days, you're not going to be back to normal in five minutes."

Victor groaned and sipped and then groaned again. Then he looked round the small square room, praying it would keep still. And then he rapped the bridge of his nose, like you do with a toaster when you can never get all the crumbs out.

"God knows how all those people in advertising do it. They must have steel-plated nostrils. Explains all the crap they come up with, I suppose. So what did the doctors say in the end. Did they say I could go home yet?"

"There's a few more blood tests to come back. But they said they'll ring us if they find anything. Otherwise we can go whenever we want.

As soon as you feel steady enough. I think you should take your time and not rush."

Victor checked his watch, which said 7.32. At least the second hand was now moving at its normal speed again. And someone had helpfully put his heart back inside his ribcage. That feeling he had that suddenly all his hair was growing back on his head, but inwards, had also now passed. If this was cold turkey they could keep it.

The last few hours had all been a blur. Why that lovely big ice palace had come down he had no idea and didn't like to ask. Something to do with that man in the car he nearly hit, at a guess. From the council maybe, turning up with a demolition order. All hell had broken out after that. Squad cars and ambulances and BBC helicopters – all the first responders – arriving in seconds. Victor had been promptly whisked off to A&E, and subjected to much poking about and a barrage of questions that threw him completely, till his wife turned up with most of the answers.

"So will you need any help getting your trousers back on?"

"I think I'll manage. You can pass them across if you like."

Margaret passed them across. Then sharply perked up as a text appeared on her phone.

"Ohhhh! Thank goodness, thank goodness."

"What's that."

"Jean! She's alive and OK, by the looks of it! They found her in a ditch, tied up in a sack. The poor woman, she must have been terrified out of her wits!"

"Oh dear."

"I mean, can you believe this person? I still can't get my head round it. The whole thing's been a nightmare. And didn't I tell you, at the time? We should have got shot of him the minute we found him there. Dossing down like that in *our* garden shed!"

"Oh yes, I distinctly remember you saying. What if he turns out to be a local drug dealer on the run who's planning to hide two bags of cocaine inside some Phostrogen boxes. Why is it? You try and do your best for people and this is what happens. I don't know why I bother."

Margaret crossed the room and stood gazing out of the window. Outside the hospital chapel two men in shorts with very fat legs were watching *Peaky Blinders* on their phones. There was a sound of people sobbing. Not just here but all over the world. Having seen what lay beneath, the darkling sky was keeping its distance. And something in the air made her shiver.

"Yes, it's been a strange old week, that's for sure. And it didn't help with all that other going on. His mother next door and everything. I mean, we know it's all part of the condition, they go wandering off like that, but … what with the way you'd started acting, I was almost beginning to wonder if— well."

"Beginning to wonder if what?"

"Ohhh goodness knows. You know the way things prey on your mind. In the night especially. If I'd known at the time, it was just Mrs Aylesbury's security lights on the blink. It only took a couple of cats having a fight and the whole street lit up. She says it's all been fixed now, hopefully. And then, the most stupid thing of all, those marks in the grass, where he must have been squirting his weedki—"

"Evening Mr Meldrew! Sorry to disturb you in your underpants!"

The tap on the door was so brief and so light it might have been a fly banging its head. And then into the room, like a child's balloon, bounced the very man she had mentioned. Grinning from ear to ear and Lord knows where else.

"Ohhh! Mr Swainey!"

"I know! Is this a coincidence? I was just talking about your husband up at the nurses' station. They'd got him down as dead on arrival! If you can believe such nonsense. I don't think they're all that thorough sometimes in this place, to be frank with you. I said no, no, no, I'm sure I just heard his voice in that room along the way. Either that, or there's a very angry parrot on the loose!"

The suspicion that someone had dropped a can of nitrous oxide in the corridor was then given weight as he relished this quip, while Victor and Margaret swapped silent glances.

"So … you here today with your mother then, Mr Swainey? She's not taken a turn for the worse or anything."

"Oh! No, no, nothing like that. I'm just here to collect someone, as it happens. Mrs Akhani, in fact – the lady you very kindly picked up for us, Mr Meldrew, at the airport. Apparently she had a bit of a funny turn, and they've been keeping her in for a few days. Seems to be on the mend now, but … last time you saw her she was fine, I take it?"

"Well – yes. She seemed as right as rain, from what I remember. A bit on the nervy side, but …"

"Oh well. They'll be bringing her down in a bit, so I'd better shift myself. Bubb-bye to you both. It was nice to run into you."

Five minutes later, when Victor and Margaret left the building their neighbour was just pulling out of the car park. As he drove past he gave them a merry wave and they waved back. The Asian lady seated beside him did not wave, but seemed to stare right through them looking rather bewildered.

Margaret paused for a second as the car disappeared up the road.

"That was odd. Poor dear didn't seem to recognise you. I wonder if she's ready to go home yet. Didn't you say she lives on her own?"

Victor frowned. His own head was only just clearing, but something wasn't right here.

"I don't know about that, but … I've never seen that woman before in my life. He must be going as cranky as his mother."

"W— but why would he say such a thing. I mean, unless he got the names mixed up or something? I suppose he has had a lot of stress just lately."

"Suppose."

The two of them were about to step off the kerb when an ambulance pulled up with its lights flashing. The doors at the back were thrown open, and a trolley flew out with two paramedics attached, along with a uniformed police constable and a figure in shirtsleeves with a bullet head.

The latter had the look of a man who had seen it all and written the manual, with a glint in his eye that was licensed to kill. There was little enough got past Alan Radlett, as many a villain had found to his cost. But his patience today had worn seriously thin.

On the trolley was a twitching shape encased in a shroud of what looked like Bacofoil. Along with a nose and two eyes poking out the top the only sign of a body within was a hand, which was cuffed to the officer. The officer, clutching his cap, was then dragged alongside as the medics careened through the doors.

"Mind your backs please, everyone! Collapsed hypothermic coming through! Paging Dr Boosler! Paging Dr Boosler!"

Pausing only to grab his jacket Radlett raced after them. At the back of his mind was a Paul Daniels trick with a girl under a silk sheet that had once bamboozled him. So vigilance here was the key.

"Stay with it Ron! And keep a close eye on that wrist! He's a slippery eel this McVitie, with a lot of angles! And we've all seen *Silence of the Lambs*!"

Victor and Margaret watched this unfold with a nervous twinge. Had they really just heard what they'd just heard? Amid the din of car doors and sirens and arguing taxi drivers it was hard to tell. And in any case, McVitie was not such an uncommon name, was it?

But then again.

Margaret was already thinking back to the other night and those men in white suits. Good God, could it really be? That Tony and Betty – of all people …

And there she was the next day, on *The Six O'Clock News*: "No, they always seemed such a quiet couple. Kept themselves to themselves. Sweet little boy, always cracking jokes. We never dreamt what was under that freshly laid turf in the back garden …"

Victor's mind, also, was churning. That face in the car window was deeply disturbing, the more he thought about it. And why had Mrs Akhani always been so very, *very* jittery whenever she saw him? Like he was about to pull a knife on her or something. It made no sense at all.

Unless?

Supposing it wasn't Mr Swainey who had got things mixed up, but …

For the moment they kept their own counsel and said nothing. No doubt these issues would resolve themselves, as they always did, in the fullness of time. Either way it was beyond their control, and there was nothing to be gained by fretting about it.

Sometimes in life denial is the best policy.

*

The facts in the case of Fenella Fortune's summer house appeared to be cut and dried. Some racketeer who was fleeing the cops in a stolen car had made a detour through the grounds and veered off course. The details of his background were not yet clear, but revenge attacks were launched on local places of worship just to be on the safe side. The driver, when he did come round, was clearly still under the influence of something or other: referring the police to a small cocker spaniel for evidence of his diminished responsibility. (As it happens, Oscar had misdiagnosed an intraluminal polyp, but we won't hold that against him.) And everyone there who had witnessed the act agreed it was down to this single mad character who seemed to be hell-bent on destruction.

Everyone there except one.

Patrick alone could see past the obvious, to the lurking presence that dogged his every step. And in hindsight of course it was all clear as day. The demolished conservatory was a Meldrew speciality they should have been ready for. With a different m.o. this time to keep things interesting. Previously, in his own back garden, a cow had been dispatched to do the deed. Then later on a giant spider: cleverly planted in his wife's toiletry bag to drive him berserk. Only by the grace of God did someone else go through the window into that big glass outhouse below. But now with this latest stunt, getting out of his head to play silly buggers on a lawnmower, he'd really upped the ante. And when they asked Patrick to report what he'd seen he was naturally bound to oblige.

Fenella Fortune rang up the next day and fired him.

It turns out that while the building was fully covered against criminal damage, acts of negligence on the part of the owner or any member of staff were another matter. And when Victor's shenanigans came to light the insurance company basically told her to get stuffed. At which point Patrick, whose job security of late had relied on – shall we say – a "hands-on" approach by his boss, found that no amount of nice bottom could save his sorry arse.

Victor didn't need to be fired. For the third time in a row he had gambled with a future and lost. Thanks to whatever bastard was up there having fun with his life, his dreams of self-reliance had come to nothing.

Perhaps a short break to Neptune was the answer. It couldn't be worse than where he was now. Or maybe a weekend getaway to the Sun – though didn't someone say there was a hosepipe ban there at the moment?

Ah yes, it was that bloke Dennis, he'd run into again at the hospital; while he was taking a shortcut to the moon through Accident and Emergency. Victor said it was nice to see him again and asked how he was getting on with his shaving, then wished him a safe journey. It was, he felt, only fair and proper. Who was he anyway, to contain a free spirit? With flights of the mind it was rapidly approaching peak season; and these days it was no wonder. Show him an alternative to sanity and he was definitely up for it.

"And I mean it's not the first time, is it, you've got yourself mixed up with drugs like that."

"What?"

If Victor imagined that by holding a large book in front of his nose it would keep Mrs Warboys at bay he was much mistaken. With the pair of them seated in facing armchairs he was, in effect, a sitting duck in his own front room. Though what she was doing there in the first place he'd rather forgotten.

"I'm surprised the police didn't mention it. You'd think it would be there in their records."

"What are you talking about?"

"And I mean, we all know it wasn't your fault, but still. When they raided that young prostitute's place and found you in the bath."

"Yes, well I don't think we need go raking all that up again, do we. It was bad enough at the time."

"Handcuffed to the taps with no clothes on, wasn't it. I think I've still got the newspaper cutting somewhere. Talk about a Christmas you'd rather forget!"

"Well if you'd rather forget, what are you harping on about it for?"

In truth these events had not been far from his mind of late. When the pair of them had come across those mince pies in a students' refectory, how could they have known what was in them? A lot more than currants and spices as it happened, and the effects had been costly. But trust her to dredge it all up at this moment.

"And in any case! Who was it gave one of those pies to a gorilla at the zoo! As if there weren't enough signs up, saying *Don't Feed the Animals.*"

"Oh don't, Mr Meldrew! Please don't."

"It's no wonder the poor thing got excited."

"Mr Meldrew—"

"Knocking out his keeper and dragging you into the cage like that—"

"Mr Meldrew!? Please? It was the most horrible thing ever! And I don't want to be reminded of it!"

"Well who brought the whole subject up in the first place? Not me!"

"No, I know, but—"

"Myyy God, are you two at it again? I can't step outside for a second, can I, and leave you together."

Margaret was barely through the back door when the bickering reached her ears. Shaking her head with despair she sank into the settee between them and tried to coax a final cup of tea from the pot.

Mrs Warboys went to the toilet in contrition, while Victor pretended to read for a bit, and then asked:

"So how're things next door?"

"Well, just as you'd expect after everything. She said he's just about back to normal now, apart from waking up screaming every night. And his right hand's still basically a claw. Which they're hoping will wear off with time. I just popped round to lend her a few kitchen knives. Police are still hanging on to most of theirs for analysis. You'd think once they'd found that Mrs Khan, and heard all about your cock-up, that would be that but ... oh, and she said Josh has given up now on his comedy career. He says nothing seems funny any more."

"Huh! I know what he means."

Margaret, for all her outward dismay, allowed herself an inner smile. Until a few days ago the man she married, being full of sprightly joy, was a shadow of his former self. That glitch at least was now corrected. And from what she was hearing all was back in perfect working order.

Life, it seems, was not finished with Victor Meldrew by a long chalk. In all his years he'd never fathomed it nor reckoned he ever would. He'd never asked to be and had no idea why he was. Or why anything that was was, and why it was what it was when it could easily have been what it wasn't. When people asked "How are you?" it begged the question "How is anything anything, and to what end, or for what conceivable purpose?" "I'm good" took you absolutely bloody nowhere.

No, that question mark would go on hanging round his neck for a long while yet. Like a boa constrictor threatening to throttle him.

Rodney Carlo Willson is a name that may not mean much to anyone, though it might have meant everything to someone.

When, after new evidence was uncovered, he signed a confession regarding two counts of first degree murder in the state of Arkansas there were no celebrations in Chesney Pinkerton's cell, which the latter had long since vacated.

The news, in any case, did not travel far, which was no bad thing. Mrs Warboys and Margaret would not have taken it well.

A man who sought to have a part of himself preserved, and to pass it on to the only one who ever believed in him, had serious issues for sure. Medication might once have been the answer. But not the medication they gave him.

The convictions of those who convict had prevailed as they always do, and for those who live on the moon there is scant regard.

But you already knew that.

With one foot in the grave and counting, the world was in serious trouble. And the cry for help was deafening.

Somewhere in the south-east RAF fighter jets were scrambled, and the prime minister chaired an emergency meeting of the COBRA committee.